11/5/95

MAR

Holl

In a sequel to his "New York Times" best-seller, *GOOD FRIDAY*, Robert Lawrence Holt has written another steamy thriller. This time ...... it is Cuba, Castro, the CIA, plus Marine Harriers and one Cobra out of Guantanamo Bay.

Fidel Castro, speaking before a million people in the Plaza de la Revolucion of Havana, gets a taste of his own voodoo. CIA agent Lou Fricke, observing in Havana, gets singed by more than the tropical heat, ... and Marine Colonel Tom Hemingway again exceeds his authority in order to accomplish his mission.

If Fidel chooses to go the hard way, it could happen something like this.......

Robert Lawrence Holt's novels include:

Sweetwater: Gunslinger 201---a saga of aircraft carrier pilots on the Kitty Hawk.

Good Friday----Saudi Arabia is invaded.

Peacemaker----U.S. launches the ultimate Star Wars weapon that thinks for itself.

The Christmas Ruby--a story for the holidays that illustrates the *"the Tenfold Return."*

Mad Eagle--an environmental thriller based in San Diego County, California

*(reviewer's comments
on pages 315-318)*

Holt's non-fiction include:

The Complete Book of Bonds

Straight Teeth: Orthodontics

How Mothers & Others Stay Slim

How To Publish & Promote Your Own Book

Horio, You Next Die!---true account of survivor of World War II Jap POW camp.

*(ordering information
on final page)*

Havana Heat

By
Robert Lawrence Holt

Pacific Rim Press

Library of Congress Cataloguing in Publication Data

Holt, Robert Lawrence
Havana Heat

A Pacific Rim Press Book
I. Title
PS3592.Y38594 1994 813'.54 93-85342 93-45849
ISBN 0-930926-17-X 93.85342

Printed in the United States of America

First National Edition

Cover Design
by
Mary Settle
Artistic Typesetting
San Marcos, California

Pacific Rim Press
A Division of
California Financial Publications

(see inside last page for ordering information)

.....dedicated to the Cuban patriot, Jose Marti.
May his dreams come true.

PREFACE

This book was six years in the researching and two in the writing.

In 1991 and 1992, more than one publisher in New York City declined the manuscript of *Havana Heat* due to a fear that Fidel Castro would soon follow the footsteps of other Communist dictators in the West.

It is a measure of Fidel's remarkable staying power that he is still with us. Many people have told me Castro will fall at any time. I do not agree. After studying every available reference on the man, I am convinced he'll remain in power to the bitter end---a bitter end for his people, not for himself.

Some commentaries may suggest that this book presents a slanted view of Fidel, particularly in the prologue. Those pages attempt to portray the early traits of this exceptional man which have contributed to both his triumphs and defeats. Further in the book, one will read why Fidel is either hated or loved by his people, with relatively few straddling the fence.

I would like to acknowledge Ken Carter and Patricia Valiton. Their repeated readings of the manuscript, plus their incisive advice have proved invaluable. The counsel of Chuck Banks, publisher of my first novel, has been propitious. The fine-tooth comb of Mary Lane and Annie Flanigan has been of immeasurable value. And no writer should be without a 24-hour a day editor as talented and lovely as Barbara Fox White.

There is one person I have not met to whom I would like to express my gratitude. Tens of thousands of my readers (perhaps, even hundreds of thousands) might also be grateful to Harold N. Boyer of Broomall, Pennsylvania. He penned words which appear on the backcover, words which propelled this book into a second printing.

Havana Heat is one of the first novels to spotlight the Whiskey Cobra AH-1W---the premier attack helicopter flown by the United States Marine Corps. For assistance in accurately portraying this gunship, I thank Captain Russell "Metal" Doty---a Cobra driver on Camp Pendleton, California who actually gets paid for the privilege of flying these lethal machines. The *Snake* is pictured below.

Finally, I thank my fine friend, Frank Johnston for watching with an eagle eye as I bounce off the rocks and race down the rapids in this crazy roller-coaster profession.

RLH

The Whisky Cobra---better known as *the Muttering Death* to the Viet Cong.

Prologue

The background of this novel is basically true. If conditions in Cuba continue to worsen, much more of *Havana Heat* may become true.

It includes three real people---Fidel Castro and the two other members of his triumvirate, Raul Castro and Vilma Espin.

The following incident defines Fidel Castro quite well. It occurred on October 27th, 1962, during the Cuban Missile Crisis.

Castro was touring a ground-to-air missile site which the Soviets had just installed on Cuban soil. As the senior Russian officer (General Georgy Voronkov) explained the missile's firing sequence to him, an American U-2 reconnaissance aircraft appeared on the radar screen. Though Castro inwardly seethed, he uncharacteristically displayed no outward displeasure at the American plane's violation of Cuban airspace. The U-2 intrusion was a common occurrence during the crisis.

Proudly, Voronkov told Castro that the U-2 could be knocked down by the push of a single button. "Which one?" asked Fidel. When Voronkov indicated the button, Fidel suddenly reached over and depressed it. The rest is history.

The missile destroyed the U.S aircraft. The flabbergasted and horrified Russian general was soon recalled. Khrushchev insisted it was an accident. JFK, rather than react and thereby escalate the affair, chose to hush it. Castro was furious when Khrushchev backed down.

No one, before or since, has brought the world closer to nuclear war than Fidel Castro.

Some of Fidel's natural fury can certainly be traced to his genes.

His father arrived in Cuba as a 13-year-old orphan. Though penniless and uneducated, Angel Castro was ambitious. For a start, he sold lemonade to field workers, then peddled goods to them, bought land with his savings, labored from dawn to dusk, purloined what land he could not acquire by legal means, and eventually became a sugar baron, controlling a 26,000 acre plantation. He was known for a violent temper.

What of Fidel's mother? Lina came to the plantation as a cook, but her comeliness soon diverted the attention of Angel from his first wife. Without the benefit of marriage, Lina bore Angel three children in quick succession. Fidel was the third. She would have four more.

Does Fidel's illegitimacy account, in part, for his lifelong belligerency? His compulsion to be the best in any endeavor? And his coldblooded elimination of any competitor?

When Angel's first wife---finding her husband's arrangement intolerable---finally left, Lina displayed little interest in assuming domestic chores. Astride her stallion, Lina could be seen in the fields of the plantation each day. At the waist of her loose dress, she wore a holstered revolver. No one crossed Lina, save Angel. From her genes sprouted both Fidel and Raul.

The brothers ran wild on the estate. Fidel, headstrong and large for his age, was spoiled by the servants and other offspring of his father. Fidel was also the smartest---able to read and write by the age of four. At six, the sturdy boy enjoyed the use of firearms, practicing on hens with a shotgun. Later, cows served as targets for his pistol. His defiant tantrums led his father to banish him to a boarding school on the other side of the island. The young boy was said to be broken-hearted at his exile. Has this embitterment affected his adult life?

On the surface, Fidel's devastation was only temporary. At the boarding school, his photographic memory permitted him to recite chapter upon chapter of material. Yet, he cheated on exams, forged grade cards sent to his father, and became the bully of the schoolyard. Angel Castro, upon receiving reports of his son's incorrigible behavior, withdrew him from the private school.

His parents did not realize that Fidel, after attending the private school for three years, had come to prefer it over his own home. When their child threatened to burn down the family house unless returned to the school, his father promptly had the young tyrant reinstated.

As a college student, Fidel was an exceptional athlete whose pitching ability prompted a $4,000 bonus offer from the New York Giants. Yet, if Fidel's team fell behind, he would quit the game rather than permit himself to lose. The bonus offer was ignored, some say because the pistol-toting Fidel was too busily engaged in the violent politics of Havana University.

After receiving his law degree, Fidel married a woman of Cuba's upper class. Their five-year marriage produced one son, Fidelito. His wife, Mirta, was described by friends as a saint....for patiently accepting a husband who was often gone and paid no bills (he never sought a real job). Fidel found it more stimulating to trouble the corrupt regime of Fulgencio Batista. After divorcing Mirta, he never remarried, but did father eight more offspring---none of whom he is close to.

The adult Fidel Castro proved to be an excellent revolutionary in the field. Within two years, he and his *barbudos* (bearded ones) defeated Batista's army, though outnumbered 10 to 1 even at the height of hostilities.

Unfortunately for the Cuban people, Fidel would prove to be an abysmal administrator. A mild megalomania renders him incapable of delegating authority....and equally incapable of tolerating dissent. His compelling need to oversee all areas of Cuban government is uncontrollable; and, of course, impossible. Instead of administering his government in Havana, he prefers to travel around the island on "inspection tours." Cubans often joke that they have two governments---the crippling bureaucracy in Havana and Fidel Castro in his jeep.

Castro's rule is typical of most dictators. No one dares contradict the caudillo....but himself, which is often. In a group, no one laughs until he does. The only mistakes permissible are those by the Maximum Leader.

Within a year of Batista's overthrow in late 1958, a staggering number of Fidel's former guerrilla-fighters fled back into the mountains, unwilling to accept the emerging Marxist state. When Fidel reneged on his 1957 Manifesto promising popular elections and other democratic reforms, the armed dissidents swelled to more than 3,000 men and women. Fidel, unable to dislodge these adversaries, requested the assistance of his new ally. Soviet troops entered the mountains with heavy air support and annihilated the freedom-fighters.

Since that time, the dread of rebellion and assassination has been an obsession with the Cuban leader. For good reason. After the last of eight documented attempts by the CIA to assassinate him, Fidel publicly warned: "Behind me, come others more radical than I. And the first will be Raul."

Raul Castro. Four years younger than Fidel, Raul possesses a deceptively frail appearance. He has been described as vindictive, colorless, shrewd, and a strict disciplinarian notorious for his heavy hand and ideological inflexibility. In many ways, he is the opposite of Fidel.

A sister once described Raul as the most "tender and loving" of the Castro brothers and a good family man.

There are consistent rumors which may explain why Raul does not resemble Fidel. The rumors suggest Raul had a different father....most likely an officer in Batista's army by the name of Captain Felipe Mirabel. Early in 1959, when Batista's officers were being arrested and executed, Felipe Mirabel received preferential treatment in prison. And, though sentenced to die, he survived. Whenever the subject of Raul came up in prison, Mirabel "would become oddly cold and quiet and would not speak."

In Santiago de Cuba at this time, Raul acquired international infamy when he personally ordered the summary execution and bulldozer burial of 74 Batista officers in one night. *(Fidel was more careful to dis-*

tance himself publicly while engineering the execution of another 600 Batista supporters in Havana.)

Of the major revolutionary leaders who helped Fidel overthrow Batista, Raul is the only one still alive. Many Cubans believe this longevity is due to his subservience to Fidel and the fact that they are related.

Raul secretly remarried in the late 1980s, but his first spouse---Vilma Espin---is still his "official wife." Vilma and Raul have remained professionally close, even treating each other with affection in public....to the distress of Raul's new wife.

Vilma Espin. Like Fidel, Vilma is a person of many contradictions. In her patrician youth, she was a delicate beauty, the daughter of a pre-revolution attorney who was a director of the Bacardi rum company. A bright individual, Vilma attended the Massachusetts Institute of Technology where she studied architecture as a graduate student.

Captivated by the charisma of Fidel Castro (as were many young women of Cuba's aristocracy), she dropped out of MIT to join his struggle. In the first months of the revolution, she carried ammunition and other supplies concealed in her long skirts and petticoats. When the rebel group numbered but 20, Vilma climbed into the Sierra Maestra mountains of southern Cuba to fight alongside them. She took Raul Castro as her lover, who soon converted her to his fervent communism. A few months after the revolution, they married.

Vilma possesses a fast mind, and Fidel has often favored her judgement over that of Raul. She is a coldly self-righteous woman, whose only religion is Marxism. Even in the 1990s, she is described as "a hardline Stalinist." Vilma has been implicated in the death or disappearance of former colleagues (including Frank Pais, a man said to have refused her advances) who challenged Fidel's leadership.

She founded the 2-million member Cuban Federation of Women and was the promulgator of the most radical family legislation in the macho Hispanic world---the Cuban Family Code of 1975---which requires men to share housework and childcare with their wives.

At diplomatic functions and during visits by foreign dignitaries, Vilma has usually served as Fidel's official hostess. She can appear quite charming

Contemporary historians of Fidel Castro and his revolution are often at odds. They cannot even agree on the year Castro was born---1926 or 1927. And, the police state existing in Cuba does not encourage the dissemination of reliable information. Nevertheless, in *Havana Heat*, I have attempted to portray the triumvirate and conditions in Cuba as accurately as possible.

On April 11 of 1991, the United States angrily announced to the world that Algeria had secretly built a nuclear power plant with technology purchased from China. Algeria would be the first Arab nation to possess plutonium, the fuel for a nuclear bomb. The Chinese denied everything, as did the Algerians.

Fidel Castro, one of the first world leaders to embrace the newly independent Algeria in 1962, must have been delighted.

In 1960, he had sent military supplies to Algeria during their fight for independence from France. Three years later, Castro furnished an army battalion to assist Algeria in a border war. Cuba is one of Algeria's oldest and staunchest allies.

The sultry nature of Cuba can be seen in her shape. The curves of her coastline resemble a kneeling woman at the climax of a heated dance. With arms flung back in abandon, her body is arched in a seductive pose.

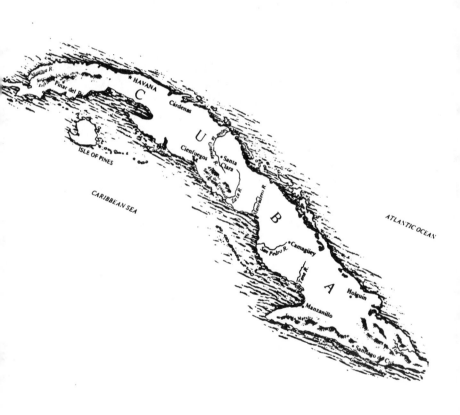

Or....might it be in agony?

LIST OF CHARACTERS

"Iron Balls" BARRAGAN---U.S. Marine Cobra pilot
Ed BELLIN---Chief, U.S. Interests Section, Cuba
Captain CARTER---CO, Naval Base, Gitmo
Fidel CASTRO---President of Cuba
Raul CASTRO---Defense Minister of Cuba
General DIAZ---CO, Central Military District, Cuba
Vilma ESPIN---wife of Raul Castro
Louis FRICKE---CIA operative
Camille FOX---employee, U.S. Interests Section
Maria GOMEZ---Cuban woman at Plaza fountain
Lt.Col. HEMINGWAY---CO, Harrier squadron
KRISTINE---student from Havana University
NO-CHIN---officer of Cuban State Security
Diego ROCA---elderly Cuban man
Edward ROLLE---Director, CIA
Allan STEINER---American President
Colonel VALDES---aide to General Diaz
Clayton WALTERS---U.S. Secretary of State

A Phantasmagoria

As the bearded guerrilla trudged down the mountain road, the haze of twilight hung like a saffron veil over the Sierra Maestra of southern Cuba. His mind lost in thought, the man's eyes followed the deep ruts of the dirt road.

A harsh screech from a hidden macaw shattered the silence.

The *barbudo*, or bearded one, looked up at the warning. Two shapes were hurtling toward him on the narrow mountain road.

"Not again," he moaned.

The barbudo wanted desperately to flee. His head whipped back-and-forth, searching the sides of the road. Tangled vines and thick undergrowth of the tropical forest blocked any escape.

As the shapes loomed larger before him, the bearded man tried to twist around. But the harder he attempted to move his body, the more he found himself locked in place by his wretched fear.

"No, not again," lamented the barbudo. He could only wait....hypnotized by the sight of the charging beasts.

The smaller creature raced ahead of the other one, which ran with a strange hopping stride. As the two shapes passed through shadowed stretches of the road, they came in and out of the man's sight.

"Go 'way!" the man tried to shout. His stricken voice, muted by a debilitating fear, was weak and powerless.

The first creature materialized before him as a black terrier. Scabby and emaciated, the small dog sprinted forward in a rush.

The bearded man felt the sting of its nip, and he stooped to feel the wound. When he checked his fingers, he saw they were smeared with blood.

Hearing a husky snarl from the other wild dog, the man wrenched himself upright.

A German shepherd stumbled to a halt before him, just beyond reach. Where the dog's ears should have been, a few ragged slips of cartilage appeared. Its coat was mottled by mange.

As the earless shepherd wavered in a wide stance, the man saw why it had run in such a peculiar stride. One hind leg was shriveled to half-size and lifted lamely off the ground.

Through the dim light, the barbudo gaped at the glazed eyes of the crippled dog. Dangling from one side of the shepherd's open jaw was a foamy mass of froth.

"Not again," groaned the barbudo with a shudder.

The rabid shepherd made a sickly cough, and the man winced again as a gob of white spittle separated from the dog's slack jaw and splattered in the dirt.

He kicked at the crazed animal.

The shepherd, ducking under the blow, snagged the cuff of the man's pants.

In a corner of his eye, the barbudo spotted the terrier angling in for another pass and he attempted to sidestep the small dog.

Instead, he felt himself begin to lose his balance....falling blindly and helplessly backwards....in an odd slow motion.

Finally, his tailbone exploded in pain on the rutted road. The man's eyes reopened to the shepherd yanking at his pant's cuff.

Jabbing his other foot at the jerking head of the animal, the barbudo managed to free his leg.

The snarling shepherd backed off as the terrier bared its teeth and charged the man's outstretched hand braced in the dirt.

Snatching back his hand, the barbudo heard the dog's teeth click shut and felt flecks of foam from its fevered mouth wet the back of his hand.

The rabid dogs circled, forcing him to rotate on the seat of his pants. As he pivoted, the barbudo flailed his arms out in all directions.

Sensing fear in their victim, the menacing dogs moved nearer, snapping at his feet and hands.

In desperation, the man began to bark back.

When the shepherd paused at the human's odd behavior, the man distorted his face to further bewilder the animal.

At a sudden stab of pain on his thigh, he chopped down at the terrier's head with his hand. It glanced off the dog, which darted away.

Scraping up dirt from the road with his hands, the man heaved it at the frenzied dogs. Again and again, he clawed at the road. His chafing fingertips burned raw before dust began to obscure the dogs' dripping jaws.

As their image faded from his view, it became quiet again on the mountain road. In the unusual stillness, the man found himself shaking uncontrollably.

From out of the void, the terrier abruptly reappeared, circling slowly before him.

The barbudo, swinging his hand to keep the dog at bay, heard a howl building behind his ear.

"No, no," he whimpered. "Not again."

The man attempted to lean away from the bellow of the shepherd, but his shoulders were frozen in place.

He forced his head around and stared into the hideous mouth of the lunging shepherd.

The dog's lips were curled back. Its teeth, drenched in saliva, were inches from his neck.

Movement slowed to an even more tortured pace.

The jaws of the rabid dog opened wider.

19

Sensing the animal's foul breath on his face, the barbudo focused his eyes on slime flowing down the shepherd's swollen tongue.

As the teeth of the beast came nearer, its howl blotted out all thought.

At the anguished scream, the door of the bedroom flew open.

Two muscular, white-uniformed men rushed in....Uzis at the ready. The bodyguards found their bearded president sitting bolt-upright in his bed.

The broad shoulders of Fidel Castro were heaving in short, shallow breaths. His face was coated with sweat.

"Commandante!" called out a bodyguard. "What is it?"

In the blessed safety of his wakefulness, the dazed president of Cuba continued to gaze at the opposite wall.

Few people knew of his recurring dream.

It always began on the same deserted road high in the Sierra Maestra. Two rabid dogs would cause him to stumble. The jaws came at his neck....and then, the merciful end. He awakened.

His phantasmagoria had begun soon after he assumed power in 1959. A friend had urged psychiatric help, but Fidel already knew what triggered the fantasy. And they occurred on the eve of each of his appearances in the Plaza de la Revolucion.

Tomorrow would be the anniversary of the first military action leading to the downfall of Fulgencio Batista's regime.

It would also be Fidel Castro's next appearance in the great Plaza of Havana.

Havana

Plaza de la Revolucion

At midsummer....on the Tropic of Cancer....what kind of man would assemble a million people under the broiling sun?

The CIA man shook his head at his own question, and again scanned the sea of people.

It was five o'clock in the afternoon, and a cruel heat beat down on the vast throng in the windless Plaza de la Revolucion. A few of the people fidgeted. Most stood like mummies.

Lou Fricke wondered whether they were raptly listening to their "Maximum Leader" or simply rendered lethargic by the baking sun. Figuring in the oppressive humidity, he chose the latter.

A miserably hot day like this, mused Fricke, *is only good for making love.* The pleasurable thought distracted him for a few moments.

The occasion for the massive gathering in the Plaza was the 26th of July---a hallowed day for those who practiced the ideology of communism in Cuba. Since the 1960s when the public celebration of religious holidays was prohibited, this date had officially replaced Christmas and Easter as the island's most festive day. It was the anniversary of Fidel's first attempt to overthrow Cuba's previous dictator---in an attack on the Moncada Barracks.

That this day should be celebrated at all mystified Fricke. After studying the CIA file on the attack, he could not fathom why Castro would choose to commemorate his most disastrous day as a guerrilla fighter.

The ill-planned and poorly-executed operation had ended in crushing defeat. Three-quarters of Fidel's men were promptly captured, then tortured to death by Batista's henchmen. Even Fidel and Raul Castro were captured, and they narrowly escaped the same fate. Nevertheless, the 26th of July was Cuba's *Revolution Day.*

Lou and Camille, his interpreter from the U.S. Interests Section, had arrived early in the Plaza. For the last three hours, they had stood in the semi-shade of a telephone pole---one of many erected throughout the 110-acre Plaza carved out of the center of Havana. The tall poles held immense loudspeakers which amplified Castro's voice.

Camille lifted her chin to Lou and accented her acid-clipped words with a glare.

"Don't blow those fumes at me!"

Clenching the offending cigar in his teeth, Lou casually admired the woman's angered face.

Her obsidian eyes glistened beneath velvet-smooth shadows of violet. The pert nose ski-jumped over her tightly-drawn lips, which---in the triple-digit heat of the Plaza---still managed to retain a flawlessly-applied layer of ruby-red.

Lou thought Camille was prettier when agitated, and for a moment he thought to tell her so. Instead, removing the foot-long cigar from his teeth, he smiled broadly.

"Sweetheart, this is a Montecristo---Castro's finest." He offered the soggy end to her. "Here.... have a pull."

Camille twisted her face away. "The stink of it could drop a horse!"

His hurt expression feigned offense.

"And don't call me sweetheart!" she added.

Lou shrugged. As Camille resumed her monotone translation of Castro's speech, he flicked off the cigar's smoldering tip to extinguish it and returned his attention to the Cuban president.

Fidel Castro was speaking from the base of the Jose Marti memorial obelisk at the north end of the Plaza de la Revolucion. The white marble column was the only monument of note in the Plaza.

Lou recalled the candid statement concerning the Cuban patriot in the CIA files at Langley. *Jose Marti was the martyred leader of the 1895-98 Cuban revolution, that culminated in the Spanish-American War---a final conflict which replaced Spain's domination of the island with that of investors from the United States.*

From a distance, Fricke and Castro did not look that dissimilar. Over the last year-and-a-half, the CIA man had taken considerable ribbing from members of The Company for letting his beard grow. When asked the reason for the whiskers, Lou had responded evasively.

In studying the Cuban leader, Lou had been amused at their shared traits. Both men were confirmed but active bachelors, somewhat overweight at six-foot-two, and prodigious readers with photographic memories. Each amused himself with unpredictable behavior and loved sports. Fricke, at 59, was eight years younger.

When a few of Lou's friends at Langley---watching his beard blossom and aware of his assignment---began calling him "Fidel," he regretfully instructed his barber to trim his flowing salt-and-pepper whiskers into a modified Prince Albert style.

Lou checked his watch.

Castro had been addressing his fellow citizens for nearly two hours. Lou knew---from reviewing past "26th of July" speeches---that the Cuban president would continue for several more hours. The previous year's speech had lasted five-and-a-half hours; while two years earlier, it had strung out a full seven hours.

The CIA man leaned against the pole at his back, letting his thoughts drift back to the dawn of the day. He'd entered Camille's studio with innocent intentions. Yet, the visit had taken a bizarre turn. As he tried to fathom the mystery of the woman, the vision of her nude figure eclipsing the rising sun kept appearing in his mind.

The dawn had begun with a hard shot to his head. Not having shaken the cobwebs from his brain yet, Lou was unable to deflect it.

Ducking as the shot whistled past, he felt it cut the air by his ear. Lou thought to tell his opponent she could've put his eye out. Instead, he gave her a disparaging glance.

"Why're you charging my forehand?" haughtily responded Camille, turning her back on him before he could reply.

Plebeian, Lou observed, *that's what she is.* The thought made it easier to lose to the woman. There was no dishonor in defeat when the other person didn't follow his rules. *Good question though,* he grudgingly mused.

He'd been embarrassing himself steadily since 6 a.m. As was their custom for the past four weeks, he and Camille had met in the early morning on the court behind the former U.S. embassy (now officially known as the Swiss embassy where the U.S. Interests Section was based). At mid-summer in Havana, the few hours after dawn were the only tolerable time to chase a tennis ball.

When volleying back-and-forth, the two of them were fairly even. However, Louis Edmonton Fricke IV had never been satisfied in simply getting the point. Triumph had to come with a flourish. Tennis.... polo.... even romance. They were all played out in the same fashion. Most people failed to comprehend his compulsive style.

Plebeians, Lou called them, in the manner of a person born to wealth. He looked down his eagle beak at those he considered ordinary, who weren't concerned with the importance of being distinctive.

Camille dipped to start her serve, then uncoiled her body in the undulating fashion of an ascending cobra. High on her toes, she cracked the ball hard with her racquet.

Admiring the woman as she followed through, Lou once more found himself entranced by the serpentine grace of her figure.

The ball was a blur when it carromed off the white line before him. Believing her serve to be out, he hadn't tried to return it.

"That was good!" insisted Camille, even though she was not entitled to call her own serves.

Lou stared down at the white line. *I'm going blind,* he told himself. Too much that had been clear a few years earlier was now just like the damned ball.

He was almost positive it had missed the line by several inches, but couldn't be sure.

He grumpily strode to the other side of his court to take her next serve.

"Thirty---love!" called out Camille, before unwinding another rocket at him.

He returned it to her backhand, which she promptly clipped into his far left corner.

Racing to the corner, Lou switched his racquet to his left hand and barely caught the ball, weakly popping it over the net.

Camille sprinted forward, but not in time to stop the ball from a double-bounce.

Catching herself at the net, she stood there, hands on hips. "I've never seen that before. How often do you switch hands?"

Lou gave her a smug smile in reply.

The last few years, he'd been changing hands with greater frequency on hard-to-reach shots to his left....and was rather proud of his skill in executing the unorthodox maneuver.

Making an annoyed smirk, Camille stalked back to her service line.

It had been five weeks since Fricke arrived in Havana. When Camille proved to be the only person in the U.S. Interests Section possessing an adequate backhand, he had curbed his caustic humor long enough to charm her onto the tennis court. There were few other daytime distractions available in Havana, particularly to a known member of the CIA. Camille had agreed to tennis in the morning, as long as it was followed by dancing in the evening.

Lou found her to be a no-nonsense player, and he was not unpleasantly surprised to find she often beat him when he let himself fall too far behind. And she didn't seem to mind the bite of his emerging wit as much as most women. He soon learned why.

Camille could exhibit a tart testiness of her own.

Lou had wondered how long he could put up with someone whose temperament was so like his.

It was part of the constant theater he created to entertain himself, though these creations often yielded less than desirable results. Three rapid and costly divorces attested to that....and convinced Lou that he was wholly unsuitable for marriage.

On the other hand, he had been well-suited for a career in the Central Intelligence Agency. As a young man, he had no need for more money, nor a quest for status. That he'd been born into.

After immigrating from Canada, the first Louis Edmonton Fricke had become one of the first shipping magnates of Seattle. The family still owned and operated the largest, privately-held importing concern in the city.

Louis the IV---due to a predilection for tennis and tequila gimlets---had been sent east to the nation's capital, where the family's contributions to both parties assured him a job in any field of his choosing. After a short stint at State, it amazed his family when Lou selected the CIA as a roosting place. But then, they had never understood their likeable misfit.

Lou had blended well into the middle-echelon of The Company. In the late 1960s, the CIA was run like a private club, not that dissimilar to the exclusive clubs which had monopolized his social life back in Seattle.

One of the few difficulties Lou experienced in his early years at Langley was a propensity to lose or misplace most of his twice-monthly paychecks. He never reported the losses. It was the payroll department who complained. Unless the checks were deposited or cashed, they couldn't make their books balance, so a compromise was worked out. Lou requested one yearly lumpsum check, for which he agreed to make a special trip to his bank.

Lou sharply undercut Camille's next serve with bottom-English, placing his shot at her feet. She returned the ball into the net, which evened the score of the game.

They then completed a long volley of hard-hit shots before Lou won the point.

Particularly pleased with their play, he casually called out: "I love you, babe!"

Camille gave him a queer look from across the net.

He'd meant: "I love playing with you, babe!" but an unconscious urge caused him to cut it short.

"Thanks, Mac," she replied with similar offhandedness and pivoted away.

He had used the same four-word compliment the previous evening after they'd completed a provocative rumba. The cool elegance of her dancing had thoroughly captivated him.

Surprised then also, she had not responded at all.

When Lou took the next point and the game, he was certain he'd distracted Camille by his words.

His opponent on the tennis court was well known to Lou long before they met. In preparing for his assignment, he'd reviewed the dossier of every American serving with the U.S. Interests Section in Havana.

Camille Fox, no middle initial, had served in the Caribbean during her entire 21-year career with the State Department. Forty-six years old, five-foot-four, trim brunette. An only child of Irish-Scot ancestry, born and raised in Maine, Princeton MA, plus a mystery the file hadn't explained---she'd never married.

The question had first arisen in Lou's mind when he scanned her picture in the file. The V-shaped face was strikingly pretty....though a bit too sharp-featured to be considered beautiful. Still, the intense face had drawn him back to her dossier several times before he'd left Langley for Cuba.

When Lou met Camille in person, he had stared a bit too long. Everything came to a point. Her chin, pert nose, high cheekbones, even her bosom. And since that first day in Havana, Lou had yet to observe her without a meticulous application of makeup.

Lou had heard Camille often voice sympathy for the common people of Cuba. That pleased him. When she insisted Fidel Castro had eradicated conditions which kept two-thirds of Cuba's population in wretched poverty before his rule, Lou was displeased. He didn't dispute her contention though. To cavil over politics with a good tennis partner would have been gauche.

Lou served well to her backhand, then boldly charged the net, intending to jam her return.

When Camille slammed the ball right at him, his racquet awkwardly deflected the ball out of bounds.

Damn, thought Lou. *I can't even charge her backhand anymore.*

After two hours of play, his trick knee was causing a slight limp, the soles of his feet were aching from the hot surface of the court, and a sore elbow was making too many of his serves half-hearted affairs.

Seeing that perspiration was causing Camille's shirt to cling to her skin, Lou knew the temperature had to be in the mid-90s already. He checked his watch, which displayed 8:15.

"Let's finish this one and call it quits," he suggested.

She nodded and proceeded to win the game..

When they returned to the embassy lobby, Camille was incensed to learn she could not take a shower. Normally, in the energy-deficient capital of Cuba, water was available only during the morning hours of 7:00 to 9:00 and again in the evening at the same hours.

As Camille seethed, Lou held up the two Perrier bottles they'd consumed on the tennis court.

"If you have another bottle of this, I could cool you with it."

Her scowl altered slightly, taking an inquisitive expression.

"Soak it in a washcloth," explained Lou.

Camille debated a moment before heading for the elevators. It sounded like an afterthought when she called out over her shoulder.

"Come on!"

Lou found her manner of speaking to him with her back turned both disconcerting and aggravating. Nevertheless, he quickly caught up. It was the first time the indifferent woman had extended an invitation into her studio apartment.

She tapped the button for an elevator, then pushed harder when no light came on.

"The electricity must be off, too," observed Lou.

It was another common inconvenience visited on the inhabitants of Cuba. For the last three years, electrical power had been cut off sporadically, though it was generally available in the evening so the populace could cook.

After waiting another minute for the elevator door to open, they trudged up the stairway.

Upon unlocking the door to her studio, Camille hesitated, debating whether to leave the door open. Lou thought she'd changed her mind....before she explained:

"When air conditioning's not available, I like to leave my door cracked while I'm home."

Relieved, Lou scanned the studio. The far side of the room, facing east into the morning sun, was filled by a balcony. Its sliding glass door was wide open. As he followed her inside, Lou was enveloped by the sweltering atmosphere of the studio. He thought the air inside the room had to be even hotter than outside. It gave him the uncomfortable sensation of having overstayed a steambath.

Lou paused....trying to convince himself the woman's company in the oven-like room was worth suffering its torrid temperature.

Camille, deciding to close the door, pivoted away toward the bathroom.

"I'll bring towels," she called out. "Why don't you take the sofa's cushions and arrange them on the floor by the balcony."

As Camille entered the bathroom, Lou could tell---by the action of her elbows---that she'd begun to unbutton her blouse. The bathroom door swung halfway closed.

What am I doing here? asked Lou of himself. *I've got a long day and night ahead of me. I should be resting now.* Lou also knew he was expected soon in the office of the Ed Bellin---the Officer in charge of the U.S. Interests Section. His curiosity concerning what might happen next on the sofa cushions kept him in place though.

It might be fun thawing this iceberg, reflected Lou, heading for the sofa. *And while she cools me, I can take a little siesta.*

Carrying the cushions to the balcony, he aligned them along the open door and started to remove his clothes. Camille reappeared when he was down to his tennis shorts.

Lou, catching a glimpse of bare hip as she came forward, realized she'd fully disrobed. One hand suspended two towels before her torso, while the other hand held a pair of washcloths.

He forced himself to stop staring and pretended to be folding his shirt.

After flipping the two washcloths beside the mat of cushions, Camille handed him a towel and deftly wrapped the other one around herself, revealing little.

"I'll get a Perrier out of the refrigerator," she said.

As he removed his shorts, Lou couldn't resist watching as Camille moved away. From the bottom of her towel peeked two slivers of stark-white skin. It was the first time he'd viewed any portion of her figure not deeply tanned by the sun.

With the opening of the refrigerator door, Camille stooped and displayed even more of her untanned derriere.

Abruptly, she twisted around with a bottle in her hand and caught him gaping.

An amused grin crossed her face before she disappointedly stated: "This Perrier is almost room temperature."

Camille took a second closer look at him and snickered. "Where'd you get those? From your sister?"

30

Lou looked down at his jockeys. The neon green briefs had come in a package of other more conservatively-colored briefs, but that didn't sound like an intelligent reply, and he used an elbow to pin his towel modestly to his hip before pushing them off.

Camille had already turned to the mat of cushions by the balcony, ignoring him as he wrapped a towel around his waist.

"You can do my back first," she announced business-like.

Reclining facedown, Camille reached behind to uncover her back and, in the process, bared most of her bun nearest him.

Lou knelt beside the half-moon of lily-white skin left by her bikini. Admiring the firm gluteus maximus and taking in her lean legs, Lou thought he might be viewing a woman hardly out of her teens.

As he reached for the Perrier, she raised an arm to place its hand by her head, affording him a generous view of her breast.

His attention diverted, Lou accidentally toppled the bottle, which bounced off her hip before he caught it. He thought to excuse himself, but she hadn't stirred and his voice would have disturbed the absolute stillness of the room.

Lou paused to compose himself and again scanned Camille's figure, deciding it had been well worth his patience. To him, four weeks had been an exceptionally long wait to reach this point.

Looking across her body, he took in the view over the balcony and mostly saw the graceful curve of the blue-green Gulf of Mexico along the shoreline of Havana. Parallel to the water was the Malecon, upon which hundreds of bicycles flowed. Along more than a mile of the famed boulevard, he spotted only two cars.

Upon arriving in Havana, Lou had been struck by the absence of big-city noise. Its population exceeded two million, yet on any day of the week, the capital of Cuba was as peaceful as Sunday morning in a small Midwestern town.

At Langley, he'd read why the city was so strangely mute....without realizing it at the time.

Cuban physicians were among the few private citizens permitted to purchase gas for their cars. Rare taxis catered to dollar-paying tourists....and Cubans only when they required a ride to a hospital or for a funeral. Most of the country's trucks and buses also were idled by the scarcity of fuel.

Returning his attention to Camille, Lou uncapped the Perrier and saturated a washcloth.

He studied her figure, considering where to begin. In the breezeless, overheated room, her back had acquired a moist glow.

Slipping his hand under her shoulder-length hair, he lifted it off the nape of her neck and drew the wet cloth across the uncovered skin.

"Hmmm," came in a low pleased murmur from the woman.

He'd applied just enough pressure to remove the sticky saltiness of her perspiration and replace it with the Perrier. And, as the carbonized water evaporated, its cooling effect created an exceptionally refreshing sensation on her skin.

Lou unhurriedly brought the cloth down the grove of her backbone and heard another pleasured purr.

After shaking more Perrier on the cloth, he spread it over her far shoulder and drew it along her ribline. At her waist, he flipped the cloth and came up in a new path. When he completed her back, Lou cleansed her arms and legs in the same manner.

With studied caution, Lou brought the cooling cloth down her backbone a second time, then angled toward the unveiled buttock. He guided his hand directly over the half-moon of bared skin with a circling motion. Sensing its sponginess with his fingertips, he started around again.

Camille squirmed, and he quickly lifted off.

When her entire body sank deeper into the cushions, Lou relaxed and reached for the Perrier again.

32

At the same time, Camille's right hand came off the mat and grazed his knee in passing before she gripped the towel still over her back and whipped it off.

Perfect twins, mused Lou. The double half-moons on her lily-white derriere starkly contrasted with the balance of her bronzed figure.

"Do my other one, too," Camille demurely requested.

After bathing the new bun, Lou gently rotated its roundness with his washcloth-covered hand. This again caused her body to stir, and Lou checked her face. Her smile had grown.

I'm enjoying this almost as much as you, he silently told her.

Lou straightened up to rest for a moment and noticed the taut dimples in the small of her back, directly above each bun. Holding up the washcloth, he squeezed drops of the Perrier into the well of each one.

As if this were a signal, Camille lazily brought her upper body off the mat and turned her face to him.

Her dreamy eyes displayed a contentment he'd not seen before. The icy aloofness was gone.

He kept his eyes locked with hers as she eased her body around faceup. When she was supine again, and only then, did Lou lower his own eyes to behold the garden of her body.

The towel was long forgotten.

Lou took it all in for a second, then jerked his eyes back to her face....to see if she was still watching him.

Her eyes were closed, and the trust they seemed to convey discouraged the man from feasting his eyes upon the figure stretched before him. Torn between two impulses, Lou looked out over the balcony again and up into the sky.

One of his fondest delights was drinking in the loveliness of a woman's figure for the first time. Now, this new reaction---the hesitation of his mind to enjoy what his instincts urged---perplexed him.

When Lou returned his attention to the face of the reclining woman, he kept his head to one side. As he dampened the cloth once more, Lou deliberately denied himself a full view of her figure.

Shifting to the top of the mat, he trailed the moist cloth along her hairline, then the balance of her forehead. He dabbed at the curve of her nose, her cheeks, and along her lips.

From Camille's measured breathing, Lou thought she had drifted into sleep as he brought the cloth under her chin, following her neck down to her shoulders.

At last, viewing her bosom....he was both disappointed and astonished. Though the breasts were well-proportioned for her figure, he saw none of the forbidden whiteness that had been so enticing on her backside.

The dark tan across all of her chest blended perfectly with that of her shoulders, and Lou recalled Camille had told him of spending weekends at Varadero---the Riviera of Cuba, some 80 miles east of Havana.

A paradise of sugar-white sandy beaches, the Varadero peninsula was peppered with luxury hotels financed by the Spanish and other European investors. The resorts were reserved primarily for foreign tourists, who spent sorely-needed hard currency, and the elite of Castro's cadre. The reports back at Langley had failed to mention Varadero's beaches were topless, reflected Lou as his eyes now scrutinized the uniquely-flawed portion of the woman's bosom.

Covering most of the surface of each breast was a circular patch of black skin that gave the appearance of being a protective shield. The immense black orbs of her areolas nearly matched the size of his palms, and their unusual size caused Lou to contemplate whether she tanned her bosom to mask the imperfection.

Placing the soothing cloth at the top of her chest, he brought it down, curling around the sweep of the nearest breast....without touching it.

When the cloth came down again, Lou lightly grazed the edge of the breast in coming round. The third time, he led the cloth fully over the tip of her breast.

The cloth's coolness instantly petrified the modified skin of her areola, causing Camille to catch her breath and shiver in the overheated room.

Following the same sequence, Lou tantalized the other side of her bosom. As she shivered once more, Camille's countenance gave the impression of being in deep concentration.

After letting her body calm, Lou traced the line of each of Camille's ribs with his cloth. When he reached her abdomen, he moved in ever narrowing circles until he arrived at her belly button.

"Again, my belly," whispered Camille when he lifted off.

As Lou repeated the circular movements, he decided it was the right time to clear up something that had been bothering him.

He spoke in a low-key tone. "I got a question."

She didn't respond.

Lou studied her tranquil face before continuing.

"We've been playing tennis and dancing now for four weeks," he told her. "Have you enjoyed it?"

A short pause.

"Yes."

Lou kept his voice light. "Well, I wouldn't have known it. You don't sound any friendlier now than a month ago."

Lou continued to massage her belly.

"I've enjoyed your company," she admitted in a toneless voice.

Lou shrugged. "I don't feel that I know you any better today than when we first met."

Her eyes still closed, Camille thought the comment over.

"The less we know each other," she finally said, "the better it'll be."

"The better what will be?"

"When you leave," the woman replied.

"Who said I was leaving?"

"When you first arrived," she told him, "I saw you enter the lobby. All you carried was a satchel and a small suitcase. I figured you for a couple of weeks to a month."

"I'm here to stay," stated Lou, immediately wondering why he'd said what he did. When the operation was over, one way or the other, he'd head back to the States.

Maybe, he reflected, *the way of life down here in Havana is getting to me.* He couldn't remember having a more relaxing time preparing for an operation....or the company of such a challenging woman.

Keeping his fingers light as a feather, Lou closed the circle over the sensitive skin of her belly several more times before speaking in a subdued voice.

"Should I cool everything?"

She said nothing. The only response he could detect was the same scant smile of earlier.

Suspending his washcloth over the fine filaments of her mons, he squeezed enough drops to fully saturate the tiny ringlets.

Lou watched Camille take several deep, silent breaths.

Opening the cloth, he spread it over her upper thigh and pulled the washcloth down to her ankles. After doing the same to the other leg, Lou felt a strain in the small of his back and decided it was time to deliver a grand finale.

Sprinkling the cloth liberally, he placed it over her nearest ankle. Holding the washcloth with both hands, he drew the cloth up her leg and onto her belly. His fingers kept the washcloth spread wide as it flowed over the swell of her breast and came off at her neck. He repeated this from her other ankle. Then draping the cloth over both ankles, he brought it up the very middle of her body.

Lou came upright to view the woman's figure.

Camille was perfectly still. Her face was serene, as if in a trance.

As she remained motionless on the mat, Lou debated. *How do I tell her it's my turn now?* He waited a minute, then another in the quiet room.

His attention drifted out over the open balcony again. The bright sunlight forced him to squint and close his eyes.

He was sitting motionless like a Buddha when spoken words snapped him alert.

"Your turn."

Lou opened his eyes.

Camille was not on the cushions before him, and he looked about.

A few feet away---framed in the azure sky---was a vision he would not forget.

She stood unclad in the door of the balcony, presenting her back to him. His eyes were level with her hips.

Camille's slender legs were drawn together as she stretched high on her toes in the manner of a ballerina, with arms raised to the sky. Her bare body eclipsed the sun, which in turn highlighted her silhouette.

As Camille held the position, Lou thought it might be how an artist would compose an ideal odalisque of a woman.

Ending her stretch, Camille reached down to pick up her towel and wrapped it about her before turning.

Lou reclined facedown on the mat and waited. He was almost shocked when the cool cloth first touched his foot. After cleansing the foot, she massaged it with her bare hands.

"After our grueling workout this morning," Lou told her, "that feels great."

Camille switched feet.

"How'd you wind up in the Caribbean?" he asked.

"I grew up in northern Maine," she replied.

When Camille offered nothing more, Lou inquired: "That's supposed to explain everything?"

Her voice was still a monotone.

"No more long, cold winters....the rain's warm down here....I don't have to scrape ice off a court to play tennis in the winter....the ocean's always perfect for swimming....the diplomatic community is full of fascinating characters. You want more?"

"Why Havana?" Lou asked.

"I particularly like the Cubans," answered Camille easily. "Most of them have an Old World graciousness about them which is not generally found in the other Latin American countries."

From his travels in the hemisphere, Lou had to agree with her statement.

"Why do you think that is?" he inquired, genuinely interested.

"Havana was the political center of Spanish America for more than 400 years," replied Camille thoughtfully. "As revolutions kicked the aristocracy out of other Latin countries, they came to Havana. Cuba was the last capital they lost."

She paused.

"The Cubans must have inherited their manners from the Spanish," concluded Camille.

She moved higher on his leg, going back-and-forth, massaging his calves, knees, thighs, and even his buns with a boldness that he found stimulating.

Camille then shifted to the top of the mat and, with a washcloth in each hand, rolled over his back muscles in long strokes.

His senses were soon overwhelmed. One moment, his muscles relaxed with the kneading; and the next, he felt his skin being soothed by cooling moisture from the cloth.

As she completed his back, Lou had a new concern which became uppermost in his mind when she told him:

"Time to roll over."

Partially raising one side of his body to her, Lou looked behind him for the extra washcloth. He noticed Camille's towel was now draped casually over her thighs.

Spotting the washcloth at her knee, he took it and mantled his tumescence with the cloth as he rolled over....to relax his mind where his body would not.

Eventually, as she worked down his face and shoulders, his concern faded and Lou could concentrate on the comfort offered by the cloth. It was not long before he surrendered to his drowsiness.

Sometime later, he was awakened by a light knock on the door. As Lou grabbed his clothes, he saw that Camille was coiled on the bed across the room, napping with a towel over her waist.

At the second knock, she still did not stir.

Lou was at the door before another rap. He opened it to find Ed Bellin, the officer-in-charge of the U.S. Interests Section.

"They told me I might find you here," commented Bellin in a low voice.

Lou sheepishly grinned.

"Washington wants you upstairs in the communications center," explained Bellin.

As Lou accompanied Bellin down the hall, the CIA man was particularly pleased with the performance in the studio. The woman had done her part well. And in his mind, Lou debated what signals, if any, had been exchanged.

Since he'd reached 50, it was his style to let the woman make the first move. The game was made more interesting by seeing how much encouragement each one required.

As he started up the stairs, Lou wondered what he might have to do in his sixties to make the chase sufficiently challenging.

At the first landing, Bellin thought to make some conversation at the expense of the CIA man.

"I didn't realize you and Camille were so close," commented Bellin.

Lou replied: "It's not what it seems."

"Camille's quite lovely," persisted Bellin. " I can see why you're attracted."

"I'm not that attracted," said Lou, emphasizing the last word.

Bellin turned an inquisitive expression to Lou. "You're not?"

Lou smirked. "She might be a Triple-C."

"A what?"

"A complainer who criticizes and gives lots of commands."

Bellin gave him a grin. "I've never heard that one before."

"You should have met my last two wives," commented Lou.

Neither man spoke again until they entered the communication room on the top floor of the building.

When Lou heard laughter course through the crowd in the Plaza de la Revolucion, he came out of his reverie and asked Camille to repeat what the Cuban president had just said.

"Castro used the word *bolas* in describing the Russians," she replied.

"What's a bolas?" inquired Lou.

"A bowling pin."

He squinted.

"Big bodies....small heads," explained Camille.

Lou nodded as she continued her translating.

The Cuban leader's angry words were directed at the Russians with a vehemence normally reserved for the *Norte Americanos*. Castro described how he had expelled all the Russians after Moscow eliminated their last subsidies to the Cuban island.

Lou snorted. "How about the technicians he's keeping at Lourdes?"

The CIA knew Castro had specifically requested that Moscow leave several score technicians at Lourdes---a communication-monitoring center on the northern coast of Cuba, originally installed by the Soviets during their pre-Glasnost era.

Thinking to relight his cigar, Lou leaned toward his interpreter. "Kim, you got a match?"

"No....and don't call me Kim!"

It was not the first time he had been reprimanded for using the shortened version of her name.

She preferred it otherwise, refusing to explain why when he'd inquired.

You sure run hot and cold, thought Lou with a raised eyebrow.

Her mellowed mood of the morning had been dispelled upon receiving instructions from Bellin to accompany Lou to the Plaza and act as his translator. Lou had mistakenly thought she wouldn't mind standing in the afternoon heat to translate what was certain to be a marathon speech by Fidel Castro.

His eyes swept down her figure, pausing in turn on her slim waist, taut hips, sprinter's calves, and well-defined ankles. The view reminded him of the unforgettable vision on the balcony, and Lou silently told himself, "Thank God, it's hot in Havana."

The crowd applauded and Lou asked: "What'd Muttonhead say?"

"Aren't you listening to my translation?" inquired Camille.

"I got distracted."

Camille paused to concentrate on the remainder of Castro's statement, then spoke.

"He promised the price of rice would be reduced 15 percent by October."

Lou chuckled. A few weeks earlier, the CIA informed President Steiner that China had secretly notified Castro that their subsidized price of rice to Cuba would be increased by 20 percent in the fall.

As Camille continued, the CIA man surveyed the crowd in the sprawling Plaza de la Revolucion. He estimated they numbered over a million. Lou wanted to check the roof of the National Theater, but scrupulously avoided looking in that direction. That he and Camille had been followed from the embassy and were being watched closely was a certainty.

The Oval Office

President Allan Steiner, seated on a sofa in the Oval Office, was hunched over a coffee table studying a map of the Caribbean. Twelve feet away on the opposite wall, Fidel Castro's face was on the TV screen. The Cuban leader was obviously speaking, but his voice had been muted on the set.

"This could backfire," stated Steiner. "Just like the Bay of Pigs."

"Mr President"---CIA Director Edward Rolle added a broad smile to his confident tone---"it won't backfire."

Rolle had visions of 22 months of work going down the drain---the length of time he'd devoted to the creation of *Havana Heat.*

"How can you be so certain?" demanded the President.

Rolle contemplated the vexed face of Steiner a moment. "Our plan may or may not succeed, sir...but it won't backfire."

"Why not?"

Rolle hesitated. At the project's inception, it had been agreed that the presidency would maintain the capability of "plausible denial." While Steiner had authorized the overall goal of *Havana Heat,* he had been deliberately kept in the dark concerning details of its implementation.

"Mr President, are you positive you want me to answer that question?"

Steiner ground his teeth. He had been voicing the same reservations for the last three months....and getting the same brick wall. On each occasion, Rolle, or someone else, had reminded him of the need for the presidency to remain unaware of the details....and therefore untainted by the covert action should it become public knowledge.

"To hell with plausible denial!" exclaimed Steiner. "How can I run this damned office if I don't know what's happening?"

Rolle raised an eyebrow, gave the President a few seconds to reverse his decision, then began.

"Sir, the equipment in Cuba can't be traced to us. Each component was made in Hungary. If Castro finds it, he'll blame them."

The revelation brought the glint of a grin to Steiner.

Rolle couldn't resist the suggestion. "Would you like us to arrange for the equipment to be found by Castro's security people....later?"

"No!" The President abruptly shook his head. "Let's not complicate this anymore."

Steiner stood and strolled to the open French doors leading to the Rose Garden. The fragrance of the roses was heady, and he was encouraged to breathe deeply of their aroma.

As he surveyed the symmetry of the garden, Steiner considered how he'd been talked into the Cuban scheme in the first place.

First, the CIA had unveiled the rumor from an Egyptian diplomat in Paris. Algeria, with its emerging nuclear capability, was planning to distribute low-yield nuclear bombs among a few of its Third World allies---a ploy to prevent their threatened seizure by the super-powers. As Algeria's oldest ally, Cuba would be an early recipient. Steiner half-suspected the rumor had been started by the CIA in Langley.

One month later, the origin of the rumor no longer mattered.

CIA Director Rolle delivered the clincher. Beyond any doubt, Chinese technicians were now helping Castro finish the nuclear power plant on the southern coast of Cuba which had been left uncompleted by the Soviets. While Moscow had made a tacit agreement with the White House to control the plutonium produced by the Cuban plant, the damn

Chinese wouldn't even admit they were assisting Castro, much less agree to withhold its plutonium from the Cuban dictator.

The volatile Castro, with the plutonium necessary to build a nuclear bomb available from his own power plant, needed only borrow the technology from his Algerian friends in order to pose another nuclear threat to the United States.

Angered at being forced to make a hasty decision, Steiner finally agreed to the CIA's covert action. The opportunity to use the *Havana Heat* scenario occurred only once a year---July 26th, in the Plaza de la Revolucion.

The CIA had maintained it was only a minor operation, hardly qualifying as a "covert action." Rolle had initially referred to it as a mere pinprick...that, nevertheless, might pop Castro's balloon.

Steiner pivoted in the doorway to face Rolle. "How did the software enter Cuba?"

Again, the CIA Director paused. Knowing the danger of revealing more, he was deliberately vague.

"The Canadians have been more than cooperative," replied Rolle.

Steiner nodded thoughtfully. "Does their ambassador in Havana know of it?"

"Supposedly not." Rolle added: "We worked with an attache."

"How'd you manage that?"

"The man's a long-time contact. And even he doesn't know what the students intend to do with it."

"Students," repeated Steiner. "How were they recruited?"

Rolle rubbed his chin and posed his own query. "Mr President, I thought you didn't want to know the particulars?"

Allan Steiner grimaced. He did and he didn't.

Among a few confidants trusted not to repeat his views, he often complained that the Oval Office was a straitjacket. There was no escape from the never-ending state of crisis surrounding the presidency. During his second term, Steiner had attempted to downgrade the number of events quali-

44

fying as a crisis, particularly those created by the press. The plan worked less often than anticipated, mostly because Steiner was ever mindful of permitting a minor problem to mushroom.

The President waved a hand as if to dismiss caution. "I think my need to know is greater than any future need *not* to know."

"It was a simple matter" began Rolle. "There are more than 750,000 Cubans in Miami and most of them have family---"

A buzzer sounded on Steiner's desk. "General Steel is here, sir."

The President leaned into his intercom. "Send him in."

Plaza de la Revolucion

Raising his wrist, Lou checked his watch. It had been 40 minutes since the sun set. Though a few stars were becoming visible in the moonless sky, the air was still stifling hot in the great Plaza.

The weak lighting strung on the telephone poles overhead suddenly dimmed significantly, indicating to the CIA man that current was being drawn elsewhere. He spoke in a friendly theatrical tone to Camille.

"A shroud of darkness fell over the crowd."

When she turned to give him a curious glance, Lou changed the subject.

"The faces out there remind me of children staring at a TV set."

"They're in an Alpha state," Camille commented, "just like the other 9 million inhabitants of this island watching on their televisions."

Not for long, Lou told himself. He glanced at the second hand of his watch again and quietly announced in her ear:

"Showtime."

Six seconds later, on a beige stone wall across the plaza, the 40-foot high mural depicting the scowling face of Che Guevara came to life.

His face was a bright yellow, accented by blue eyes and thick eyebrows. Che's fiercely handsome countenance, having moved off the wall a short distance, transformed into a three-dimensional head.

The holographic image halted Castro in mid-sentence.

"Che!" was shouted by isolated voices in the crowd.

As more of the throng turned from the muted Castro to view the supernatural image, their voices built to a chant. The phantom form suspended in air over the Plaza was that of *the patron saint* of the Cuban revolution....an icon that Castro had encouraged in order to manipulate his people. The chant became a roar.

"CHE!...CHE!...CHE!"

Cubans on streets leading into the Plaza de la Revolucion surged forward to better view the eerie incarnation.

Lou used his hands on the shoulders of those nearby to keep Camille from being crushed. Realizing this wouldn't work much longer, he reached down and gripped her arms at the elbows.

"Put me down!" she shouted as he lifted her.

Lou ignored her demand and raised the woman even higher. When her hips were even with his shoulders, he yelled back.

"Spread your legs!"

A pause.

"What?" screeched Camille.

The people around them closed the gap where she had stood, and when Camille saw it was impossible to be put back down, she permitted Lou to prop her on his shoulder.

Seconds later---upon being jostled by the unruly crowd---she fully comprehended his request. Tucking the front of her skirt between her thighs, Camille worked one leg over his head to straddle the other shoulder.

The angry face of Che began to pivot in place, as if reviewing the crowd.

The chant of his name became deafening.

On the platform of the Jose Marti monument, the people's El Commandante grabbed the collar of his State Security chief.

"Find the fool with the projector!" Castro bellowed into his face. "Find the fool with the projector!"

Castro swung back around to watch the image of Che---his former trusted aide, theoretician, and guerrilla tactician. It was incredulous to the Cuban dictator that any citizen would dare interrupt his speech with such a prank.

Fidel Castro could only watch helplessly as the throng in the plaza released their thunderous enthusiasm for the long-dead Guevara, whose hero cult exceeded even that of the Cuban President.

The aberrant image suddenly vanished.

In a matter of seconds, the chanting also died away. It was replaced by an excited murmuring in the plaza. Castro approached his bank of microphones again, to regain the crowd's attention. He planned to praise his former comrade-in-arms. And to ask for even greater sacrifices of all Cubans, pointing out that Che had made the ultimate sacrifice.

Just below him, Castro saw that his TV cameras had reversed their direction in order to film Che's appearance. He thought to shout to the TV crew and demand they return to him, but decided that wouldn't be necessary. The cameramen would come back when they heard his voice.

Leaning into his microphones, Castro looked out over the crowd and opened his mouth to speak....and froze.

Che had reappeared. His face was still yellow, and highlighted by a bluish silver. The 40-foot tall hologram of the revolutionary martyr had moved higher, to a position above the center of the great square.

Che's voice boomed over the Plaza of the Revolution.

"CUBANS!"

A pause electrified the air, and Lou felt Camille's legs tighten in fear around his neck.

"WHAT ARE YOU DOING....TO DEFEND THE CONQUESTS....FOR WHICH WE GAVE OUR LIVES?"

In the sudden quiet, Camille bent down to whisper into Lou's ear.

"That's a quote from Emiliano Zapata, the Mexican revolutionary."

"I know," Lou whispered back.

Che's voice---louder this time---repeated its challenge to the paralyzed crowd.

48

The press of woman's thighs tightened even more about Lou's neck. Their warm lushness felt good, and he almost regretted he'd have to pry her knees apart if she panicked further.

After another short pause, Che's face pivoted to face the Jose Marti memorial and Castro.

"FIDEL, MY BROTHER! WHY HAVE YOU TAKEN AWAY OUR FREEDOMS?"

The crowd took in a collective gasp.

Until now, they had believed Che's appearance was a planned part of the evening's choreography. The public challenge to their president was unprecedented.

Castro felt a constriction of his legs, as if the hands of Che were clutching his ankles. The sensation immediately reminded him that the hands of Che, in reality, were only a few feet away.

Within a small room inside the Jose Marti monument---directly below the spot where Castro stood---a grisly display could be seen by selected guests. Enshrined in this room were the amputated hands of Che Guevara. A military shirt of the dead guerrilla leader had been found, and the severed hands were fitted into its sleeves.

Stepping away from his lectern, Castro again grabbed his State Security jefe and shrieked into the stricken man's face:

"*Kill* the fool with the projector! *Kill* the fool with the---"

His voice was drowned out.

"FIDEL....RETURN OUR FREEDOMS!"

In a rage, Castro swung around to glare at his former partner.

Che shortened his call.

"RETURN OUR FREEDOMS!"

The three words came again and again until the throng in the Plaza de la Revolucion magnified the voice of Che to a crashing crescendo of their own.

Finally, Che's words abruptly stopped and his image faded into the evening sky.

Within minutes, every room in the government buildings bordering the Plaza was occupied by members of Cuban State Security searching for a projector....or any other device which might have created the hologram. They found nothing.

Had they looked as rapidly in the nearby National Theater just off the Plaza, they might have caught two students scurrying down stairs into the basement. The pair carried electronic devices which were secreted in one of hundreds of trunks containing costumes in a labyrinth of storage rooms.

Several long blocks away, the Cathedral of Havana was soon filled with people, most of whom had not entered its sanctuary in years. Many religious Cubans---being a superstitious lot---mixed their Catholicism with a liberal dose of ancient voodoo. *Surely, tonight, the martyred hero of their revolution had appeared before them.*

Citizens reveled in the streets, celebrating the return of Che, who had been killed by Bolivian army forces in the hills of that country 28 years earlier.

Reluctantly, Lou had taken Camille off his shoulders after leaving the Plaza. He was in no hurry to return to the embassy, though Camille prodded him in that direction. The CIA man was more interested in observing the reaction of the Cuban populace in the aftermath of his show.

The inflamed citizens of Havana appeared to be of two minds, depending on their participation in the largess of Cuba's one-party system.

Government ministry employees, officials of the 40,000-plus Committees for the Defense of the Revolution, Communist Party members, Rapid Action Brigade thugs, and those who held lucrative jobs in the state-controlled distribution of goods and services defended the status quo. They had much to lose.

Others in the poorly-lighted streets of Havana displayed a deep-seething anger. Their personal freedoms had been restricted for decades....their poor quality food was severely rationed....their consumer items, also rationed, were shoddy and rarely available....and decent shelter required years of waiting, provided one was politically connected.

The unprivileged majority throughout Cuba suffered a daily reminder of their privations whenever they turned on their television sets and viewed the programs beamed from Miami by the U.S.-sponsored TV Marti. The majority had everything to gain.

Confrontations between these two factions were evident on every street corner. When they became increasingly vocal and violent, Lou assented to Camille's request and the two of them ducked into the open door of a cabaret. Over the door was a neon sign advertising El Pollo.

✈ ✈ ✈

El Pollo

Lou and Camille paused just inside the entrance of El Pollo, letting their eyes partially adjust to the cabaret's darkened interior. A thick haze of cigarette smoke hung in the air, further obscuring their vision.

Most of the light came from a floorlamp used by the three-piece combo playing in back. Lou's attention also was drawn to a dying fluorescent tube overhanging the bar to the right of the door. The flicker of the tube kept tempo with the spasmodic efforts of the combo. In the weak light, Lou thought the cabaret to be nearly empty.

"Let's stay close to the door," implored Camille.

"Sure," replied Lou. Putting out a hand to check for obstructions, he guided her through a maze of chairs to a booth. Lou took the side giving him a view of the entrance to the cabaret, letting Camille face the dance floor.

When his knees hit hers in sitting, Lou repositioned his feet and put his hands out to where a table should have been. His hands wandered in thin air.

"Where's the table?" Lou inquired.

Camille hesitated to explain. In their haste to get off the streets, they had selected one of the many cabarets in the Vedado district of Havana which offered an optional amenity to customers. In the mid-1960s---to accommodate the needs of their customers---these cabarets had removed the tables in their booths. This was due to an increasingly severe shortage of housing in the Cuban capital. The deliberately dark cabarets offered an inexpensive alternative to young couples seeking a certain privacy.

"Let's get another booth with a table," suggested Lou, looking over his shoulder. It was too dark to see distinctly into the next booth.

"I doubt if any of them have tables," Camille replied.

"Why not?"

"This is a place for lovers," she explained.

Lou glanced aimlessly about. "What's that have to do with no tables?"

"For a widely-travelled man," said Camille in an amused tone, "you're rather naive."

Getting her point, that the booths doubled as beds, Lou asked: "Why don't lovers just go to a motel?"

"They do," she replied. "The government runs a large chain of special motels that rent by the hour. They're called *posadas.*"

"So why do lovers come here then?"

"I've heard waiting in line for a posada," explained Camille, "is usually longer than the stay."

Lou chuckled. Another fact the CIA files hadn't mentioned concerning the inconveniences of Castroland.

The entrance to El Pollo was less than 20 feet away, and he could still hear the angry shouting from the street.

Camille reached over to the inside wall of the booth and rapped on the wood. "This is where we put our drinks."

Extending his hand, Lou found a four-inch ledge he hadn't noticed before.

"Buenos noches!"

Lou, flinching at the sharp greeting, turned and found a vague outline of a man standing over him.

The waiter leaned into the booth to speak. "I heard your English. Are you from Canada?"

"We're Americans," announced Camille.

"We're *all* Americans," amended the waiter in a friendly tone. "What would you like to drink?"

"A bottle of Hatuey," Camille said.

"Make it two," added Lou.

Cigars and the frothy amber beer were among the few consumer items of quality produced on the island. Hatuey resembled the dark Dos Equis of Mexico in taste and was often smuggled aboard homeward bound flights by tourists.

"Do you wish cushions?" inquired the waiter matter-of-factly.

"No!" Camille's curt reply dismissed the waiter, who sank back into the inky gloom.

Lou started to ask, "Why the cushions?" but a figure at the entrance to the El Pollo diverted his attention.

In the light of the open door, a gaunt man wearing a panama hat had appeared. The CIA operative recognized the yellow-banded hat with its brim bent down all around. Back in the Plaza de la Revolucion, its owner had hovered behind them.

The thin man drew hard on his cigarette, and the resulting flare revealed a chinless face with sunken cheeks.

Camille, noticing Lou's concentration on the newcomer, asked: "Who is that?"

"No-Chin's been following us since the rally," replied Lou. "He's with the local SS."

"The what?"

"State Security," explained Lou.

No-Chin eased into a chair near the bar as the three-man combo suddenly discovered a rhythm.

Promptly, a couple sprouted from the booth behind Lou which he'd believed to be empty. The man wore baggy trousers and an open shirt. His tall blonde partner adjusted her mini-skirt and yanked her tanktop down as they headed for the small circle of marble which served as a dance floor.

"I'm getting a headache," said Camille.

"Must be the air in here," ventured Lou.

The band had slipped into a sassy mambo, encouraging a second couple to step onto the marble circle. The new female sported short-shorts and a black band of silk for a halter, while her partner was dressed in white. Lou thought both couples moved with the grace of professional dancers.

He was straining his eyes to admire the muscled thighs of the women when a bright light momentarily blinded him.

A single powerful strobe flashed over the dancers, freezing their limbs in a different position every half-second.

By the stark patches of new light, Lou observed that the cabaret was actually two-thirds full. He was amused to see couples scrambling in every booth to adjust their clothing and come to upright positions.

"Geez!" he exclaimed. "Sex must be the national pastime in this country."

"They don't have much choice," replied Camille in a sardonic tone. "Everything else is either not available or too expensive."

Lou's attention returned to the long legs of the blonde. With each flash of the strobe, her mini-skirt edged a bit higher, revealing nothing but skin to his eyes.

After a quarter-minute, the harshness of the strobe blurred the repeating images of the dancers. Clamping his eyes shut, Lou was certain the blonde wore nothing at all under her skirt.

Looking again, he saw that one side of the mini-skirt had ridden all the way up her hip. Flawless, mused Lou, at the rippling muscles of the woman's thighs. The strobe served to accentuate their definition.

He rubbed at his eyes. Back in the Plaza during the rally, he'd observed an unusually large percentage of women with equally stunning legs.

Glancing to Camille, he realized she'd been watching him stare at the dancers. He felt compelled to explain his attention. "The ladies on this island have terrific muscles....I mean, legs."

"Do you know why?" she asked.

Lou shook his head.

"Two years ago," Camille began, "Castro decreed that anyone who travelled to work less than 12 miles had to use a bicycle."

"Great idea," declared Lou. "We should do the same in the States."

They silently watched the dancers. Though the couples swayed in harmony on the marble dance floor, the strobe gave them a highly-charged, convulsive character.

When the mambo faded, the combo took on a heavier beat and both couples immediately repositioned themselves. The men stood behind their partners, who began to gyrate their hips in a circular movement. Each man began to punch his pelvis forward, and the combined movements of each couple became highly suggestive.

"Is that a dance?" Lou inquired.

"It's called El Pollo," said Camille, translating: *"The Chicken."*

Lou squinted at her. "Why?"

Her grin was made wicked by the flashes of light.

"You'll see."

Lou continued to stare at the dancers.

"Is the blonde wearing anything?" he ventured.

"A thong," said Camille.

He eyeballed the blonde again.

"It's skin-colored," explained Camille.

The beat of the combo quickened, and the male dancers now held the shoulders of the women as they thrust their hips forward.

"Have you see this before?" asked Lou.

Camille didn't answer immediately. "Once....at a party."

The distance between the dancers narrowed, and the males began to jerk their heads in the manner of a strutting rooster.

"I don't remember anything like this the last time I was in Havana," observed Lou thoughtfully.

"When was that?" inquired Camille.

"Before Castro took over."

"What were you doing in Havana?" she asked.

"I was an information officer with the embassy. Spent most of my time bailing drunk Americans out of jail."

The distance between the dancers had nearly closed, and the men's hands had dropped to the waists of their partners. A second orange-colored strobe began alternating with the white one.

Though the constant shock of the strobes pained his eyes, Lou still attempted to focus on the

56

surrealistic scene.

The bodies of each dancing couple appeared to collide as the male dancers---with a combined forward and upward motion---bumped their partners.

The band gained volume, and the male dancers began bouncing their partners completely off the marble floor. Patrons of the cabaret, caught up in the dance, cheered each thrust.

Due to the blurring of his vision, Lou had to look away. He rested his eyes by watching the repeating image of Camille's face made by the strobes. She appeared mesmerized.

Lou eased out of their booth, blocking her view. "Let's go," he told her.

Outside the club, the crowds had lessened and Camille asked: "Why'd we leave in the middle of the dance?"

Lou had her hand as they hurried down the street. "I don't feel like having a chaperon anymore," he replied. "No-Chin's busy watching the show."

After a brisk half-hour walk, they reached the embassy. In the elevator, Lou told her: "I have to go topside and make a report."

Camille pulled the front of her blouse off her clammy skin. "I need another shower and I'm certain the water's off now."

Her voice was not angry as it had been in the morning, and Lou decided her words might be more of an invitation than an offhand comment.

"Have any Perrier left?" he cautiously posed as the elevator door opened.

Stepping out, Camille spoke over her shoulder: "You're first this time."

The door closed before Lou could reply. At the top floor of the building, he entered the Communications Room to prepare his version of the evening's events for his superiors back at Langley. The first stage of *Havana Heat* had proceeded as planned, and Fricke strongly recommended the next stage in his written report.

Twenty minutes later, he pushed the elevator button for Camille's floor. As the elevator descended,

Lou leaned wearily against a wall. This island's getting to me, he thought. I'm devoting as much time to romance as to my work. It's too hot to sleep now anyway, he told himself.

Standing before her door, he raised his hand to knock before realizing it was already ajar a few inches. Lou pushed it open to peer inside. No lights were on in the room, and a sparse light shone from the open balcony.

"Come in," encouraged Camille.

At her sleepy voice, Lou stepped inside and closed the door. He shuffled his feet in the direction of the balcony where her voice had come from. A hand caught his leg, and below him, Lou recognized Camille's uplifted face.

"Lay down on the cushions," she encouraged him, "and I'll do you."

Lou paused at the softly spoken words.

"I have two bottles of Perrier this time," she said.

45 Minutes Earlier

GITMO

'Gitmo' is the nickname for the oldest overseas military base held by the United States, and the only one on hostile soil. Seven thousand Americans---Marines, Navy, and Coast Guard---occupy Guantanamo Bay Naval Base. Located at the southern tip of Cuba, its boundaries are roughly 9 miles east-to-west and 6 miles north-to-south.

Some refer to Gitmo as "the Country Club." If you play golf, your scores will improve remarkably at this isolated military post. Tee-shots drive an extra 50 yards on the dry fairways. Ever since Castro's guerrillas contaminated the outside water supply in 1958, all water for the base is manufactured in a desalinization plant.

The base was originally leased from the newly-independent Cuba in 1903, after the Rough Riders helped kick the Spaniards off the island. When Fidel Castro came to power, he stopped cashing the yearly checks ($4,000), declining to recognize the lease agreement.

Colonel Thomas Hemingway---commanding officer of all Marines stationed on Gitmo---lounged before a TV in the bedroom of his residence.

A few years earlier, Hemingway had distinguished himself as a Harrier pilot in the Persian Gulf War. A general's star might have resulted if he hadn't been a party to the violation of General Order No. 1, which had been issued out of respect to local Muslim religious leaders in that field of operations. No alcohol was to be consumed by American servicemen in Saudi Arabia.

Hemingway picked up his promotion to full colonel, but he knew that was the limit. Instead of a desk job in Washington with a future, he was given the Marine command on Gitmo. It included VMA-223, the "Bulldog" Harrier squadron. Since half of VMA-223's 20 AV-8Bs rotated every three months with the other half at Cherry Point, North Carolina, his duties were quite tolerable. Most Marine personnel considered the Caribbean base a choice duty assignment.

Three hours into Fidel Castro's July 26th speech, Hemingway was in sole command of the remote control to the bedroom TV set. His Swedish-born wife, Sandi, also reclined on their king-size bed, reading a book. In the sticky heat, he wore skivies. She wore nothing.

With his left hand, Tom roughly worked the sore muscles of his right shoulder, moving his arm in a circular motion.

His actions jiggled Sandi across the bed.

"When're you going to stop playing that silly football?" she chided.

"It's not silly."

"Tom"---she looked him directly in the eye---"when you play against men more than half your age, that's *exactly* what it is!"

Two weeks had passed since Hemingway returned from the annual Alumni-Varsity game at The Citadel, with his usual array of injuries. At the age of 41, Hemingway was still starting the linebacker position he'd played there as a student two decades earlier. After the game, the varsity quarterback had crossed the field to congratulate Tom on the three times he'd been sacked by a man twice his age. Sandi had been standing beside her husband when he received the compliment.

At the time, Hemingway had told no one of the muscle tear he suffered late in the third quarter. He'd heard the tissue rip and prudently used the other shoulder to finish the game. Within ten minutes of the game's end---as his body cooled---the tear totally immobilized his shoulder.

So far, Tom had regained 60 percent use of the arm on his injured side. He'd still told no one other than Sandi of the tear, as it had not been incurred in the line of duty and he didn't wish to be grounded by the flight surgeon. The monthly flight pay came in handy.

His injury aggravated Sandi far more than it did him. She was impatient to resume their racquetball. Since they had left Saudi Arabia, she'd put on some pounds and depended on their daily play to not gain more.

As she turned a page of her book, Sandi glanced at the TV, then to her husband. "Why're you still watching the Castro rally?"

Tom paused. A top-secret order had been relayed to the base---all field-grade officers were to watch Castro's speech. He repeated his earlier response to her.

"Fidel fascinates me."

"Is he saying anything interesting?"

"Of what I understand," replied Tom, "it's pretty monotonous."

"How much do you understand?" she asked.

"Two-thirds," offered Tom. "Cuban Spanish is more rapid-fire than the Spanish I learned in San Diego. Cubans drop their endings."

"Oh." Sandi went back to her book.

Tom shifted positions in order to use her bare hip as a headrest, then gripped one of her calves with both hands and kneaded it.

"You watch too much TV," she told him without looking up.

A hand eased over her knee.

"You should read a good book once in a while," she continued.

Half-listening to the TV, Tom inquired: "What're you reading?"

"Hanto Yo." After a pause, Sandi added: "A spiritual story."

"What's it about?"

"The Sioux Indians," she replied.

"I'm not too interested in cowboys and Indians."

"There're no cowboys."

"Then"---he palmed her underthigh like a football---"I'm definitely not interested."

"I think you could be."

"Doubt it," he replied.

While Sandi started backtracking through the pages she'd already read, Tom lightly traced the skin of her thigh with his fingertips.

As she fished through pages, Sandi pushed his roving hand down to her knee again.

"Here," she said, smoothing the book pages. "This is what the Sioux do on the morning of their wedding."

She began to read.

"As he sang he pushed back her hair and lifted water to her face. Next he moved around her and washed her shoulders and back. And then, turning her to him, he carefully thoroughly bathed the front of her---"

Tom interrupted. "I thought you said this was a spiritual book."

Sandi skipped down a few paragraphs.

"And when she seemed at ease again, he pushed her gently down against the water, his fingers carefully spreading the mysterious warm lips his hand had covered; he invited the power that moved the waters to touch upon the woman's sheath and help her reach wonder and marvel."

Looking up from the book, Sandi repeated the last line of the paragraph.

"And so this man bathed the woman he would make his wife."

Tom raised an eyebrow, his attention still on the TV screen. "Who wrote that?"

"A woman. It took her 20 years."

"Long time."

"It was translated from modern English into a Sioux dialect by a medicine man after she wrote it....then re-translated back to English using an 1806 Webster dictionary, retaining the Indian idiom."

"Interesting," Tom said in a deadpan. "When's the movie coming out?"

Sandi tapped him over the head with the book. "You boob!"

"Hey," protested Tom, raising a hand in self-defense "The book sounds good, but I gotta listen to Castro right now."

Sandi bent over to kiss the spot she'd hit, playfully placing a breast in his eyes.

On the TV screen, the cameraman clumsily panned the crowd in the plaza. Tom held her breast as he moved his head away to better see the television.

At the touch of his hand, Sandi suggested: "Let's make a baby."

"There's something happening," said Tom.

Sandi came upright, her voice testy. "You watch too much TV."

"They're doing a light show with Che Guevera."

"A what?"

"Shh."

Sandi rolled away in a pout. "Don't shush me!"

Tom was busy with the remote control, increasing the sound. He came off the bed and crouched before the set. Seeing how serious her husband was, Sandi joined him.

At the conclusion of Che's appearance, she asked what it meant.

"It could be a beginning," Tom told her.

"Of what?"

"A revolution," said Tom.

A pause.

Sandi looked confused. "I thought they already had one."

"So did they."

Midnight

Swiss Embassy

Lou disrobed in silence, wondering how much better Camille could see than he.

Glancing out over the balcony, he spotted a few isolated buildings in the distance with burning lights. They were tourist hotels which stood out like bright islands in the otherwise blacked-out city, and Lou recalled with nostalgia the 1950s when Havana had been the premier playground of the Caribbean. Its nightlife had been as garish and radiant as Las Vegas in the 1990s.

Since the light in the deeply-shadowed studio was so poor, he decided to recline on his back first.

Camille applied a wetted cloth, refreshing his face, shoulders, and arms in quick order. This time, she did not bother to knead the muscles beneath, but she did pause to manipulate his fingers. As she worked each one separately, Lou thought it was the most pleasurable of all her touches that day.

He was only half-awake when Camille finished his fingers and moved to his abdomen. The soothing cloth described several circles about his belly before unexpectantly grazing his groin in making a path down his thigh. This caused him to come alert, and Lou debated whether she'd deliberately meant to tease him....in the same way he'd teased her earlier in the day. When she reached his foot, Camille lingered on his toes as she had on his fingers.

Lou was completely relaxed when she started up his other leg. As the cloth reached his thigh, he tensed in expectation....and was rewarded with another bold pass of the cloth.

So, it wasn't casual after all, Lou told himself. *And she's done twice what I dared only once in the morning.*

"Roll over," Camille gently murmured.

His body seemed heavy as Lou lifted himself to turn over. He'd barely settled when he felt Camille moving over him to straddle his legs. He stiffened as she adjusted herself into a sitting position over his thighs.

A moment later, both her hands compressed the small of his back. In each hand was a washcloth, and as she pushed her hands toward his shoulders, her cheeks gradually came off his thighs.

With the return of her hands to his waist, her loins melted back into his legs, giving him a sublime sensation. He wanted to tell her how fine it felt, but his mind was completely obsessed by the repeating release and press of her loins to his thighs.

Camille suddenly stopped.

Disappointed, Lou anxiously searched for the right words to request she continue. Before he could express himself, she shifted. To reach the very top of his shoulders with her hands, Camille had moved higher on his body.

Her precious loins now flattened over his own, their touch electrifying his entire body. A moment later, when they lifted off, as her hands again flowed up his back, Lou breathed again.

As Camille returned and sank back into him, the contact triggered an involuntary tightening of his hips.

This is backwards, he thought. *This time, I'm the one having a meltdown.*

Lou found his mind and body entering a state of absolute acquiescence, and he could not recall when his senses had been so wonderfully overwhelmed by a woman. As their loins blended again and again, Lou felt each time an immensely-satisfying union with the woman.

When Camille paused to rest directly atop him, she reached behind to knead a strain in the small of her back. In doing so, she unwittingly made a small grinding motion with her torso that drove her buttocks even deeper into his, rendering Lou numb with renewed pleasure.

You can stop it in a year, he silently mouthed.

For some time, Camille alternated the massaging of his back and then resting upon him.

Later, when she eased entirely off to kneel beside him, he found his whole body stiff with a tension that was almost painful. As she massaged down the back of his thighs to his feet, the tenseness slowly unwound.

Finishing, Camillé asked: "How was that?"

"Finest kind," he told her, rolling onto his side and facing the balcony.

The moon had peeked over the horizon of the Gulf of Mexico; and, in the newly-emerging light, he glanced down his torso to a minor problem.

"Now, it's your turn," said Camille, "to do me, too."

"Can I rest for a minute?" asked Lou, thinking time might dissipate some of his tumescence. As he remained on his belly, his thoughts drifted to another persisting problem that had troubled him off and on since his arrival in Havana.

Before most field operations, Lou was accustomed to having a few qualms, but his mind had always managed to rationalize them away. This time, however, the doubts had remained....and he couldn't decide which one bothered him the most.

In his mind, each of the compelling factors furnished to the Oval Office to gain approval of *Havana Heat* was sufficient in itself to justify the mission....though each factor was based primarily on conjecture. On this occasion, unlike 1962, there was no hard evidence....no aerial photos of missile sites....or hostile ships bringing in missiles. A preponderance of circumstantial evidence had swayed President Steiner. However, lacking total confidence, Steiner refused to make a full commitment and approved only a scaled-down operation.

Still, the doubts kept coming back. Would Castro's State Security discover the small ring of university students? To what length would the Cuban president go to protect his position? How many people might die? Was it worth toppling the Cuban dictator, who was still a hero to a major segment of his people? Or might the aging Castro fall of his own accord soon?

Why am I so worried? wondered Lou. It's only a minor operation. Hell, maybe nothing more will come of it than what's happening in this room.

He raised up on an elbow and glanced to his waist. It was safe to move, and Lou exchanged places with Camille.

The rising moon cast its light directly into the studio, giving Lou a snowy view of her figure. He wetted an edge of cloth and dragged it down her backbone, lifting the cloth off at her waist.

Encouraged by the intimacy Camille had demonstrated, Lou placed his lips inches from the nape of her neck and let his warm breath announce his presence.

Noting the perfumed scent of her hair, he nuzzled his nose within it; and, but for a moment, he touched his lips to her neck. Then, wishing to taste of the woman, he lightly led the tip of his tongue down the length of her backbone.

His tongue caught and savored the faint residue of salt that had gathered in the groove of her spine. As he again nuzzled the nape of her neck, Lou decided how best to surpass that which she'd done to him.

With an edge of his chin, he came down her spine again, gently massaging each vertebra. At the small of her back, Lou kept contact as he cut sideways to the dimple above her left bun. After kneading the indentation a moment with his chin, Lou shifted to the dimple over her other bun. He casually moved back-and-forth between them.

In doing so, he inadvertently brushed her skin with his beard, and the touch of his whiskers tickled like tiny feathers, causing her buttocks to nervously jump in small contractions.

Enjoying the effect of his whiskers, Lou gave her several more passes before he wetted a cloth and cooled each of her legs. When he completed her backside, Lou tucked her arms close to her sides, crossed her legs at the ankle, and gently rolled the woman over.

With a new cloth, Lou cleansed her face at an unhurried pace, then moved to her chest. One at a time, he draped the wet cloth well above a breast and drew it down to her waist, enjoying how the cool friction brought her nipples alive.

Having deliberately left the hollow of her bosom untouched, Lou lowered his head and, in a single motion, swept his tongue up, capturing its salts.

The second time his tongue came up the hollow, Lou curved over her heart and circled a wide areola. As he went round, Lou fastidiously remained on the edge of the great black orb. Not until he saw its center engorge to maximum height did he neatly lift off.

Lou started up the hollow again, curving left to devote equal attention to the other black orb. This done, he switched back to the washcloth and cooled her belly with the same circling movements he'd used in the morning.

Noting her dreamy expression in the improving light, Lou shifted his position to her knees. He took a cloth in each hand and, firmly grasping round a thigh, he drew both his hands down with a steady pull all the way to her ankle. After doing the same to her other leg, Lou straightened his back and stretched his arms to yawn.

He glanced at her face and caught the hint of a smile on her lips.

"Just a hint." Lou was reminded of the three terse words spoken by President Steiner in dismissing the Algerian factor.

According to Lou's briefings at Langley, the Egyptian diplomat in Paris had demanded $350,000 before divulging his rumor. The diplomat then insisted Algeria already was building low-yield nuclear bombs, and Cuba would be the first Algerian ally to receive one. The Egyptian had refused to divulge his source, claiming it might compromise him. Since some of his past information had proved reliable, the rumor was forwarded to the Oval Office.

Lou, having been involved in a few covert operations which were founded on faulty information, wondered if this might be another. The White House had not been told the Egyptian was a heroin addict.

Shaking off the thought, Lou brought himself back into the present.

He placed both his hands beneath Camille's nearest knee. Gingerly, he raised the knee until it was propped in a inverted V position.

Lou set his own knee beside her raised thigh to keep it in place. When he felt her leg relax against his own, he wetted one of the cloths. Starting at the inner ankle of the upright leg, he brought the cloth up the inside of her calf, to the knee, and then down the inside of her thigh. At the thigh's end, he rolled the cloth up, over, and off her leg....and started over again.

In the relative darkness of the room, Lou could not be certain the cloth did not stray beyond bare skin; and he attempted to err on the side of discretion whenever the soothing cloth neared the end of her thigh.

He came up and then down the bridge of her leg....moving at an ever slower pace. Each time he passed the top of her upright knee, he could feel her leg stiffen against his own propped knee....and she would not relax again until the tantalizing cloth lifted off at the end of her thigh.

Lou glanced at Camille's unsmiling face, and he thought she appeared fully absorbed by the movement of his hand. He continued to work the upright leg for some time before switching sides.

Lou left the second leg in a reclined position as he cleansed it. The gradual march of the cloth from ankle to thigh again caused a hastening of Camille's respiration. He was thoroughly enjoying his power over the woman when he lifted the cloth from her body for the last time.

Holding her upright knee with his hand to keep it in place, he lowered himself and slipped his head within the inverted V of the leg.

He paused a moment, waiting for possible discouragement from the woman. When none came, Lou eased the cheek of his face onto her opposite thigh, luxuriating in its plushness.

The perfect pillow, mused the man.

The thought reminded him of the first time he'd fallen asleep in his cherished niche. The woman had also dozed; and, when she'd fidgeted in her sleep, Lou caught a knee in his Adam's apple. He napped lightly after that.

Lou closed his eyes to rest, giving Camille time to find whatever state of relaxation his new position and her expectations would permit.

As he patiently waited for her breathing to return to a semi-calm state, Lou debated whether he dare caress her even more intimately. While concerned for her immediate reaction, he was even more wary of the complications which might follow. After considering the possibilities, his mind wandered to a more important dilemma.

With Castro's increasing paranoia of being overthrown, his tolerance for dissent had declined, resulting in the formation of Rapid-Action-Brigades. These brutal para-military goon squads were formed to instantly silence any form of dissent, even that of a single person.

The prevailing opinion at Langley was that Castro's creation of the RAB squads proved the common people of Cuba were ripe for rebellion. However, a strong minority at Langley felt the RAB squads had instilled so much fear in the citizenry that they would be afraid to express further dissent. Which assessment was correct? Was the current situation worth risking the new network of university students, or was it better to wait? Fricke had been torn between the two factions

He was particularly concerned with losing the student network. If they were lost, there would be no other group available to exploit another opportunity in Cuba, if one occurred in the near future.

When Camille's breathing had slowed again, Lou found his position irresistible....as usual.

Gently, he lowered her upright knee so it rested upon his shoulder. Then, keeping his cheek to her leg, he played his tongue along the skin of her inner thigh.

Through his cheek, he felt the layered muscles of her leg begin to harden. The opposite leg on his shoulder also stiffened.

Partially lifting his head off the bed of her thigh, Lou reached lower with his tongue. When he found the margin where the pale skin of her inner thigh met the darker wineskin, he gradually traced its entire length up to the open expanse of her belly.

Lou found the saline tang of the woman's earthiness almost sweet. And, with satisfaction, he noted her torso was now rigid as stone and her breathing had turned shallow....expectant.

Placing the tip of his tongue on the smooth surface of her belly, he moved down an inch, reentering the vale of her thigh. After a pause, he came back in the other direction half the distance he'd traversed. In this overlapping manner, he unhurriedly found his way back down her wineskin to where he'd begun.

His course completed, Lou once more sank his cheek fully into her thigh and remained motionless, waiting for her muscles to go slack again.

When her other leg rested with more weight across his shoulder, Lou came off his perfect cushion and traced the same path a second time, even more slowly, overlapping in both directions.

On his third repetition, Lou swept his tongue up and down in one clean stroke. As the nib of his tongue ended its journey, Camille stiffened, causing her right leg to draw tighter about his shoulder.

Coming alive, thought Lou with an aficionado's pride.

He resumed with shorter caresses, spacing out his touches. For some time, he used this teasing manner....until her body relaxed somewhat.

Pausing for a long moment to take in the twin peaks of Camille's heaving bosom, Lou lifted his head off her thigh and led his tongue up in a broad sweep along the verge again. At her belly, he glided across to the opposite hipbone. Lou knew the other side of her wineskin---in anticipation---would be extremely sensitive and he began to nibble with his lips at the tender skin just below her hipbone.

Moments later, he pursed his mouth and blew warm breath into the vale of the new thigh. Then, his tongue made contact and skimmed down the fringe of her waiting wineskin.

Camille was unable to control her shivering.

Lou paused to enjoy her helpless state, but his pleasure did not last. The silent tremble of the woman's body reminded him of his own similar reaction when he first learned of the Cienfuegos contract.

A scant two months earlier, the CIA confirmed that Chinese technicians were completing the Cuban nuclear power plant south of Cienfuegos. The Joint Chiefs of Staff promptly recommended a preemptive air strike to destroy the nuclear facility, much as the Israelis had done to the Iraqi plant in 1981.

However, the CIA was unable to confirm that fuel cells had not been inserted in the Cuban reactor already. The Chinese were predictably noncommittal on the subject. Unwilling to risk a Chernobyl-type disaster that might spread radiation over Florida and nearby states, Steiner reluctantly had agreed to the CIA's covert operation.

Resuming his attentiveness to Camille, Lou alternated between the brief teasing passes and unexpected sweeps, which each time solicited yet another exquisite quiver of her entire being.

Halting the divine torment, Lou shifted back to her other side, where he would be more comfortable.

Time, he told himself, *for the coup de gracilis.*

He explored along the verge of her wineskin until he found the Gracilis---a narrow tendon aptly named by an ancient Greek physician, for it led to the most superb grace of all. The slim, taut muscle extended with some prominence from her inner thigh directly into the center of the pubic arch.

With little flicks, he played along the tight tendon. The tempo of his tongue quickened until Camille could no longer distinguish between each of the touches.

Primed with most infinite care, the body of the woman suddenly arched, stiffened, and shuddered all in the same instant. An animal-like moan ripened into the release of a sigh as she came off the peak of her meltdown.

Camille promptly coiled her body, drawing her legs up and away from the man.

In the clear moonlight, Lou watched her clinch herself into a tight ball. After a few seconds, he shifted his body around to protectively hold the woman in her curled position.

You've done it again, maestro, he congratulated himself. *Now, watch out.*

As he rested beside the motionless woman, Lou began to ponder what he would be watching in the morning. The uncertainly was not as unsettling as the fact that he knew the CIA was being forced to play with less than a full deck again. This concern---the lack of total commitment by the President---was his biggest qualm. It had been the fatal flaw in the Bay of Pigs. Would it doom this operation, too?

Within the confines of Langley, the Deputy CIA Director had actually argued against *Havana Heat* unless there was total commitment. But others had prevailed. Obtaining approval from the Oval Office for any Cuban covert operation was rare; and, as Fricke had agreed at the time, the CIA had to take the opportunities when they came.

It was twenty minutes later when Camille twisted around, reaching her arms out for him. For the first time, they kissed.

By the hunger of her lips, Lou knew what must come next. He withdrew from her first, then peppered her face with his lips. Each time her eyes opened, he returned to kiss them closed again.

When her hands began wandering about his body, Lou gathered them up and brought her finger-tips to his lips.

Camille shifted nearer and spoke haltingly.

"I'd like...."

"Later," interrupted Lou.

When he remained majestically silent, she quietly asked: "Is something wrong?"

"I like to go slow," Lou stated with practiced nonchalance.

He pondered how to explain his feelings, afraid that in sharing them that he would not be understood, or worse, his sensations would be dampened. Increasingly over the last decade, he'd found the pleasure of expectation to be as good, if not superior, to the ensuing reality.

Moving at a measured pace in a new relationship afforded him time to better gauge the nature of his partner....particularly her potential for patience, a trait Lou too often found lacking in the women to whom he found himself attracted.

Though Lou relished the feverish passion of a high-strung woman, finding it immensely satisfying to trigger, he also was understandably hesitant to suffer her inevitable sting.

Still, to him, the sensual stretching of the senses was theater of the finest kind. And he hadn't found a woman yet who didn't respond in the same fashion to the distended pleasure.

Camille, relaxing her hands within his, gazed into his eyes and asked:

"Can't we---"

Lou again cut in. "No, babe."

He paused before once more touching his lips to her fingertips.

When Camille's face contorted in confusion, Lou snickered to himself and spoke disparagingly.

"Honey, I'm just a jaded Scorpio."

It was a fair warning he issued to any woman who got close. Instead of acting as a caution though, as he'd meant the words to be taken, he generally found they acted as an encouragement.

"Why don't you turn around?" suggested Lou. "I'll hold you again while we watch the lights."

The moon now shone brightly over the balcony as they silently watched the islands of light in the warm tropical night.

Camille did not talk further, and Lou hadn't expected her to say as much as she already had. A woman seldom spoke afterwards, preferring instead to retain her quintessent state as long as possible.

As Lou played his hand in soothing circles about her soft belly, he pondered what had brought him to Havana. The CIA had waged its private war with Fidel Castro for 35 years.

Lou inwardly grinned at the thought of how friendly the CIA had been toward Fidel during his guerrilla years. Via the American consulate in Santiago, they had smuggled a radio transmitter into the Sierra Maestra for Fidel, who used it to broadcast propaganda across the island. The same operative also channeled $50,000 in cash and other supplies into the mountains for the rebels.

It was not uncommon for Langley to take both sides of an unpredictable conflict....as insurance. When these favors later backfired so miserably in Cuba, the CIA leaders felt they'd been betrayed and vowed revenge. The Bay of Pigs only added to their embarrassment and hostility.

This enmity helped explain why the two nations had managed to remain in contention for almost four decades. There was no precedent for such enmity with a neighbor of the United States, and Lou wondered whether his presence in Cuba would inflame the unnatural hostility between the two countries or help extinguish it.

A half-hour later, when Lou gauged it was cool enough to fall asleep, he excused himself with the statement that he needed sleep before dawn.

The Next Morning

Oval Office

"Fidel must be having a fit!" CIA Director Rolle concluded his comment with an unholy grin.

Rolle sat at the north end of the Oval Office in one of two sofas before the fireplace. Both sofas had been turned to face a large television screen built into a bookcase on the west wall. The set was displaying the signal of Cuba's sole TV station. Sitting on the other sofa was the Chairman of the Joint Chiefs of Staff, General J. Robert Steel.

President Steiner, who paced nearby, locked eyes with Rolle. "How certain are you that Castro's coming on?"

"According to Fricke in Havana," replied Rolle, "all Cubans have been alerted to watch their TVs at 10 a.m."

Steiner glanced at the grandfather clock in the northeast corner of the room. "That was 15 minutes ago."

"I think Castro will appear," persisted Rolle. "He reacts the same way in every crisis. Within 24 hours, he appears on television to mollify his people."

After a pause, Rolle continued: "I imagine his telecast has been delayed because he fired his television crew last night. Word has it Castro sent them all to the Isle of Youth. The new people probably haven't figured out how to use the cameras yet."

"I thought his prison island was called the Isle of Pines," said Steiner.

"A few years ago, Castro changed the name for cosmetic purposes," said Rolle.

The President turned to General Steel.

"Robert, how many times have we tested your new satellite?"

"More than a dozen, sir."

Three months earlier, the Air Force had placed a military communications satellite into geodesic orbit (stationary at 22,800 miles over the equator), in a direct line south of Havana.

"How much time will Castro have before he's cut off?" asked Steiner.

"Twenty-eight seconds, sir."

"We got him!" exclaimed Rolle, pointing to the TV screen.

It exhibited the grey-bearded face of Fidel Castro, who fumbled for a moment with a microphone attached to the lapel of his military uniform.

With a remote control, Rolle flipped on the voice synthesizer which instantly translated Castro's Spanish into English.

"Comrades."

Castro spoke in his customary manner, a deliberate and painfully slow pace which he used at the beginning of all his speeches. It accentuated the fever pitch to which he often built.

"Last night....the images we saw of Che Guevara....were false fabrications....of the Yankees. They were a sacrilege to his memory."

The seething rage on Castro's face did not match the calm modulation of the computerized voice synthesizer.

"Che was a brother. If he were alive today.... he would support our ongoing revolu---"

For two seconds, the TV screen filled with horizontal static.

A new face appeared before a dark-red background. The computer-created image of Che Guevara looked real. Mesmeric black eyes glared out of his intense face.

"Men and women of Cuba," began Che's impassioned voice. "In a true socialist state, certain freedoms must exist. Freedom of speech....freedom of the press....freedom of choice in all personal matters."

He paused.

"Do these freedoms exist in Cuba?"

The face of Che gave a knowing look to his audience, then twisted its lips into a sneering grin before becoming serious again.

"In 1886," he resumed, "slavery was abolished on this island. Yet today, the state controls where you live....what you eat....even where you work. Now, *all Cubans* are slaves!"

Che's image paused again.

"At one time, this island grew its own food. Today, every type of food is rationed. We wait a month or longer for one chicken. Cuba is the only tropical island in the world where fruits are difficult to obtain. This need not be. Stop the special food privileges of the elite and tourists. And stop exporting your best foods to foreigners! *Cuban food for Cubans!"*

The face of Che visibly calmed.

"Men and women of Cuba, perhaps, it would be well if I told the truth of myself. Do you remember when I disappeared in March of 1965? For six months, no one heard of me. Even when my mother called for me from her deathbed, I remained incommunicado. How did this come to be?"

Che exhibited a smile of resignation.

"The answer is simple---I dissented."

Raising his eyebrows, Che asked: "And what was my sin? I proposed free elections for a full-time national assembly. It is my belief that only freely-elected leaders will be responsive to the needs of the people."

Che again smiled. "Yes, Fidel....you tell us that Cuba already has an assembly. But what kind of assembly is it that meets only four days a year? What kind of assembly is it that automatically rubber-stamps all your programs?"

Che nodded his head from side to side disapprovingly.

"Both Fidel and Raul strenuously objected to my proposal. I warned them I would take the issue to you, the people. And for that, I was isolated."

For a moment, Che dropped his dour eyes.

"During those six months, I had only one visitor....but he came often. Finally, he---Fidel---convinced me that I must leave Cuba. Together, we wrote my farewell letter. Secretly, I went first to the Congo to organize rebels; but that was a hopeless venture. Bolivia was next. Six months after my arrival there, supplies and other support from Havana mysteriously ended. The rest is history."

Che's face hardened.

"I was betrayed....just as you have been. Today, the resources of Cuba are wasted in maintaining a bloated bureaucracy....whose main goal is its self-perpetuation."

The life-like image of Che deliberated a moment, then drank from a glass of water.

"My friends, do not deceive yourselves. Cuba is no socialist state. It is a dictatorship....of one man....however benevolent he may appear. And, as we have seen in Russia and Eastern Europe, no autocracy can resist the will of its people."

The face of Che loomed larger on the screen.

"Beloved Cubans! Believe in yourselves! *Demand your freedoms! Cuban food for Cubans!"*

With the final exhortation, Che's image faded from the screen.

The TV screen in the Oval Office---as did those in Cuba---remained grey.

In the ensuing quiet, Rolle offered: "Well, the match is lit."

✈ ✈ ✈

Havana

Lou rapped on the door of the women's powder room off the lobby of the Swiss embassy. He'd been impatiently stalking the door for over eight minutes. Pushing the door open an inch, he shouted inside:

"Let's go!"

After watching Castro's interrupted TV appearance with Camille and other members of the U.S. Interests Section, Lou was anxious to observe the action on the streets of Havana.

Getting no reply, Lou opened the door wider.

"What's keeping you?"

From inside, Camille responded in a calm, even voice. "I'll be with you in a minute."

"What're you doing?" demanded Lou, pushing the door wide open. He could see her at a mirror, applying lipstick with a tiny brush.

"I can't believe this," groused the CIA man. "At a time like this, who's going to care whether or not you're wearing lipstick?"

The diminutive woman wheeled around. She'd painted her lower lip a bright red. Her upper lip was still plain, giving her the appearance of a pouting child. But her eyes were smoldering and the voice was firm.

"I do."

Lou debated whether to go in and pull her out. Instead, he spoke in a jocular tone.

"Camille, you must be the first woman who ever put on makeup before attending a riot."

With finite care, Camille continued to paint her upper lip.

Realizing that his nice approach wasn't working either, Lou sauntered into the powder room and quietly stood beside her. In his opinion, the brightness of her lipstick---combined with a heavy application of black on her eyelashes---was giving her face a hard edge. To hasten the woman, he considered telling her not to go overboard with the makeup, but Camille spoke first.

"What makes you think we're going to a riot?" she inquired.

Lou folded his arms, thinking. He wasn't certain they were. There were no shills in the crowd this time.

In the late 1980s, the flamboyant Cuban double-agent, Juan Camejo, had compromised the majority of the CIA's contacts in Cuba. Dozens of Havanans had disappeared overnight. They had not been replaced in significant numbers yet. Recently, a small network of students had been established on the campus of Havana University, working through student exchange programs from Eastern European countries now friendly to the United States.

"Wouldn't you be inspired to some domestic disorder," inquired Lou, "if you were Cuban and saw Che's speech?"

"Maybe." She gave him a condescending glance. "And maybe not."

"What do you mean?" Lou inquired.

She stopped applying lipstick and spoke to him through the mirror.

"I think a fair percentage of Cubans are just plain lazy. They prefer their easy-going lifestyle of minimal work and generous leisure under Castro. They may have relatively few consumer choices, but no one's starving and who needs a lot of clothes in this climate?"

Lou did not choose to dispute what she said. The Cuban experts at Langley had expressed similar views; which, of course, had been omitted from the briefings given President Steiner.

In any case, what the majority of Cuba's citizens wanted for themselves was considered irrelevant by the Latin American specialists at Langley. As a rule, they knew the majority of any country generally waited to see the direction of the wind before taking sides during insurrections.

Three decades in the CIA had taught Fricke that a small minority could efficiently carry a rebellion from beginning to end. All that was required was a tight nucleus of radical visionaries...usually young, and foolish enough to offer their lives for ideals. Fidel Castro's own assent to power in 1959 was a textbook example of this precept.

"I'm ready," Camille announced and she walked out of the restroom ahead of him. As they left the embassy, Lou glanced at its facade and observed:

"This place always reminds me of a Holiday Inn back in the sixties."

The structure exhibited an ugly, squarish, six-story facade. It was located at the far west end of the Malecon, which ran the length of Havana's two-mile shoreline.

Lou noted his tail---the chinless man who'd followed them into El Pollo---keeping pace about 30 yards back. An unlit cigarette dangled sloppily from No-Chin's mouth.

In the plaza the previous evening, Lou had not found it difficult to pick out the man from State Security. He was the only person nearby who could be seen chainsmoking---a sure sign of privilege in Cuban society. In the cabaret alone, Lou had counted eight cigarettes being lit up by No-Chin. The official ration in Cuba was only two packs, or 40 cigarettes a month.

Lou and Camille walked a half-mile along the Malecon before pausing to cross the boulevard. It was full of bicyclists going both directions in all its lanes, irrespective of the normal flow of traffic.

As Lou stepped off the curb, he took Camille's hand. After crossing the boulevard, he held onto it and was pleased when she made no attempt to withdraw her hand.

"You been married?" he asked, already knowing the answer from the files at Langley.

"Blunt, aren't you?" she responded.

"Well?" Lou looked away, not wishing to meet her eyes.

"Well, what?"

"I was just wondering," he persisted.

"Why?"

Lou had a sense he was being bluffed by a tough opponent in a poker game.

"You're blunt, yourself," he countered.

"Why are you interested?" expanded Camille.

Lou scrunched up his face for a moment, wondering why was she being so difficult?

That a woman in her forties might be hesitant to admit she hadn't experienced marriage yet did not dawn on the man.

"I feel sorta close," he awkwardly began. " I mean, we....uh....were somewhat intimate last night."

"Somewhat?" she sarcasticly repeated with a quick grin that he missed.

"I thought so," stated Lou with conviction.

Camille's voice became casual. "We were just cooling off each other." After pausing, she charitably added: "It was nice."

Feeling chagrin at the minor praise, Lou considered whether to ask if that's all it had been to her.

"I haven't married," she told him, saying the words as if they meant little to her.

Lou knew better than to be blunt again in asking the real question on his mind. Now that he had met the woman in the captivating photograph in the Langley file, he was more curious than ever to know why she'd never married. He decided to go in the backdoor, using a compliment.

"Amazing," he mildly exclaimed. "You're extremely attractive, smart, and a damned good tennis player."

"What does that mean?" replied Camille, having heard similar comments before. She was curious to know what he was getting at.

Lou seethed for a moment.

"Damn it," he exclaimed under his breath. " It means I'm interested in you!"

His unabashed reaction surprised her, but Camille still gave him a mocking smile. She liked his bluntness. It was a trait of her own, and she gave it back to him.

"I'm not interested in marriage."

Well, mused Lou to himself, I'm not sure I am either.

"Long-term relationships always bore me," she continued.

I can't believe this, Lou thought. This woman thinks like I do. She can't be for real. But he knew she was. In his entire life, he'd seldom met a woman who stated her preferences and views as candidly. Camille was specific, clear, and knew what she wanted every minute of the day. Lou found it refreshing.

"So," he began, "how long is long?"

"Anything over two years," she said in an off-hand manner.

"Two years," repeated Lou, thinking that his own relationships seldom lasted more than a year.

"You dating anyone right now?" he asked.

"Off and on," she said.

Lou liked her answer. "Who is there to date around here?"

"There's plenty," she replied. "The diplomatic corps is full of bachelors. They're well-educated, sports-minded, and seldom in Havana longer than two years."

"Sounds like the perfect setup for someone like you," observed Lou.

"It is."

Lou hesitated. "I can appreciate your attitude toward relationships. It's similar to mine."

Camille inwardly smiled. It was the normal response she got to her two-year comment. Men are all the same, she told herself, including this bozo.

"How about when you get older?" Lou posed.

His question threw her. The subject had been in the back of her mind a long time, and she preferred to keep it there.

"I've been married," began Lou in a meditative voice, "and divorced three times....in my younger years. The experiences convinced me to think as you do---"

Camille turned her head to study him as he spoke, beginning to take him seriously. The man was relating circumstances not unlike those of her mother and older sister. Their multiple marriages had been as sour as their divorces were ugly. To Camille, it seemed easier to avoid the heartache in the first place.

"---but now I'm thinking of the future. I'd like to find a woman who keeps my interest up."

As Lou finished his words, he wondered why he was sharing them with this woman who had already expressed an aversion to lengthy relationships. Maybe, he thought, I feel safe in talking with her.

"If such a man existed," countered Camille, surprising herself at her comment, "I'd like to meet him."

As they walked, Lou and Camille alternately eyed one another, he with a nervous smile, she with skepticism.

Lou debated whether this woman could be a possibility. She certainly had plenty of mysteries to unravel.

He broke the silence.

"You're weird," grinned Lou, giving her hand a squeeze so she wouldn't take his words the wrong way.

She squeezed back.

"You should talk, Mister Scorpio!"

They both laughed, and Camille decided to ask her own pointed question.

"How come you haven't made a pass at me yet?"

He gave her a foolish grin, then shook his head at the craziness of the question.

"I'm beginning to think you're gay," continued Camille, unsuccessfully trying to keep a straight face, "especially with those neon-green shorts you favor."

Laughing again with her, Lou decided to pass on the question. The streets of the city were getting thick with people. A fair number of Havana's citizens were watching from crowded windows and wrought-iron balconies overhanging the streets.

Spectators, thought Lou, waiting like everyone else to see what will happen.

Pressing deeper into the city, they passed boisterous groups of youths, acting as if they'd been drinking. Glancing behind him, Lou noticed that No-Chin had closed the distance to about 20 paces.

As they approached a crowded intersection, Lou held Camille's hand tighter to pull her along more quickly. He was certain that somewhere in downtown Havana the people had to be creating a disturbance or protest of some sort, and he wanted to be there.

"Why do you want me with you this morning?" asked Camille as they hurried around a corner.

"For your pleasant company," responded Lou.

Camille planted herself and yanked him to a halt.

"Wait a minute!" she said. "I have to tie my shoe."

Though his reply was true enough, he had a far better reason for asking her to accompany him. Her presence---that of a "diplomatic person" immune from arrest---made it less likely Cuban State Security would detain him or take any other hostile measure against his person, a known CIA operative.

As Camille tied her shoelace, Lou couldn't help but admire the ample cleavage created by her hunched shoulders. Though he'd seen her full figure in the moonlight, that had been a static display and masked by opaque shadows. Now, in daylight, the tease created by the partial view of her embracing breasts encouraged his imagination. In his mind's eye, he saw himself reaching down to lightly trace the luscious valley of her bosom. Someday, Lou told himself, I'm going to do it. He didn't spot No-Chin until almost too late.

The Cuban, rushing around the corner and into Camille, would have bowled her over if Lou hadn't thrown his hand out to stiff-arm him away.

Shunted aside abruptly, No-Chin caught his falling cigarette in mid-air as he recovered his balance.

"Hi!" Lou grinned at the stunned man.

The Cuban's eyes bugged out.

"Camille, tell this guy it's okay to stay closer to us."

She came to her feet. "Who is he?"

"The man in the cabaret," said Lou.

Not having seen No-Chin clearly the previous night, Camille blankly stared at him.

"My official escort," continued Lou, "courtesy of the Cuban government."

"Oh," acknowledged Camille.

"Just tell him to stick with us," prompted Lou. "That way, he won't be running over you anymore."

Camille started talking in Spanish, but the man raised a hand to halt her.

"I speak English," revealed No-Chin.

"Good!" exclaimed Lou. "What's your name?"

The Cuban hesitated, surprised at the familiarity posed by a member of a hostile intelligence agency.

"Okay, Pedro," grinned Lou. "Try to keep up."

Giving the CIA operative a strange look, the Cuban kept a few paces behind as they marched deeper into the city. When they reached Galiano, the main thoroughfare of Havana's shopping district, Lou spotted a commotion down a side street. A small crowd had gathered at a storefront.

"We've finally found something," said Lou with relief. He took Camille's hand again and pulled her toward it.

"It's a food-rationing outlet," she told him when they were close enough to read the store's sign.

Through a broken window, Lou saw youths inside the store tossing cans out onto the sidewalk. He thought the oldest boy in the store looked to be no more than 14. As the cans rolled into the street, they were being snatched up by men and women.

The CIA man was amused to see that most of the women who wore skirts were holding their hems up high in order to carry more of the cans. Modesty appeared to be of little concern to the women, who were more intent on getting their share of the unlimited and free food. The people were in a festive mood, shouting encouragement to the boys in the store.

On the fringe of the crowd, Lou noticed a policeman, seemingly unconcerned by the ransacking. One woman, spilling cans from her over-stuffed skirt, approached the policeman and invited him to pick out a can. Graciously selecting one from the basket of her skirt, the officer tucked it within his jacket and nodded thanks.

Lou pivoted to No-Chin and waved him forward. "Go get some, yourself. We'll wait for you."

After studying the idea a few seconds, the gaunt man looked away, drawing deeply on his cigarette.

Camille squeezed Lou's hand and pointed down the street in the direction they'd come. A second policeman---pistol in hand---was running toward them.

At the broken window, the new policeman waved his weapon and shouted to the youths inside. First one can, then a barrage of cans flew out the window, forcing him to retreat. The crowd cheered.

Facing the crowd, the irate police officer stepped toward the jeering people with his pistol upright. Those nearest backed away, while others only hooted at him. Confident he was secure from the unruly crowd, the policeman started to turn back to the youths in the store....and caught a can on his ear.

Staggered by the projectile, the officer went to a crouch and made his way back to the broken window. The cans of food were still flying.

With the report of his pistol, a scream was heard within the store and the cans stopped.

The policeman, bleeding heavily from his ear, took careful aim and fired several more times. Some of the crowd shouted for him to stop shooting at the youths.

Lou watched with heightened interest as the first policeman broke though the crowd and ran to the window. He seized the other officer's forearm which held the pistol. When the two men grappled and fell, Lou heard another report from the weapon.

The policeman who'd tried to stop the shooting rolled away into the gutter.

"My god!" rasped Camille. "I think he's dead."

Infuriated members of the crowd began hurtling their cans at the second policeman, who was still sprawled on the sidewalk. As the cans pelted him, he pointed the gun at his nearest assailant and attempted to fire it.

The gun was empty though; and, the crowd realizing this, closed in to heave their cans with even greater fury. The officer soon collapsed under the onslaught.

Lou pulled at Camille. "Let's scram!"

They ran back the way they'd come, No-Chin huffing behind.

Before they reached the end of the block, a white police van---siren screaming---passed them, heading toward the store.

"They'll find the dead policeman," shouted Lou, "and think the crowd did it. Keep running!"

At the next intersection, they heard shots behind them.

Lou looked over his shoulder and spotted No-Chin, head-down and well behind them. Lou took a quick right into another side street filled with milling people. Many of them were running with fresh produce in their arms.

Great, thought the CIA man, *it's happening everywhere.*

At the open door of a restaurant, Lou saw people hauling out large chunks of raw meat, along with crates of vegetables and fruit. One looter had managed to wave down a dilapidated taxi, whose driver waited patiently as his seats were jammed with the stolen food.

Lou paused briefly to watch.

"That's surprising," he commented to Camille. "Even the restaurants are getting hit."

"That's a tourist restaurant," she countered as Lou pulled her along. "Few Cubans can afford to buy meals in such places."

"Why's that?"

"They take only dollars and charge exorbitant prices," Camille explained, "even to the tourists. That's one of Castro's clever tricks. He lures tourists to Cuba with cheap hotel rooms, then overcharges for their meals and other services."

More sirens were heard over the din of the plundering. When Lou looked again for No-Chin, he spotted him a half-block back leaning against a streetlight to catch his breath.

"Let's return to the embassy," urged Lou. "I want to report what's happening."

When they were a block from the Malecon, No-Chin was no longer visible behind them and Lou altered direction to enter the gardens behind a seaside hotel he knew to be the Hotel Nacional. It was the most elegant luxury resort in Havana, with spectacular views of the sea.

"Look at that." Lou pointed to the elaborate rear entrance of the hotel.

Cubans were running out of the building and cutting across the spacious flower gardens, carrying a wide variety of items. As Lou and Camille approached the high-arched back entrance, they saw as many people pushing to get in as were scrambling to get out of the jammed opening.

"They're emptying the dollar-shops," observed Camille.

Dollar-shops were specialty shops which catered only to tourists and the few Cubans who could pay for their purchases with U.S. dollars.

"I didn't think they'd go that far," commented Lou.

The two of them stood to the side of the archway, watching looters leave the hotel with camcorders, miniature color TVs, toaster ovens, fans, and other consumer goods. The pockets of the looters bulged with smaller items.

"Most of what they're taking," observed Camille, "is not available in Cuba except in the dollar-shops."

They saw people begin to carry out whole turkeys, plus baskets of lobsters and shrimp.

"Looks like they found the hotel restaurant," commented Lou.

"Those meats not available to Cubans at all," she told him.

Lou guided Camille around the abandoned swimming pool of the hotel to its front, where they crossed the Malecon and headed west along the waterfront. They'd gone only 400 yards when Lou indicated a narrow-based, but tall building up ahead with broad balconies offering views over the Gulf of Mexico. People were milling about the towering structure, and Lou could see items dropping from the windows of its lower floors.

"What's that building?" he asked.

"Apartments for the Chinese and North Korean technicians who replaced the Russians," said Camille.

"I want a closer look,"

As Lou stepped off the promenade along the waterfront to recross the Malecon, horns blasted him back onto the wide sidewalk. A convoy of military vehicles roared past, using all four lanes of the boulevard. Lou decided to continue along the promenade until they were opposite the apartment tower.

Several hundred Cubans surrounded its base, while others had forced their way into the building. Lou saw jubilant Cubans leaning over the balconies of floors near the ground, heaving a wide variety of food and household items to their friends below.

He wondered why some of the military troops did not stop to halt the rampaging crowd. Their trucks continued east along the Malecon, oblivious to the disturbance.

"Up there!" exclaimed Camille.

Lou followed her gaze to one of the middle floors of the tower. Over a balcony railing, a man had propped the unmistakable muzzle of a rifle.

The panicked North Korean pointed his AK-47 out over the shoreline and released a short burst. The detonation of automatic-rifle fire momentarily froze the crowd.

"Get me out of here!" ordered Camille.

"Sure," Lou instantly replied.

As they hurried down the Malecon, Lou couldn't resist observing: "Well, the Cubans aren't so lazy after all."

Camille, giving him a brief glance, did not reply.

Upon their arrival at the Swiss embassy, Lou spotted No-Chin loitering in the parking lot. Waving to his tail, Lou received a brief smile in return from the Cuban....who was genuinely glad to see his charge again.

Palacio De La Revolucion

The triumvirate was in session.

One of them spoke in his usual high-pitched voice, while the other two---Raul Castro and Vilma Espin---mostly listened. Accustomed to the lengthy monologues of the Cuban president, Raul and Vilma waited for Fidel to talk himself out.

Fidel, as he alternately raged and then spoke in a calmer manner, paced in the plodding gait of a portly man. His once athletic build had expanded with his increasing isolation in the 1990s. Of the major nations, only North Korea and China still shared his dogma. Many Cubans now referred to their Commandante as *El Gordo*....The Chubby One.

The three members of the triumvirate were in the spacious but spartan presidential office on the third floor of the Palacio de la Revolucion. The building was a sprawling structure built by Castro's predecessor, Fulgencio Batista, to house the Cuban Supreme Court. After exiling most of its judges in 1959, Castro had renamed the building and made it his headquarters.

Making himself comfortable on a couch some 20 feet away was Raul Castro, Defense Minister of the Cuban state and heir-apparent to Fidel. He sat sufficiently distant to not be bothered by the pungent smoke of the first cigar Fidel had lit in eight years.

As Defense Minister, Raul was ostensibly in charge of the armed forces of Cuba. Since the mid-1980s, his primary activity was the "defense" of drugrunners who used Cuba as a safe haven and bridge into the United States. A fee---payable in dollars---was levied on the value of every kilo of drugs passing through Cuba. These funds had substantially improved the country's hard currency reserves in the 1990s.

Raul knew what bothered his half-brother the most, and it was a subject which Fidel had yet to mention. It was not Che's upstaging on television.

Nor was it the food riots, which had finally petered out once the stores and restaurants were emptied of their supplies.

"The problem is," stated Fidel Castro, wagging his finger at his two listeners without even looking at them, "most of Che's statements were partially true. Yes, we often disagreed. Che and I might have quarreled over the means; nevertheless, our goals were always the same. Che did not understand that fully free elections would be an anathema. They would---"

As he spoke, Fidel checked Vilma first, then Raul. She was paying attention, but Raul's eyes were raised to the ceiling as if admiring its ornamental trim. Fidel moved toward Raul to punch his shoulder, a frequent habit of the Cuban president whenever he caught someone daydreaming during his extended monologues.

Fidel was only a few feet away when Raul spotted him, became properly attentive again, and avoided a bruise.

"---but when has the populace *ever* elected honest leaders?" demanded Fidel, with a broad sweep of his arms. "Cubans cannot be trusted. They have always elected corrupt men. Che never denied that fact!"

It was an accurate claim that Fidel had made over and over to Che during the latter's six months of isolated re-education.

"Che maintained television would make Cubans better informed and more likely to elect honest officials," commented Fidel thoughtfully. "But that is not true. Look at the thieves and murderers who are routinely elected in Haiti, in Puerto Rico, in Mexico....even in the United States!"

Pleased with his statement, Fidel drew at length on his cigar before he went on.

"As for freedom of the press, the reporters of Havana's newspapers before the Revolution were *bought* by Batista and his predecessors through subsidies and bribes. The people were fed lies all the time!"

Facing Vilma Espin, Fidel jabbed his cigar in her direction.

"It was a lie," he told her, "that Che's farewell letter was co-written. Yes, we discussed its substance beforehand, but Che wrote it. He was always more clever with words."

Fidel swung around to his brother to see if he was daydreaming again. He wasn't.

"Raul! When did Che first bring up his Bolivia scheme?"

While Raul searched his memory, Fidel answered his own question.

"It was late 1964, when we saw LBJ begin the buildup in Vietnam. Che thought Washington would be too preoccupied with Vietnam to care about our dealings in Bolivia."

Pausing before the broad window of his office to gaze out over the Plaza de la Revolucion, Fidel reflected for a moment.

"Che brought up Bolivia," Fidel went on. "I did not agree with him at first. Bolivia's poor were not ready to rebel. And unlike the Spanish peasants of Cuba, they were Indians who cared little to improve their lot. I did not encourage Che."

Neither did you discourage him a year later, Vilma Espin silently thought to herself. She also vividly recalled when Fidel had returned ecstatic from one of his sessions with Che. Sending Che to Bolivia was a way out of the dilemma. Che could leave Cuba and its politics behind, while Fidel would give the appearance of supporting Che in a new Bolivian adventure.

"I did not encourage Che," repeated Fidel, as if attempting to convince himself.

While Che Guevara lived, Vilma Espin had treated him with a respectful reserve. She knew Che was idolized by Cubans on a par with Fidel. They were like two kings. And no island....no country could be ruled by two kings.

Vilma had another reason to be cool towards Che, for she was then the wife of Raul Castro who might someday compete with Che for dominance.

"I did not rejoice," began Fidel, "when Che was killed in---"

Fidel halted mid-sentence, reminded of the Nixon comment: "I am not a crook."

Am I protesting too much? Fidel thought to himself. And he decided that he was.

"I deeply grieved for Che in 1967," began Fidel anew, also recalling the sense of relief he'd felt with the knowledge that Che was no longer alive to embarrass him.

"I saw to it that many monuments were erected to Che's revolutionary spirit," said Fidel firmly. "I renamed numerous schools for him. I made a cult of Che. Even now, his likeness is plastered on the walls of every city in Cuba."

Until now, Castro had felt secure from the influence of Che. A dead man could not hurt him....he had believed.

Che did incite the food riots though, Fidel told himself. *But I was too smart for him.*

Remembering the lessons of the violent upheavals in Eastern Europe, Castro had instructed his State Security units to use minimal force on the food rioters. He had believed the rioters would leave the streets after they were permitted to take their food home. And they had.

Fidel swung around to his half-brother again.

"Raul, why did you not remove General Diaz years ago?"

Now, it starts, thought Raul.

General Carlos Diaz, commander of Cuba's Central Military District, was the subject for which Raul had been patiently waiting.

Raul did not respond to Fidel's charge, even though it was unfair. It had been Fidel who insisted on retaining the crusty general, after Diaz uttered questionable remarks in the aftermath of General Ochoa's execution in 1989. Because Diaz had played a pivotal role in defeating the Bay of Pigs invasion, Fidel had chosen to ignore the reports of his general's privately-stated remarks.

"Why could you not persuade Diaz to come to Havana last night?" demanded Fidel. "Each of my other commanders came to pledge support."

In a show of force for Fidel, the commander of the Cuban Air Force had sent three squadrons of MiGs---every plane available---to buzz Havana immediately prior to Fidel's morning TV appearance. The television newsmen had filmed General Rodriguez of the Western Army District dispatching troops to safeguard Havana's airport. General Pina of the Eastern Army District also had appeared on the TV screen to encourage Cubans to remain calm.

On the other hand, General Diaz of the Central District had displayed a definite reticence when summoned by Raul to the Cuban capital. Diaz claimed his presence was required where he was---at Camp Cienfuegos---in order to quell continuing disturbances in his district.

However, both Fidel and Raul were fully aware of the real reason for Diaz's hesitance to come to Havana.

A few months earlier, Fidel had let it be known that he had a new general in mind for the Central command. It was a favorite tactic of the Cuban president when discharging a key minister or general.

After receiving such a notice, the individual to be replaced could chose to retire or resign in advance of a formal dismissal. The charade gave the appearance that Castro ruled with a light hand.

"We did not kill General Ochoa well," remarked Fidel, thinking of another dead man who had returned to haunt him now.

Fidel pointed his finger at Raul.

"And it was *you* who insisted on a public trial, as an example to other ambitious generals," said Fidel. "If I had let Ochoa die quietly instead, then we would not have the problem with Diaz today."

This time, Fidel's words were neither unfair or inaccurate. The disloyal remarks made by Diaz in 1990 had been to a supposedly trusted member of his staff. They concerned the immensely-popular General Arnaldo Ochoa, a highly-decorated hero of the Angolan and Ethiopian conflicts, who had been tried and executed in 1989 on the trumped-up charge of aiding South American drugrunners.

The trial had accomplished two goals for the Castro brothers. Ochoa, a popular general mentioned in some circles as a possible successor to Fidel, had been eliminated. And the world watched Cuba pretend it opposed drug-running. It was another charade.

After the demise of Ochoa, General Diaz had not criticized the need for the Castro brothers to eliminate his fellow general. What Diaz questioned was the manner in which it was done. Ochoa's excellent military reputation and family were ruined by the false charge. It would have been far better, Diaz maintained, if Ochoa had simply lost his life in *an accident*---a subterfuge the triumvirate had often utilized in the past.

"Diaz is no fool," said Fidel. "He knows what I have in store for him if he comes to Havana now."

"We must destroy him quickly," urged Raul.

A man of few words, Raul Castro said no more.

"Yes," agreed Fidel. "But, let us be careful. We need only neutralize General Diaz for now. The Air Force can destroy his tanks."

Raul thought to protest, for he believed it would be better to first send State Security units in an attempt to arrest and assassinate Diaz.

"Order the Air Force to do that now!" commanded Fidel.

Raul went to Fidel's desk and did as told. After the Air Force made short work of the tanks, then he could suggest that State Security finish the job.

Vilma Espin came to her feet, indicating that she wished to speak.

She was a stout matron with gray hair and glasses, the grandmother of three. Though Raul had secretly remarried in the late 1980s, Vilma Espin Guillois was still his "official wife" and fully retained her position as the First Lady of Cuba. Some said she wielded more power than Raul.

"When we turned off the television transmitter," Vilma stated in a bitter tone, "Che still
continued. Therefore, his signal must come from the
TV Marti blimp."

She referred to the blimp over Miami which
beamed telecasts financed by the U.S. government,
specifically aimed at the Cuban populace. It broadcast
both news and entertainment, often designed to
disrupt the Castro government.

"If we cannot stop Che's interruptions," suggested Vilma, "then let us order all TVs in Cuba
turned off."

"How could such an order be enforced?" posed
Fidel.

Vilma thought for only a moment. "Let the CDR
leaders relay the order. If necessary, they can rip the
antennas off the roofs."

Every block in Havana had a sign designating
the office of that block's *Committee for the Defense of
the Revolution.* These CDRs had been established by
Fidel in 1960---the year after he took power---to
counter sabotage. Their para-military function had
expanded to include block cleanups, vaccination cam-
paigns, and political lectures....but their prime
purpose was to serve as a constant monitor of
dissident individuals. They were the eyes and ears of
State Security.

Thirty-one years later, it was from CDR members that the Rapid-Action-Brigades were formed.

"I agree," added Raul, hanging up his phone.

Fidel nodded. "Yes, do it."

Vilma Espin went to Fidel's desk to relay the
TV directive.

"I have it!" exclaimed Fidel, freezing Vilma as
she'd picked up a phone receiver.

"I will call a rally in the Plaza for this
afternoon!" he told them.

"Why not wait until tomorrow?" suggested Raul.
"So we can organize it."

"I must speak to my people immediately!" thun-
dered Fidel.

Raul checked his watch. "Then speak to them tonight. That will give State Security sufficient time to arrest the 10 thousand most prominent dissidents and---"

"No!" exploded Fidel. "There is no time."

Fidel knew his brother was good at executing an order....and he often wished his brother could think as well.

"If we wait until nightfall," explained Fidel, "the Americans can use their holograms again."

"A hologram is visible in daylight, also," contended Raul.

"Yes," agreed Fidel, "but not as much. And we must not give the Americans time to set up another one."

Vilma spoke. "The CDRs can bring everyone in Havana to the Plaza!"

"Yes," said Fidel, "and we will use them to lead the crowd in spontaneous cheers."

"My Federation of Women will sing patriotic songs," added Vilma. "A hundred-thousand voices."

"What of security?" said Fidel. "There may be a few demonstrators."

"Shoot them!" exclaimed his brother promptly.

"No," countered Vilma "If everyone is ordered to the Plaza, many children will be present."

Fidel shook his head at Raul's suggestion and calmly observed: "I would not have the firing of guns as I speak."

There was a lengthy pause in the room.

"Why not *knives*?" suggested Vilma. "They would be silent."

Fidel's frown gradually became a grin, and he folded his arms over his broad chest.

"Excellent!" exclaimed the Cuban president. "Knives will not disrupt my speech."

"We can instruct the Rapid-Action-Brigades to bring knives," offered Raul.

Fidel raised a finger to his brother. "But they will not be used unless I give approval."

↣ ↣ ↣

U. S. Naval Base - Guantanamo Bay

"Hemingway! Get over to my office, pronto! A Cuban colonel just dropped in."

The abrupt, fast-spoken words of Captain Ken Carter automatically caused Hemingway to reply in the calm drawl which he customarily assumed in a tight situation.

"What do you mean....dropped in?"

"He landed on my airstrip in a single-engine plane that's all shot up," answered Captain Carter. "He's being escorted to my office."

"I'll be right over."

In response to the summons from the commander of the Naval Base at Guantanamo, Colonel Thomas Hemingway was in a Huey helicopter and airborne inside of 40 seconds.

He arrived at the white-washed headquarters of Guantanamo Naval Base in time to see three Shore Patrol jeeps roar up with their prize. No officer of the Cuban military had been allowed on the American outpost in more than three decades.

Hemingway entered Captain Carter's office as the Cuban was being frisked in the hallway.

Carter shot a stern glance at his Marine commander. "Tom, you speak Spanish, don't you?"

"Good enough, Ken."

A Shore Patrol officer poked his head in the door. "He's clean, sir."

"Bring him in," snapped Carter.

The Cuban colonel strode into the office, checking out both Hemingway and Carter. The former was outfitted in his flightsuit, Carter in Navy whites. Knowing the Navy commanded Guantanamo, the Cuban saluted Carter.

"I am Colonel Antonio Valdes, Chief of Staff to General Carlos Diaz, commander of the Central Military District."

Rising from his desk, Carter briskly returned the salute.

"I'm Captain Carter, commander of the base. This is Colonel Hemingway, CO of the Marines on board."

Valdes nodded to the Marine and faced Carter, speaking in fluent English. "General Diaz requests your assistance."

Carter waited for more.

"We are being bombed by our own planes," continued Valdes. "Castro has ordered his Air Force to destroy the tanks of the Central District."

Carter lost his placid expression. "Why?"

"Because," Diaz pridefully smiled, "General Diaz declined Castro's order to come to Havana." After a pause, he added: "My General prefers to wait....to see what the Cuban people do next."

"Interesting," nodded Carter. "So what kind of help does your general wish?"

"Air cover," said Valdes quickly, "to stop the destruction of our tanks."

Carter briefly grinned. "That's not likely."

"Without tanks," stated Valdes, "we cannot support an uprising."

Carter glanced to Hemingway a moment. The invitation to participate in a Cuban insurrection was totally unexpected. While both men had been ordered to watch Castro's speech of the previous evening, neither had been told why or alerted to this possibility.

Carter rose from his chair and faced the wide wallmap of Cuba beside his desk. "And what are your Western and Eastern District commanders doing?"

"General Pina, the Eastern commander, flew to Havana," replied Valdes, "but he is also a close friend to General Diaz. I do not know the disposition of General Rodriguez, the Western District commander."

Colonel Valdes knew very well that Rodriguez and Pina were actively supporting Fidel Castro, but he did not wish to discourage the Americans by telling them so.

The island of Cuba was divided into three military districts---the Western District encompassing Havana, the Central District headquartered at Cienfuegos, and the Eastern District abutting Gitmo.

"I'll send your request to my superiors," said Carter.

"How soon will permission come?" pointedly inquired the Cuban officer.

Carter's eyes narrowed. "Colonel, I would not assume we'll get permission. And if we do, I have no idea how long it will take to arrive."

Carter expected that even a speedy reply could require more than an hour. The message would first go to the commander of the Atlantic Fleet in Norfolk, Virginia. After deciding whether to recommend approval or rejection of the request, the Fleet Commander would relay his endorsement to the Chief of Naval Operations. The CNO would determine his own recommendation before going the Chairman of the JCS, who would then contact the President. It might easily be a good 45 minutes before the White House even learned of the request. And how long President Steiner would sit on it was impossible to predict.

"Half our tanks are destroyed already," exaggerated Valdes.

Carter checked his watch. It was a few minutes before 3 p.m.

Hemingway spoke up. "Ken, why don't I take Colonel Valdes to Leeward? If permission comes, we can be airborne in seconds."

Receiving no objection, Hemingway left with Valdes for Leeward Point---the Marine airfield on the west side of Guantanamo Bay. As they ran to Hemingway's Huey, Valdes shouted: "It would be prudent if insignias on your aircraft were painted out."

Hemingway nodded. He had the Huey pilot radio ahead instructions to prepare his eight available Harriers. As the U.S. insignias were sprayed over, each was to be outfitted with four AIM Sidewinders and two 300-gallon auxiliary fuel tanks.

When the Huey hit the tarmac across the bay one-and-a-half minute later, each Harrier AV-8B was surrounded by crewmen.

Noting the Harriers were one-seaters, Valdes asked: "How will I go with you?"

"Good question," replied Hemingway.

"I *must* accompany you," emphasized Valdes.

"I agree," Hemingway replied. "I'll give you this Huey for transportation."

"If possible," said Valdes, "I would like to contact General Diaz now."

"Follow me," Hemingway told him.

They entered the commshack for Marine aviation on Leeward Point and raised General Diaz on a frequency provided by Valdes. After briefly listening to his general, Valdes broke off to reveal:

"Camp Cienfuegos is under air attack again!"

Valdes held the earpiece to Hemingway, who could heard explosions in the background. He asked Valdes: "Find out what type and the number of aircraft doing the bombing."

After a moment, Valdes replied: "Approximately 20 aircraft---a combination of MiG-23s and MiG-29s---are arriving every half-hour.

To Hemingway, this meant the entire Cuban Air Force of some 60 aircraft was probably engaged in the operation against the Central District.

Concluding his conversation, Valdes told Hemingway: "General Daiz says the MiGs are bombing our barracks also. It will take an hour for your planes to reach Cienfuegos. That means two more unopposed strikes....even if you took off right now."

Hemingway kicked at the leg of a chair.

"We may arrive in time to bury Diaz," Valdes sourly observed.

Turning away, Hemingway started out of the commshack. At the door, he stopped, turned around and grabbed a phone to raise Captain Carter.

"Ken, I'm thinking of running a training exercise the coast, staying over international waters. You got any objections?"

Hemingway heard Carter's breathing over the phone.

"I'm not sure that's a good idea, Tom."

Hemingway wondered whether it was the "base commander" speaking or the "go-for-it Naval aviator" that he knew Carter to be.

"So what would you do in my place, Ken?"

Once more, Hemingway heard only breathing. Finally: "I don't know."

Or, thought Hemingway, you don't want to say.

"Ken, my men need to get their flight hours in. That's what we're paid for."

"I'll have to report your flight immediately, Tom."

"I hope you will," replied Hemingway. "I always like my friends to know where I am...in case I need a pitstop."

Carter understood the message. *Pitstop* was the call-sign for the USS Tarawa, currently cruising near the Cayman Islands, due west of Gitmo and some 250 miles south of Cienfuegos, Cuba. After the mission, heading for the helicopter carrier to refuel would be shorter than returning to Gitmo.

"Roger that," said Carter, adding an unnecessary caution. "Stay well out in international waters, Tom."

Hemingway made a mental note to buy a bottle of premium Bacardi for Carter. As base commander, he could have grounded the Marine aircraft if he'd wanted to thoroughly cover his ass.

"Thanks, Ken. Call me if you hear any news."

Carter immediately sent two more coded messages, the second one to the Tarawa. His brief words alerted its task force commander that eight Harriers were conducting a training mission in waters along the southern coast of Cuba. Though it had the appearance of a routine message, the Tarawa promptly pointed northward and stepped up to full-speed. A training flight would rarely involve every available Harrier at Leeward Point.

Hemingway had more difficulty as he explained to a Marine captain why it was necessary to commandeer the young officer's Harrier. Hemingway, as CO of the Marine airfield at Leeward Point, no longer flew an AV-8B on a regular basis, though the

aircraft had been his specialty since it'd been intro-
duced to the Marine Corps.

As the disappointed captain stalked away,
another pilot ran up.

"Colonel, I heard you're going fishing."

Hemingway winced. He'd recognized the voice
before he pivoted to face Captain Ramon "Iron Balls"
Barragan.

A variety of minor disciplinary problems and
communication shortcomings with superiors had
encouraged the Marine Corps to plant Barragan in
Gitmo, hoping to isolate his peccadillos. Though the
bachelor captain didn't encourage female attention,
he also didn't decline it or discriminate between
single and married admirers, causing considerable
havoc wherever he was based. Hoping to minimize
the problem, Hemingway had banned Barragan from
the Officer's Club....in vain.

Barragan's dilemma was not uncommon among
the rare recipients of "the blue ribbon sprinkled with
white stars." That he seldom wore his decoration was
uncommon. Most men proudly displayed evidence of
their valor. As one of only three active-duty Marines
entitled to wear the Congressional Medal of Honor,
Barragan assumed (and accurately so) that his flying
reputation preceded him. He'd earned it several
times over Iraq. His last feat had been taking his
Cobra into a hornet's nest to singlehandedly shield
survivors of a crashed B-52. While waiting for arrival
of rescue aircraft, he'd destroyed three tanks and
chased off an Iraqi battalion which had attempted to
interfere. Before having his Cobra shot out from
under him, Barragan managed to gather the survivors
and see them aboard the rescue helicopter, which he
barely got aboard himself. The flying that day also
earned him his indelicate sobriquet.

Hemingway glared into the contagious grin on
Barragan's face.

"Doesn't your Huey need a shotgun?" inquired
Iron Balls.

The Marine colonel had to give the Cobra pilot credit. He himself hadn't thought to give the Huey an escort.

"I'm available," announced Barragan. "And they don't come any better."

Hemingway winced again. It was the same well-known line the cocky, slim-hipped pilot used on the ladies.

Barragan got serious. "I'd sure like to get off the base, sir."

Now that's a fine idea, thought Hemingway, deciding the flight-time would keep the maverick out of trouble for a short while.

Hemingway nodded. "Why don't you saddle up a Sidewinder on your Cobra, Captain."

"It's happening, sir." Barragan had already taken the precaution of readying his AH-2W attack helicopter.

Changing his mind about putting Valdes in the Huey, Hemingway added: "And dump your gunner. The Cuban officer will be riding with you instead. Put on an aux fuel tank, too."

Barragan's Cobra could travel at 235 mph, nearly double the top speed of a Huey. Hemingway, working figures in his head, determined the Cobra would put Colonel Valdes into Cienfuegos some 70 minutes after his Harriers arrived in the area.

Iron Balls gave the smartest salute he'd executed since arriving in Guantanamo three months earlier....and was wisely out of sight before Hemingway could change his mind.

Hemingway's briefing to his Harrier pilots was short. Codenamed *Jai Lai*, the mission---if approved by higherup---was to eliminate MiGs over Camp Cienfuegos. They would maintain radio silence.

The eight Harriers and Cobra were heading out to sea three minutes later.

Palacio De La Revolucion

The triumvirate had completed their planning for the mass rally---a precise schedule of events meant to appear as a spontaneous demonstration.

Their 11-page scenario was sent to every CDR office in Havana, exhorting the Communist cadre in each block of the city to bring every available citizen to the Plaza de la Revolucion by 3 p.m. All factories, stores, and government offices would be closed. Henchmen from the Rapid-Action-Brigades, spread throughout the crowd, would handle any protestors.

Members of State Security would be at the front of the Plaza---forming a buffer between Castro and his people.

This routine was similar to that of all major speeches by Fidel Castro held in the Plaza....with two exceptions. Today, RAB members would be armed. And the rally would not be broadcast on Cuban TV. Fidel's message would reach his countrymen by radio only. If the Americans attempted to substitute another message, all Cuban radio frequencies would be jammed promptly.

After Vilma Espin departed to make arrangements for the participation of her Federation of Women, the two Castro brothers began a discussion on the deployment of the Special Forces Brigade of State Security and army units at the nearby Camp Columbia.

The Special Forces Brigade---a modern-day *Praetorian Guard*---consisted of 5,000 hand-picked men from the provinces of the island. This unit acted as a "bodyguard" for the Cuban government in Havana. It was equipped with the best armor, helicopters, and other aircraft available to the Cuban military.

Its members were selected from the provinces as a precaution in case they were needed to quell civil disturbances in urban areas such as Havana. Fidel had learned this lesson from the Chinese, who found it necessary to bring in troops from outlying areas in order to quell the 1989 "pro-democracy" demonstrations. The army units stationed near Beijing had been too reluctant to open fire on the students in Tian An Men Square.

Raul Castro was having some difficulty keeping the discussion on the disposition of the Cuban army units, as his brother kept digressing to a more personal subject.

Fidel paced as he spoke.

"The Romanian dictator, Nicolae Ceausescu, was a fool! Each man and woman he shot on the streets became an instant martyr."

Fidel paused to stroke his beard thoughtfully. "In two days, Ceausescu created 6,000 martyrs."

Raul, recalling Vilma's caution concerning children at the Plaza, commented: "Many of those Ceausescu killed were children."

"It makes no difference!" glared Fidel, shaking his cigar at Raul so hard that it dropped ashes on the rug. "They are all the same. Never kill your people in the open!"

The remark struck Raul as being rather callous. He remained silent, thinking. Raul himself had a reputation for ruthlessness, which he deliberately fostered as a means of instilling discipline among his underlings and fear in his enemies. Yet, he considered himself far more sensitive than his older brother....particularly when it came to children.

Before the Revolution, Fidel had a son by his only wife, Mirta---whom he soon divorced. The boy was named Fidelito. Raul often counseled his brother to give more attention to Fidelito, but the suggestion had little effect. Fidel virtually ignored his other eight children (fathered out of wedlock) also.

"It's better to send troublemakers to work farms," continued Fidel. "And let the worst of them rot in prison....until they die of their own accord."

"Of course," nodded Raul.

Fidel abruptly halted his pacing and, staring at the floor, he observed in a subdued voice:

"Ceausescu died poorly."

Raul nodded again.

"He led his country for a quarter-century," continued Fidel. "Ceausescu kept Romania independent of Moscow....and for all that, he was shot in the head."

Fidel resumed pacing.

His voice anxious, Raul cut in. "We must decide what to do with the Special Forces Brigade and army units at Camp Columbia," he reminded his brother.

"That's what I'm talking about," Fidel replied irritably.

Raul turned away to hide his own anger as Fidel stopped at one of the broad windows in his office. Gazing out onto the Plaza de la Revolucion, Fidel spoke in a wistful tone.

"I am concerned for the quality of my immortality."

He pivoted around to Raul.

"I want to be remembered like Che. Look how he moved the people yesterday. And he's been dead 37 years!"

So even my brother believes the CIA voodoo, thought Raul, pulling at the cloth of his military blouse. He debated whether to remind Fidel that it was the Americans who spoke through the hologram, not Che.

"When I'm gone," continued Fidel, "how will my people remember me?"

After a long silence, Raul realized that his brother wanted a response this time. Caught off-guard by the vague question though, Raul studied his brother as he considered his reply.

Fidel glowered back.

Raul shrugged and spoke in a small voice. "A fine monument in the Plaza, perhaps."

"A monument is nothing!" sneered Fidel. "Ho Chi Minh had a city!"

Raul regretted not replying by posing a question of his own. It was usually safer to pick his brother's mind for ideas than to offer new ones.

Fidel turned to the window, his voice pensive again.

"The dogmas of the quiet past are inadequate to the stormy present. The occasion is piled high with difficulty....and we must rise with the occasion."

Raul had heard the Lincoln quote recited by his brother many times, usually during periods of crisis. He waited patiently for Fidel to complete it.

"As our case is new, so we must think anew, and act anew. We must disenthrall ourselves."

Raul remained silent a full minute before venturing to speak.

"Fidel, how should I deploy the Special Forces Brigade and my army units."

His brother walked from the window and sat at his desk. He spoke without looking up.

"Do you think I should retire?"

Raul cocked an eye at his brother. Recently, Vilma and he had discussed such a possibility. After their quiet divorce---still unannounced in Cuba---the former husband and wife had found it convenient to remain professionally close. Both of them had been concerned for their personal safety in the event that Fidel left office unexpectedly. And they concluded that their own survival depended on an orderly transition of power.

In the past, when Fidel complained of the burdens of his office, Raul usually suggested a slower pace or some shifting of responsibilities to others. But Fidel would have none of it. Everyone knew he thrived on a hectic pace....and would trust no one's judgement above his own.

"If I stepped down," posed Fidel, "would the Cubans remember me as they do Che?"

"More than Che," offered Raul.

Fidel ignored his brother.

"I named an airport for Jose Marti. And built a fine monument for him in the Plaza de la Revolucion."

111

After a lengthy silence, Raul asked: "What has this to do with preparations for this afternoon?"

"Everything!" shouted Fidel.

Fidel looked in consternation at his brother, then shook his head in disbelief. Raul was so shallow. Everything had to be spelled out for him. Fidel tried to keep his voice calm.

"If I unleash force against those who oppose me in the Plaza....and lose....I could be buried soon....in a common grave. Then, I will be *nothing!*"

Finally getting some of his brother's drift, Raul thought to reassure him. "The people love you," he insisted. "You will see that at 3 o'clock."

"Yes, my people love me." Fidel grimly smiled at the thought. "But not as they did. Two years ago, they would cheer my face when I appeared on the news reels shown in movie theaters. Now, they sing a jingle of insult."

The jingle was a line to a popular song: *"The man is a little crazy."* It was also one of the reasons that most of Havana's movie theaters were now closed, and the few which remained open only showed films on Saturday and Sunday.

Fidel methodically jammed his cigar in an ashtray, came ponderously to his feet, and walked directly to Raul. Gripping his brother's shoulders, Fidel told him:

"Promise this, Raul. If anything happens to me, give the university my name."

Raul squinted, immediately concerned for his own status in the event that his brother was deposed. Misunderstanding the confusion on Raul's face, Fidel repeated his request more clearly.

"I would like it renamed the University of Fidel Castro."

Raul awkwardly nodded. "Of course."

Fidel pointed to the Plaza de la Revolucion. "And erect a statue twice the size of Marti's. Put it at the opposite end of the Plaza, behind the dolphin fountain."

"Yes, a taller statue," agreed Raul.

"Good!" Fidel gave his brother a brief hug. "It is done."

"Now, the Special Forces," began Raul once more. "What---"

Fidel interrupted. "Keep the Special Forces Brigade behind me at the Plaza, a few blocks away, out of sight. And send some of its units to protect the radio and TV stations."

"And the army?" queried Raul.

"Go to Camp Columbia," said Fidel. "Make sure General Rodriguez is fully cooperating. His units are to back up the Special Forces by patrolling the streets of Havana."

Fidel paused to study his brother a moment. " I will come with you to Camp Columbia, too....if you need me."

"I will not need you," said Raul hastily.

As his brother stalked out of the office, Fidel was both pleased and disturbed. That Raul felt confident of the army's cooperation was good. That Raul might feel too confident of himself was another matter.

Fidel was well aware that behind the back of the two brothers, Cubans often referred to Raul as "the Little Squirt."

The Oval Office

The second message from Guantanamo Naval Base sped through the chain-of-command considerably faster than the first one.

The fact that a flight of Harriers was skirting the southern coast of Cuba caught up with General Steel, the JCS Chairman, just as his helicopter touched down on the White House pad. Upon entering the Oval Office, Steel found the President, CIA Director Rolle, and Secretary of State Walters leaning over a map of Cuba. Steel informed the President of the Harriers without offering his own assessment of the flight.

"Gentlemen," promptly responded the President, "all I've agreed to do in Cuba are the Che messages."

Secretary of State Walters fixed Steel with a frown before speaking. "If there's any evidence that our military is intervening in Cuban affairs, Castro will use it to rally all Cubans to his side."

Embarrassed by the Harrier flight and feeling defensive, General Steel chose to remain silent.

Walters continued. "If those planes caused an incident, Castro could compare it to the Bay of Pigs in 1961. It would play right into his hands....if he's hoping to get a bomb from the Algerians."

CIA Director Rolle was anxious to speak, but held off at the mention of the 1961 CIA fiasco and was immediately thankful.

"Mr President," began General Steel in a calm voice, "the Bay of Pigs was ill-planned and poorly executed because it was a military operation run by *civilians*."

President Steiner half-grinned. "Are you saying the Bay of Pigs would have succeeded if it'd been executed by the military?"

"Sir," replied Steel firmly, "if the Pentagon had been in charge, there would have been no invasion at the Bay of Pigs. That was an exceptionally inferior location to invade the island."

General Steel squared his shoulders. "If President Kennedy had ordered a military intervention, the contingency plan at that time was to eliminate Castro's airpower first. After---"

Walters cut in. "Isn't that exactly what the CIA people tried to do?"

Rolle quickly took the opening. "You're correct, Clayton. Five of Castro's 13 planes were destroyed. The remaining 8 could have been eliminated also....except President Kennedy arbitrarily reduced the 16 B-26s available to attack the Cuban airfields by one-half the day before the invasion. As a result, Castro's surviving aircraft were able to sink one of our ships and drive the others out of the Bay of Pigs....dooming the men already ashore."

There were a few seconds of silence before General Steel resumed.

"After completely destroying Castro's aircover, the 101st Airborne would have landed east of Havana, the 82nd Airborne at the airport to the south, and the Marines would have gone ashore to the west. Castro was to be overwhelmed, thereby discouraging any serious resistance."

Steel paused for but a moment.

"However, I doubt if that strategy would work today. With an active military of more than 130,000 and another 400,000 combat-experienced reserves, Castro possesses the largest and best-equipped military force in Latin America. It could be a long, hard fight if we went in now."

Even though General Steel had turned negative, CIA Director Rolle decided to speak out.

"Mr President," Role began, "this situation reminds me of a somewhat similar one in Panama."

"How's that?"

"Sir, do you recall when a handful of rebel Panamanian officers temporarily captured General Noriega in a coup a few months before we invaded that country?"

Steiner nodded.

"It has always been my contention," observed Rolle, "that we could've avoided the need for that invasion and its subsequent casualties if the White House had quickly supported those rebel officers."

President Steiner contemplated Rolle with a steady eye. Steiner knew there had been several conflicting intelligence reports. By the time the reports from Panama became convincing and the White House had ordered military support, troops loyal to Noriega were rescuing him.

Rolle continued. "Noriega got the upper hand again and personally executed those rebel officers. The opportunity was lost. Later, our failure to act on a timely basis cost the lives of 27 Americans and 475 Panamanians during our invasion."

Steiner frowned. "So, you think this is another *timely opportunity?*"

Realizing he was prodding the President hard, Rolle selected his words with care.

"It could be, sir."

Walters piped up in a pinched voice. "Edward, what you propose is unplanned and dangerous!"

Rolle pivoted to face Walters. "You're partially correct, Clayton. Most opportunities like this are unplanned."

"Mr President," continued Walters stridently. "I recommend against aiding General Diaz."

Steiner picked up the messages on his desk and reread the second one.

"General Steel," he inquired, "how many Harriers are in that flight?"

"Eight, sir."

"Will Castro's MiGs have air-superiority over them?"

"That depends, sir," replied Steel. "If the MiGs engage from a distance with air-to-air missiles, yes....they would be superior. However, since the MiGs are making bombing runs, they may not be carrying those missiles."

"So our Harriers would be gambling the MiGs are not carrying missiles?" posed Steiner.

116

Steel met the President's eyes a moment before reluctantly answering. "Yes, sir."

President Steiner rotated the chair at his desk and sat down, leaning back in a contemplative pose. He well knew how a small military operation could escalate into the chaos of a major commitment. It was far better to plan a large operation in the first place, when its full effectiveness could be controlled. That had been the foundation of the Persian Gulf strategy in 1991, and the maximum deployment of weaponry had delivered the goods.

Steiner shook his head without speaking. Dumping Castro is not worth it, he told himself, unwilling to unleash a major offensive against the Cuban isle.

"General Steel, I'm not in a gambling mood. We stick to the game plan. Recall those planes."

Over The Caribbean Sea

The eight Harriers flew in a modified *loose deuce.* Their combat spread consisted of tight pairs 50 feet off the deck. Each pair maintained an interval of 300 feet, while the distance between the four pairs was roughly one mile. Colonel Hemingway's duo was nearest the Cuban coast.

Their close proximity to the water decreased the chance of being detected on coastal radars. And, at mile intervals, a Cuban naval vessel might sight no more than one pair of AV-8Bs at a time. The need to stay over international waters extended the 360-mile distance between Guantanamo Bay and Cienfuegos to 420 miles.

Colonel Hemingway had kept the flight at a steady 550 knots---the equivalent of 632 mph, under the Harrier's maximum speed. It would take only 40 minutes to reach the coastline off Cienfuegos.

At the 32-minute mark, Hemingway watched the peaks of the Loma San Juan range pass by on his right. The summits---some 55 miles distant---gave the appearance of volcanic islands. Like the Sierra Maestra near Guantanamo Bay, the steep mountains displayed a dried pistachio shade of green along their slopes.

Their color reminded Hemingway of the Sierra Nevada pines at the north end of Lake Tahoe. After the Iraqi War, he and Sandi had climbed a bluff north of the lake that offered an eagle's view into the next state. Then and there, Hemingway made a promise to Sandi. At an even twenty, he'd walk away from the Corps. With only a year-and-a-half to fill it out, he'd get a 50 percent pension. Thinking about that Sierra bluff started to raise doubts about his "training mission."

Cuban politics had never been a great concern of his. And, Hemingway told himself, I'm not looking for any more glory. Downing a pair of Mirage fighters over Baghdad was a nice enough cap to any flying career.

Hemingway also wasn't interested in receiving another "administrative letter" in his personnel jacket. After the liberation of Kuwait, a sergeant in his squadron had rescued three dozen cases of San Miguel beer from an abandoned Iraqi command bunker. When asked what to do with the forbidden alcohol, Hemingway had told his enterprising NCO to "get rid of it." A media guest had written up the ensuing squadron victory party....to the immense displeasure of General Schwarzkopf.

General Boomer---commanding officer of all Marines in the Gulf---had been forced to relieve Hemingway as CO of his squadron, in addition to issuing the written censure.

Later, the Corps compensated Hemingway by awarding him Gitmo as his final duty assignment. Still....the relief as CO had been distasteful; and, now, Hemingway knew he was exposing himself again.

His earphones came to life....the words in Spanish.

"Jai-Lai Uno, Cinco. Bogeys right, 2 o'clock high, 6 miles!"

It was a message from Hemingway's wingman.

Scanning right, Hemingway barely spotted the specks of silver coming fast out of the green background of the mountainous coast. At six miles, the aircraft were still too far away for identification or an accurate count.

Watching the Cuban aircraft come closer, Hemingway debated exactly how far his AV-8B was from the coast. Cuba claimed a 50-mile limit for territorial waters. Though he knew his Harriers were at least 50 miles out, Hemingway decided to be cautious. He spoke in Spanish.

"Jai-Lai flight, Uno. Alter course 10 degrees left."

The eight AV-8Bs adjusted slightly. By the time the Cubans closed up, Hemingway computed he'd be 60 miles from the coastline.

At one mile, the specks enlarged to bug-size. Hemingway was pleased to note there were only six, and they were MiG-23 Floggers, not the newer MiG-29s received by Cuba in 1989.

The six Floggers were at 2,000 feet when two peeled off, the other four maintaining their heading out to sea.

The two MiGs swung around to Hemingway's rear, looking to assume a superior position.

It was common for Floggers and the newer MiG-29 Fulcrums to escort Harriers off the Cuban coast. Occasionally, they initiated mock dogfights where opposing sides attempted to fix their fire-control radar on the other's aircraft for practice....and aggravation value. The harsh buzz made in a pilot's earphones when hostile radar locked on was obnoxious....and meant to be.

Hemingway wasn't especially worried about such games, though. Under the wings of the Cuban aircraft, he had observed large bombs, the weight of which would seriously inhibit the MiGs' agility. In addition, the configuration of a Flogger's cockpit gave it limited downside visibility, and a mediocre turn rate made the aircraft a poor dogfighter at low altitude.

The Flogger had been designed primarily to engage aircraft with medium-range missiles....which were not evident under their wings.

Hemingway assumed the MiGs were from the airbase just north of Santa Clara, 105 miles northeast, and had been on a mission to bomb General Diaz's units when sidetracked to check out unknown aircraft off the coast.

A hard voice in his earphones stiffened Hemingway. It was his wingman.

"Uno! Bandits dropping hardware!"

At his wingman's warning that the Floggers were releasing their bombs into the Caribbean, Hemingway silently told himself: "So, they want to play."

He decided to make the game a bit more complex. "Cinco, Uno. Reduce speed to 100 knots."

Hemingway's instructions were directed to his wingman, but were heard by the other AV-8B pilots as well.

One of the two Floggers streaked over Hemingway's canopy.

He grinned at the frustration of his Cuban counterparts. If they'd attempted to remain behind the Harriers long enough to get a radar fix, their engines might have stalled. And without elevation, the Cuban pilots would've slammed into the water before they had time to restart their engines.

As the two Floggers banked and picked up altitude to come back around, Hemingway chuckled to himself. It was fun making your own rules in a mock dogfight....and no fixed-wing aircraft was more adept at controlling the parameters of aerial combat than an AV-8B.

The Marine Corps officially designated the Harrier a ground *attack* aircraft (for hitting ground targets)....as denoted by the first letter of *AV-8B*. The air-superiority features of the Harrier against *fighter* aircraft were an unintended by-product of its adjustable exhaust nozzles.

In flight, the direction of their vectored thrust could be altered from the horizontal (rearward in normal flight) to the vertical (as far as 9 degrees forward if necessary). This also permitted the aircraft to take off or land vertically like a helicopter---the prime reason the Marine Corps acquired the Harrier, as it was meant to serve in close-support of ground troops.

After the MiG pilots lined up again to the rear, they came in at 60 feet off the deck....10 feet above the Harriers' altitude. A higher elevation would have caused the Cubans difficulty in maintaining visual contact with the Harriers.

This time, the approach of the MiGs was also slower. When they were directly overhead the Marines, both hit afterburner, throwing turbulence into the paths of the American aircraft.

"Take it up!" shouted Hemingway to his wingman.

Both pilots goosed their engines to push themselves higher and out of the disrupted air.

"Keep it at 100 feet!" instructed Hemingway. "If they come up on us like that again, we'll split out diagonally before they pass over."

Hemingway searched his mind for some way to return the treat. As far as he knew, this was the first time Cuban pilots had ever tried to shove Harriers into the water. It was a dangerous stunt.

As the MiGs approached for a third flyby, Hemingway kept glancing at his rearview mirror. The speed of the MiGs was slow as before. They were 500 feet away when Hemingway called out:

"Cinco, Uno. Split turn---go!"

The Harriers banked in opposite directions.

A shadow zoomed over Hemingway, too close for comfort. The Flogger had almost rammed him. Hemingway considered other evasive maneuvers as he watched the Flogger circle for another pass. Getting fancy would expend precious fuel though, and he dropped the idea. Better to let the Cuban hotshots play their games.

Hemingway's wingman returned to his port side, keeping their conservative 300-foot interval.

Thinking the MiGs' harassment was meant to chase his Harriers further from the Cuban coast, Hemingway decided to order his flight an additional 10 miles out to sea. He was keying his mike when a flash of light caught his eye.

The shock wave of an explosion shuddered his Harrier. He glanced left and saw no aircraft where Cinco should have been.

Banking hard right, Hemingway looked over his right shoulder and spotted boiling foam in the water where the Harrier had plunged. Hemingway's first thought was that a MiG had accidentally rammed his wingman. He looked again where the Harrier hit water. The absence of a second spot of boiling foam meant only one thing. A MiG had opened fire.

This was confirmed by the poc-poc of a 23mm shell passing through his canopy. The MiG round entered his cockpit in front of his right eye and exited behind his left ear---leaving thumb-wide holes in the canopy.

"Jai-Lai, drop your tanks!" shouted Hemingway, adding: "Arm your missiles and defend yourselves!"

Near-empty fuel tanks instantly dropped from under each of the Harriers' wings, giving them greater maneuverability.

A quarter-mile distant at 300 feet off the deck, Hemingway spotted both Floggers curling away from one another, each inscribing the far end of a figure-eight pattern as they circled to come around again. At their current speeds, Hemingway figured the Flogger most distant---the one which had downed Cinco---would come into strafing position within another 11 to 12 seconds.

With two bandits on your case, the book dictated disengagement---to get the hell out of the way of a superior force. But a Harrier could not outrun a Flogger, and Hemingway had nowhere to run if he could. At least, he thought, the Floggers are within Sidewinder constraints.

Giving his throttle full-military-power, Hemingway turned with the nearest Flogger and flipped the master-arm-switch on his weapons control panel. Five seconds later, he got a growl in his headset. The heat-seeking sensor at the tip of one of his Sidewinders had registered the hot exhaust of the Flogger.

Hemingway released the missile.

White smoke ignited at the Sidewinder's tail as it dropped from his wing....for a moment, assuming the Harrier's 350 mph speed. Two seconds later, the 85-pound, 9 1/2 foot missile made the AV-8B look like it was standing still.

At the end of the Sidewinder's run, the missile was traveling in excess of 1800 mph. After a lock-on, the kill-rate of the Ford-manufactured missile was 90 percent.

Hemingway's attention was split between the speeding missile and the second MiG. Consequently, he didn't see the Sidewinder's proximity fuse explode in the exhaust of the bandit. His next view was of a Flogger---minus its tail assembly---flying out of an expanding cloud of smoke and debris. Hemingway also missed the pilot's ejection.

He was concentrating on the second Flogger, having banked his Harrier right and reduced his throttle.

At an elevation of 400 feet, the Flogger was coming out of the far side of his figure-eight, unaware of the fate of his partner. The advantage was no longer Cuban.

The remaining Flogger came dead straight for Hemingway from one mile out, its twin-barrel cannon spouting lead.

This time, Hemingway followed the book. Selecting full-power again, he descended to a mere 15 feet off the deck and began the game of chicken.

The Cuban pilot, due to poor downward visibility, had to nearly point his aircraft into the water to align his 23mm cannon for a meaningful shot.

The combined speed of the two aircraft was just under 900 mph. Their gauntlet would last five seconds.

Hemingway saw tracers streaking past his eleven o'clock and slid slightly right. As he realigned head-on, Hemingway unleashed his own 20mm cannon without aiming. The burst served its purpose.

Tracers leaving the Harrier distracted the Cuban pilot, whose next flurry hit the water well to Hemingway's left. Another flurry was better aligned, but chopped into the water in front of the Harrier. The MiG pilot was now so close that he could no longer see his target.

Hemingway took up half the slack on his trigger-control....waiting for the MiG to pull away. It would be a critical shot. If too early, Hemingway knew pieces of a disintegrating bandit might fly right into him.

As the Cuban began nosing up, Hemingway concentrated on keeping his aim just before the Flogger. When the Cuban plane was fully committed to its new flight path, Hemingway took up the rest of the slack.

He watched his 20mm shells ricochet off the rear of the MiG's armored belly, to no apparent effect.

The MiG whizzed past, 40 feet overhead.

Hemingway promptly brought his aircraft up to 50 feet and let up on his throttle, yanking the AV-8B's exhaust nozzles to breaking position. The four nozzles went from horizontal to vertical.

The combined effect was instant deceleration. For a short moment, the powerful exhausts escaping the nozzles created a rooster-tail in the water below. In less than three seconds, Hemingway had reined in his plane, which now hovered nearly motionless in the air.

Swinging his nose around, he selected another AIM-9 on his weapons-control panel.

Though the Flogger was three-quarters a mile away and gaining elevation, the American pilot got the treasured aural tone. He started to squeeze off another Sidewinder when the MiG-23 began yawing to starboard.

Hemingway watched as the MiG gradually lost its aerodynamics. The aircraft began a barrel roll and proceeded into a rapid descent.

Got a hit after all, mused Hemingway, thinking a round or two must have interdicted a hydraulic line of the MiG's tail assembly.

When the Flogger was little more than 150 feet from the water, Hemingway saw the pilot's seat come off the plane. The American almost looked away at what came next. The doomed plane had been on the underside of its roll when the pilot separated; and in the process of trying to right his aircraft, the Cuban had lost his own equilibrium. The seat, occupant still attached, smacked into the surface of the ocean at more than 300 miles an hour.

Death had to be instant.

Hemingway made a wry grin. It was the same Cuban who'd nailed his wingman without warning.

Staying on the deck, Hemingway changed course to a northwesterly direction. In the distance, he'd observed a sky filled with jinking planes.

He hadn't seen a furball since the first day of the Persian Gulf War. Then, as now, if it weren't for radically different colors of opposing aircraft, it would have been difficult to tell friend from foe. The darker Marines were in camouflage green, grey, and tan. The Cubans were in silver. Hemingway quickly counted six Harriers and three MiGs....and assumed another MiG had been downed.

The Harrier pairs followed one another in a stack of closed circles, daring the faster MiGs to attack. The Cubans flew in a broader band around the Harriers, like Indians circling a wagon train.

Remembering how quickly the Iraqi pilots had skated out of dogfights, Hemingway banked right, placing himself between the furball and the Cuban coast, where he could cut off any MiGs trying to hightail it home. The fewer stories told about his Harriers, the better.

He watched an impatient MiG---foolishly diving on a Harrier in a circle---immediately draw the attention of a second Harrier. The Cuban pilot sprinted by the first Harrier, throwing out a stream of tracers.

As the MiG sped away, the second Harrier pilot left his protective circle to take up pursuit behind the intruder. Almost immediately, the AV-8B released a Sidewinder. Spotting the missile, the Cuban pilot made his second mistake---attempting to outrun it. The MiG pilot streaked toward Hemingway, who eased himself higher in case he was forced to initiate evasive action from the missile himself. One afternoon over Baghdad---before tactical air controllers had limited American aircraft above the Iraqi capital---an Air Force plane had accidentally downed its own kind in a furball.

When the panicked Cuban pilot finally started evasive maneuvers, the missile dove with his aircraft. Popping magnesium flares to decoy the missile, the Cuban pulled hard out of his dive. He lost the Sidewinder, which flew through the flares and into the sea.

Seeing the MiG rapidly ascend to his starboard side, Hemingway came around to it. The MiG was a good mile distant when Hemingway saw the pilot come over the top of his loop....upside down. The MiG started an inverted flat spin toward the sea. Hemingway backed off, knowing what had happened.

In looping to evade the Sidewinder missile, the obviously-inexperienced MiG pilot had pulled too many G's and lost consciousness.

Watching the twirling MiG, Hemingway hoped the pilot would regain his senses. When the MiG-23 instead pancaked into the Caribbean, the sight turned the American's gut. It was a fate feared by pilots of all high-performance aircraft.

Switching his attention back to the dogfight, Hemingway made out a Harrier two miles distant limping toward land.

A moment later, he saw a Flogger sweep down through the sky and---looking for a kill---rake the AV-8B. The Cuban pilot, anxious to finish the crippled Harrier, wasn't watching for company.

Hemingway came in fast at a diagonal to the path of the damaged aircraft, so his missile would not select the wrong target. As the MiG turned sharp to get back to its victim, Hemingway fired his second Sidewinder without waiting for a lock-on.

The Cuban spotted the Sidewinder midway in his turn, four seconds from interdiction. The AIM-9 traveled at twice the maximum speed of a Flogger, but the stubborn MiG jock hit afterburner and turned even harder. The missile met the MiG like a blocking fullback.

It reminded Hemingway of the time---back at The Citadel---when he'd delivered a flying block on a cornerback near midfield. The defensive player was the last man chasing the ball carrier down the sidelines. The hit bowled the cornerback over, rolling him out-of-bounds and up to the feet of Hemingway's coach.

The Flogger was still flying....in two pieces. The rear of its fuselage spun skyward as its port wing sliced through the air like a boomerang. The balance of the plane pitched gracelessly forward. When the pilot's seat ejected from the fuselage like a secondary rocket off a firecracker, Hemingway mumbled to himself:

"Good luck with the sharks, sucker."

Remembering the crippled Harrier, Hemingway raced to catch up. As he sped over water, Hemingway considered the ease in which the four MiG-23s had been downed. It was his first encounter with the Floggers, and reports of their limited maneuverability had been telling, in addition to the inexperience of their pilots. Hemingway figured the best Cuban pilots were probably flying the newer MiG-29 Fulcrums.

Approaching the tail of the crippled Harrier, Hemingway detected neither smoke nor fire, yet the aircraft was losing altitude steadily.

Hemingway keyed his mike. "Quatro, Uno. What's the problem?"

No reply came.

Moving in closer, Hemingway spotted part of the problem. The tip of the plane's aluminum tailfin---containing its UHF/VHF and L-Band antennas---had been shot off. He also saw gaping holes in the fin's graphite-epoxy rudder, which flapped uselessly behind the tailfin.

Motioning with his hand, Hemingway indicated to the other pilot to follow him.

Hemingway sped toward the Cuban coast, angling at the foothills of the Loma San Juan mountains south of Cienfuegos. He wanted a hiding place for the aircraft. If he found one, he'd call in a Sea Stallion from the Tarawa to recover both Harrier and pilot.

As Hemingway grazed a coastal road, he spooked a team of oxen pulling a wagon of steaming manure. The dozing driver tumbled backward onto his load.

Hemingway overflew several small valleys leading up into the foothills from the coast. He was looking for a grassy surface the size of a tennis court, isolated from view. When he pinpointed one, Hemingway went back for Quatro's aircraft.

128

Using hand signals, Hemingway again indicated for his pilot to follow. After watching the pilot make a safe vertical landing, Hemingway headed out to sea. Over water, he keyed his mike.

"Jai-Lai flight, Uno. Check in."

"Uno, Dos," reported his senior pilot. "Circling at 2 K. All but one bandit is in the drink."

"What is status of the last bandit?" asked Hemingway.

"Ran like a rabbit," was the reply.

Hemingway started to grumble disapproval, but thought of a more important subject.

"Fuel check!"

As Hemingway expected, the fuel levels of the 6 remaining Harriers were low after the fight.

When he'd joined up with his Harriers, Hemingway conducted a missile count. There were 11 Sidewinders left, out of the original 24....not counting what might be recovered from the disabled Harrier on land.

"Jai-Lai One, Fronton." The words from the U.S. Naval Base back at Guantanamo Bay repeated.

"Jai-Lai One, Fronton."

With the second transmission, Hemingway recognized the voice of Captain Carter. He keyed his mike and responded. "I have you, Fronton."

"Mission denied. Repeat, mission denied. Return to Fronton."

Hemingway wanted to tell Carter that the message denying permission to assist General Diaz was a bit late. For a moment, he debated how much to reveal over his radio concerning the downed MiGs. Deciding that it would not be a secret to the Cuban military much longer, he keyed his mike.

"Fronton, Jai-Lai One. Six bandits initiated engagement over international waters. Defensive measures taken. Five bandits in water. Jai-Lai down one....another crippled."

Carter's reply was immediate. "Roger, Jai-Lai One. Return to Fronton."

Hemingway glanced at his fuel gauge again. It was a ridiculous request. There was no way his Harrier, or any of the others, could make it back to Guantanamo Bay on their remaining fuel. He keyed his mike.

"Fuel too low. Where is Pitstop?"

There was a pause, then Carter replied: "Pitstop, 180 degrees....for 190."

The USS Tarawa was due south, at a distance of 190 miles. Hemingway debated whether to risk flying out to sea, hoping the fuel of each Harrier would last until they found the Tarawa. From their reported fuel levels, he knew three of his Harriers were definitely marginal.

"Fronton, Jai-Lai One. Pitstop also too far."

After a short silence, Hemingway heard:

"Roger. Wait one."

Hemingway knew the commanding officer of Guantanamo Bay was going higher-up. As any smart Navy captain would. Let an admiral take the responsibility. Except the admiral in Norfolk was having none of that. The CNO in Washington made the decision.

Carter relayed it. "Jai-Lai One, Fronton. Make Pitstop. Repeat: make Pitstop."

Hemingway had been thinking of several matters in the interim. The three MiGs he'd blown out of the sky---added to the two Mirages shot down over Baghdad---made him an *Ace*. The thought might have been cause for some elation if he had not been considering the possible consequences now of his decision to run a "training flight." More than a few Marine generals and Navy admirals would hold him fully responsible for one dead Marine pilot and his Harrier....plus another on land if not recovered.

And rightly so, Hemingway told himself. The pilot wouldn't have died without my decision.

Hemingway knew his career would end unceremoniously as soon as he returned to the jurisdiction of the Navy Department---whether it be Guantanamo Bay or the deck of the USS Tarawa. He keyed his mike one last time.

"Fronton, Jai-Lai One. Negative your last."

✈ ✈ ✈

3:00 PM

Plaza De La Revolucion

The mid-afternoon sun threw a fierce heat down upon the great Plaza. Yet, the citizens of Havana did not have the same docile nature which they'd displayed the previous day.

Lou was pleased to observe animated discussions going on about him. The faces of the people had an air of expectancy, an electricity that he'd seen before in other restive crowds.

He had rushed with Camille to the Plaza de la Revolucion when word came of the mass rally. All Cuban workers in Havana, including those at the Swiss embassy, were notified to attend. Every government ministry was closed down, as were all the schools, factories, and stores.

This time, Lou hadn't found it difficult to persuade Camille to accompany him, though she had requested that they remain at the rear of the Plaza.

While Camille still exhibited her normal tense expression, her voice had lost some of its edge and was no longer brisk. Lou had been pleased when she reached out to hold his hand on the way to the Plaza.

For the last hour, the two of them had been peeling oranges to quench their thirst, while sitting on the rim of a circular pool surrounding a fountain.

The fountain consisted of a shoulder-high marble bowl upon which four life-size dolphins perched on their tails. Before the 1990s, water had spouted from the mouths of the dolphins into the pool below. The fountain stood at the opposite end of the Plaza from the Jose Marti memorial platform--- where Fidel Castro would speak.

Shortly after Lou and Camille arrived, five university students---four males and a female with a videocamera---waded through the algae-covered, knee-deep water of the pool and climbed atop the fountain. One of the young men carried a Cuban flag on a short pole, which he tied to a dolphin.

The flag reminded Lou of the state flag of Texas. A single white star was displayed in a triangle of red, with blue-and-white stripes running horizontally across two-thirds of its length.

On Camille's left sat an elderly man wearing a straw hat. When he'd sat beside her, she had noted with a quick glance that his worn clothes had been patched in several places. For a moment, she thought to move away; but, catching a whiff of his pleasant cologne, she took a second look and realized his clothes were cleanly-washed.

Seated on the other side of the old man was No-Chin. He occupied himself by rolling cigarettes from a pouch of tobacco. Each finished product was placed in a thin, silver cigarette case. One of the crimped cigarettes dangled unlit from his lower lip.

Earlier, Camille had pointed to the Ministry of Interior building bordering the Plaza and commented that its three-story mural of Che Guevara---from which the holographic image had come alive the previous evening---was now covered by over-sized Cuban flags. Lou only nodded in response.

Neither of them commented on the highly-visible men wearing red armbands of the Rapid-Action-Brigades, who constantly patrolled in scowling trios through the crowd. Many of these men sported machetes on their waists.

As a pair of neatly-dressed teenage boys with close-cropped hair and wearing orange armbands passed by, Lou asked of Camille:

"Who are those kids?"

"Cadets from the Young Communists," she told him.

Lou's eyes followed two attractive women in blue skirts who were hurrying a group of white-shirted children by the fountain. He estimated the youths ranged in age from about 7 to 13. Each wore a blue-and-white scarf.

"Those are Young Pioneers," offered Camille. "They're like our Boy Scouts."

"Not exactly," Lou replied in a low voice. "I understand most of them can assemble an AK-47 blindfolded within a minute."

She gave him a quizzical look. "Where'd you hear that?"

Instantly regretting his knowing observation, Lou shrugged and changed the subject. "There's almost as many kids here as adults."

Camille's eyes roamed the crowd, observing that fully a third of those nearby appeared to be in their teens or younger.

"How many bodies do think are in the Plaza?" Lou asked.

"Castro usually draws close to a million for a major rally like this," she replied.

The crowd was more numerous than the night before, and Lou glanced behind him, wondering how much protection the fountain might afford if they became unruly.

The elderly Cuban beside Camille leaned forward and gave Lou a friendly smile, then spoke in a barely-accented English slurred by a mouth missing most of its teeth.

"Only when Fidel first appeared in Havana after the revolution were there as many people here as we see today."

Camille returned the man's smile. His face had the deeply-wrinkled tan of someone who'd worked in the sun all his life. Her gaze was drawn to the clarity of his coffee-brown eyes.

The old man wistfully bobbed his head up and down. "All of Havana was here that day....and many more from the countryside. Fidel spoke more than six hours."

Lou chuckled. "I don't know how people can listen to him for so long."

"Do you understand Spanish?" politely asked the elderly man.

Lou pointed to Camille. "She interprets for me."

Glancing at her ringless left hand, the man gracefully doffed his straw hat.

"Good afternoon, senorita. My name is Diego Roca. I am pleased to share a seat at this fountain with you."

When he also offered his hand, Camille took it. His leathery palm felt like coarse sandpaper to her as he wrapped thick, muscular fingers about her hand.

"Thank you," she smiled. "My name is Camille Fox."

Lou extended his hand. "I'm Lou Fricke," he said, then pointed to No-Chin. "And this is my official government escort."

Lou thought it prudent to warn the Cuban citizen of the presence of a State Security agent.

In the middle of rolling another cigarette, No-chin simply nodded to Diego.

Diego came back to Lou. "If you understood Spanish, perhaps you would know why it is easy to listen to Fidel for six hours."

Lou thinly grinned. "No American politician would dare talk that long."

Diego returned a wide smile. "You speak hastily, sir."

The CIA man cocked an eye at the chiding words. Seeing the gentle expression worn by the old man, Lou lost his ire.

"Some years ago," Diego continued, "you had such a man."

In the ensuing silence, Camille inquired: "Who was that?"

"A man of color," replied Diego, "who lives no more."

"Martin Luther King?" offered Lou.

Diego acknowledged with a nod.

Lou tried to recall another American who could mesmerize an audience as well as the famed civil rights leader. A few men came to mind who could speak as well, but Diego was right. None could spellbind as long as King.

"The common people of Cuba love Fidel as your own loved Martin," said Diego.

The observation gave Lou pause. As was the experience of many whites, it had been many years after King's assassination before he came to fully appreciate the significance of King's accomplishments.

Lou shrugged. "I don't understand how Cubans can love a dictator."

Diego reacted with a wide, gaptoothed laugh. "Dictators have been our natural form of government for centuries."

No-Chin was leaning forward, taking an interest in the discussion.

"There is much that you Americans," continued Diego in a patient voice, "don't understand about Cubans."

"If Castro is loved so much," challenged Lou, "then why is his schedule never announced in advance.....except for a major event like this? Why does he have to shift back-and-forth between so many different homes?"

Diego was taken aback for a second.

"Perhaps," he suggested, "if your Martin had been equally clever, he would still be alive today."

Lou got a hard look from Camille. As a State Department specialist in Caribbean affairs, she was fully aware of the numerous CIA-sponsored attempts on Castro's life during the first decade of his rule. In her opinion, the question was in poor taste.

"Men of vision," commented Diego, "are often silenced by the blind."

Lou studied the downcast face of Diego, wondering where such a ragged, weather-beaten man had learned to express himself so eloquently.

Diego raised his head and spoke slowly. "Yes, President Castro is careful, but not so careful that he does not visit every town on this island each year."

The old man paused. "I myself have personally seen him nine times."

Impressed, Camille asked: "Have you ever spoken to him?"

"Once in 1967," nodded Diego. "Fidel even hugged me."

"How was that?" she inquired.

"I had thanked him for sending the high school students into the countryside to teach the peasants to read in 1961. It was a precious gift to me, for until the age of 42, I could not read or even sign my name."

Diego's account brought another to the mind of the CIA man. In a Langley file he'd reviewed, Cuban political prisoners described Castro's visits to their work-farms. Mingling among the prisoners, the unarmed Cuban president would openly engage them in political debate for hours on end. It had struck Fricke as unusual behavior for a dictator.

Shaking his head at the thought, Lou said: "It's amazing Castro has lasted so long."

"As I said," responded Diego, "Fidel is clever. He has many homes, but that is only for his safety. None of them are large. Unlike those before him, Fidel is not interested in wealth."

Lou smirked. Several years earlier, he had been present during a debriefing when a Cuban defector described how he'd made a $4.2 million deposit in a Swiss bank account under the name of Castro.

Diego spoke firmly. "I believe Fidel is not interested in money for himself. When I have seen him, he is in an open jeep....and sometimes he even drives it about Havana himself."

Lou debated whether to mention the Cuban president's three stretch-Mercedes limos with blacked-out windows. They were known as Castro's night transportation. Foreign reporters who'd shared them with the Cuban leader, particularly those who were attractive women, often commented on the luxurious appointments of the vehicles. And there were also the Rolex watches and lavish cars which Castro customarily awarded to each of his new ministers.

After a short silence, Camille asked a question to which she knew the answer, thinking it might prove enlightening to Lou.

"Mr Roca, why do your people always call President Castro by his first name?"

The reply came quick. "Because he keeps himself on the same level as his people. Even at 67, Fidel still works two weeks every year in the fields at sugar harvest time. On television, we see him swinging his machete and sweating like the rest of us."

Lou spoke mockingly. "He probably works in front of the camera for ten minutes."

"No!" No-Chin sharply protested, pointing a finger at Lou. "That is untrue! Fidel sweats a full two weeks! And he takes all the government ministers with him to work the sugar harvest. I have seen this with my own eyes."

Diego raised a hand to calm his countryman, then turned to Lou and asked:

"Do you know how smart our president is?"

Lou silently met the old man's eyes.

Diego Roca slyly grinned. "No one criticizes Fidel more than Fidel himself. He openly admits his mistakes. Then, when he tells us he will try harder....this encourages us to all try harder with him."

Lou noticed Camille giving a concerned look at the sky. He glanced up himself and saw thick cumulus clouds making domes to the north.

"Cubans admire a humble man," continued Diego. "It is part of our Spanish heritage."

Thinking the two silent Americans might have been offended by the conversation, Diego paused until Camille's attention returned.

"Senorita, you have Latin eyes," he told her. "Black pearls of the sea."

An embarrassed smile enveloped Camille's face, and she touched the old man's arm appreciatively. "You speak English well. Where did you learn it?"

Diego drew up his chest proudly. "For 21 years ---until the Revolution---I worked at a sugar mill owned by Americans. Because I could not read, I developed a good ear."

Lou leaned into the discussion again. "Were you treated well by the Americans?"

The CIA man waited for the elderly man to admit how much better off the people of Cuba had been when the Americans controlled most of the sugar mills.

Diego's eyes narrowed as he studied his hands. He wanted to tell his truth, but was uncertain how to say it without offending.

"I was more fortunate than other peasants in the country," he began. "The American sugar mill which employed me gave me work for half the year. I believed my life was good. There was enough money to feed my family...."

Diego paused thoughtfully, not noticing the smug smile building on the CIA man.

"Like other peasants in the country," continued Diego, "my family lived in a hut with a dirt floor and no electricity. We had a well outside, a small garden, and a few chickens. We were happy."

Diego looked up.

"My wife and I were blessed with three boys and two girls. We lost one of each when they were babies to an epidemic. There were no doctors in the countryside. There were no schools either, and my children worked in the fields as soon as they were able. When my boys reached 13, they joined me at the mill. My daughter married at 15."

Diego faced Lou.

"Yes, the Americans treated us well....but the peasants in the fields worked only a month or two. After the sugar cane was harvested, they had to survive on their small gardens. As I said, I was fortunate to have worked in a mill."

Lou vaguely recalled reading something about the Cuban sugar harvest being a short season. And the large landholders (as Castro still did) preferred sugar as their sole crop.

"My eight grandchildren, all born after the Revolution, were luckier than my children," observed Diego. "Of the eight, five have received free university educations. They all have jobs year round. None died of disease, as doctors have been in the countryside offering free care since 1959. Their apartments have free electricity, and even telephones cost nothing."

The face of Diego became apologetic.

"Yes, the Americans treated me well," he said again. "But life is better now."

When Diego saw Camille's troubled expression, he thought to cheer her up. Raising his arms in an expansive manner, he laughed amiably.

"Everyone should be able to retire as I have. I spend my time going to baseball games and other sporting events, for there is no admission charge. Most of my food, I raise myself in a community garden, and what little else I require is very cheap. I do not even need all of my small pension. For an old man, it is a fine life."

Camille wondered what had become of the man's wife, and she was about to inquire when Lou distracted her.

With a resigned expression, he had removed a foot-long Montecristo from his shirt pocket and placed it between his teeth. As Lou searched for his lighter, the cigar was ripped from his mouth.

Before he could react, Camille also snatched the two other Montecristos from his breastpocket. She dropped the first cigar into the stagnant water behind her and extended the remaining two across Diego's lap to No-Chin.

"Would you like to have these?" she asked the State Security agent.

No-Chin stared open-mouthed at the pair of premium cigars. Montecristos were a forbidden item to Cubans, as they were manufactured for export only. It had been years since he smoked a decent cigar, as each Cuban citizen was rationed one small cigar per month, made from the poorest grade leaves.

He wavered between accepting the cigars from an American.

Lest No-Chin refuse the gift, Camille briskly stuffed the Montecristos in his shirt pocket.

Lou, confounded by the woman, angrily whispered in her ear.

"Why'd you do that?"

Looking him square in the eye, she smiled: "I don't like the way they smell."

Lou watched helplessly as No-Chin offered one of the precious cigars to Diego. The old man accepted the gift, bringing the fine cigar under his nose to savor its special aroma.

To calm himself, Lou came to his feet and stretched. Across the sea of heads stretching to the other end of the Plaza, he saw wisps of steam curling off the crowd. He squinted to look again across the Plaza.

The torrid sun had baked the hundreds of thousands of people until a steam arose from their bodies, creating a shimmering mirage above their heads.

Pivoting to sit again, Lou found that he'd lost more than his Montecristos.

A blonde woman with a baby had taken his place on the pool's edge. The hair of the child was lighter than that of its mother, who looked to be no more than 18 or 19. Her brief outfit---white shorts, a red band of elastic around her full bosom, and white tennis shoes---set off her golden skin in dramatic fashion. Lou thought she might have been descended from the Castilian Spanish, who had dominated Havana society since its founding.

The baby's father spoke in hurried Spanish to his wife, causing her to shift closer to him. Smiling up at Lou, the man then patted the open space she'd created for Lou to sit.

Lou nodded thanks and squeezed between Camille and the young mother.

When the baby promptly started to cry, Lou--- out of the corner of his eye---noticed the blonde drop the other side of the red elastic band and latch the child to her swollen breast.

Lou couldn't resist peeking at the nursing baby.

The child, catching the curious man's eye, returned his gaze. When Lou winked, the baby came off its mother's nipple to stare back.

Lou's attention went to the tiny hands of the child which still clutched the alabaster-white breast.

The baby, losing eye contact with the man, again threw its mouth around the rosy nipple and resumed feeding.

Sensing Lou's scrutiny, the mother turned to give him an engaging smile. Her rounded face had appeared attractive to Lou until she'd smiled. Lou caught himself staring into the wide gap between the woman's two front teeth, and he switched his attention to her blonde hair which flowed in generous waves over her bare shoulders.

Lou nudged Camille and said: "Ask her how old the baby is."

The mother spoke first.

"I understand you," she replied with a slight lisp. "Seven months."

"Beautiful child," commented Lou, glancing at it again.

"Thank you," replied the mother.

A tall, middle-aged woman---wearing a faded purple mini-skirt---brusquely interrupted them by thrusting flyers into their faces as she stalked around the perimeter of the fountain. Her arm displayed a yellow CDR band. As she moved away, Lou's eyes were riveted to the woman's well-shaped legs, which had fared better with age than to her bulky torso.

"This is the order of the rally, Romeo," began Camille, aware of Lou's distraction.

Lou looked at the flyer. "What's this?"

"The schedule of events," said Camille.

"Another spontaneous rally, eh?"

Camille gave him a disapproving look.

"What's first?" he asked.

Camille put her finger at the top of the sheet. "The Young Communists start with 'Viva Cuba.' Then the Pioneers do 'Viva Fidel.' The Federation of Cuban Women sing the revolutionary anthem. Castro speaks. Then, Communist Party members will---"

Lou raised his hand. "Enough."

He was concentrating on the purple mini-skirt, which had come full circle and was now only a few feet away. The zipper of the CDR woman's mini-skirt was not meshed....affording a generous display of black lace and bare skin. One button and a safety pin were doing a mediocre job of holding the zipper together.

The nursing mother beside Lou loudly observed: "Fidel is wrong to give a speech at this time of day!"

Pivoting around with a sour face, the tall CDR woman barked out: "Watch your tongue!"

The young mother glared back with equal defiance. "Fidel should not subject children to this heat!"

Studying the baby a moment, the CDR matron contemptuously turned away.

Lou's gaze was irresistibly drawn back to the nursing breast. Satiated by the warm milk, the baby had fallen away from it with closed eyes.

"Would you like to hold him?" the mother asked Lou.

It was too late to pretend disinterest and when Lou failed to decline her offer, she handed the sleeping baby over. As he tried to balance the limp child on his forearms, its mother brushed the hair off her child's forehead before covering her open breast.

"What's your baby's name?" inquired Camille.

"Miguel," said the mother. After a pause, she bent over to massage her calves. "Before coming to the Plaza, I stood in line two hours to buy his first pair of shoes."

Lou raised his brow. "Two hours?"

"That is nothing," said the blonde. "This morning---for my family's monthly ration of coffee---I stood for more than three hours."

"How much do you get?" asked Lou.

"Two ounces."

"For a few cups of coffee," grimaced Lou, "you'll wait three hours?"

"And we don't even drink it," the mother ruefully grinned. "We need it to trade for other food. What bothers me even more is the quality of what they give us. Look at this."

She raised her hand to the red elastic band and pulled it away from her chest. "After only one month, the elastic is giving out."

Lou marvelled at the openly-displayed bosom, thinking the mother must be exceptionally proud of her figure. When Maria released the band, it fell back, leaving a nipple exposed. Hitching the band up again, she commented:

"It's been five years since any store in Havana carried a bra."

Camille debated whether to offer help in finding a bra for the mother. A simple call to a friend in Miami would have one on the way overnight.

The blonde laughed. "Last week, I stood in line all morning to buy an electric toaster. Now, I have three."

"Why do you need three?" inquired Lou.

"I don't. Last week was the first time in years that toasters were available. I saw the line, so I got in it. I will trade my extra toasters for---"

Diego Roca leaned forward to cut in. "Would you like an electric fan?"

She shook her head. "What good is a fan if the electricity is off during the hottest hours? What else do you have?"

He thought. "A small cassette recorder."

"What kind?"

"Russian."

"No! Nothing Russian. What else?"

"A new blanket," offered Diego.

"What color?" asked the mother. "And how big?"

"Blue," said Diego, holding his arms apart to show their width.

The blonde looked to her husband. When he nodded, she came back to Diego. "Done. My name is Maria Gomez. My husband is Alex."

After they'd exchanged addresses, Maria took her sleeping child back from Lou.

Several youths---Lou guessed them to be college students from Havana University a few blocks away---ran by the fountain, tossing green leaflets into the air.

Catching one, Lou held it before Camille so she could read it. Half the sheet was taken up by the face of Che Guevara.

A commotion nearby drew their attention. Two cadets of the Young Communists were grappling with a female student who'd been distributing the green leaflets.

Tearing the leaflets from her hands, the cadets began ripping them up.

"What are you afraid of?" shouted the girl.

One of the cadets---putting his hand in her face ---roughly shoved her backwards. The girl stumbled, but kept her feet.

Disapproving comments came from people nearby, yet none moved to defend the girl.

She came back to the Young Communists and shouted into their faces. "Are you afraid of Che?"

"Shut your mouth!" snarled the cadet who'd shoved her.

Snickering, the girl put her hands on her hips. "For a few special privileges, you sell your souls to the devil!"

Before the cadets could react, the girl ran into the crowd.

Lou, folding one of the green flyers and tucking it into a pocket, picked up another one at his feet.

"What's Che say this time?" he asked Camille.

Lou knew what it said already, still he'd spoken loudly enough so No-Chin could readily hear him. Camille read outloud.

"Stop Giving Our Food to Foreigners! Cuban Food For Cubans! Free Speech! Free Elections!"

In smaller print, there was a quote beneath Che's face. Camille brought the leaflet closer to read it. "This is a quote from Che," she began, "from when he was Cuba's Minister of Industry."

"Why is it that men's shoes, which are made with the same materials and by the same methods as before the Revolucion, soon lose their heels; and that women's shoes often become unusable after being

worn for one day; and the Coca-Cola now tastes un-pleasant and contains all sorts of impuri---"

The green leaflet was ripped out of Camille's hands. She and Lou looked up.

A burly man and his two companions---each wearing a red armband---had already moved to the parents of Miguel and grabbed their leaflets as well. No one protested. Each of the men had a knife on his belt.

Lou made the glint of a smile. The basic message on the leaflet was brief. And most of its viewers would have adequate time to read it before they were confiscated.

Diego Roca leaned forward and spoke apologetically to the two Americans.

"The young people are a problem in Cuba. They do not know what it was like before the Revolution. Their leaflet was false. We do have free elections for our National Assembly."

Maria bent forward, directing her words at Diego.

"The National Assembly is a national shame! Its members must be nominated by the Communist Party, and it meets only twice a year for two days to approve whatever Fidel gives them."

Diego straightened at the woman's truthful rebuke, then looked over his left shoulder.

Lou, hearing the loud and growing whir of a fast-approaching helicopter, instinctively hunkered down and turned his head in the same direction. A military helicopter flashed by....no more than 15 feet above their heads. It swept the length of the Plaza before curving around the far side of the Jose Marti obelisk, and depositing Fidel Castro behind the raised platform.

Camille gripped Lou's forearm.

When he turned his head to her, she whispered. "Why don't we leave?"

Near Cienfuegos

Deciding it was time to contact the helicopter bringing General Diaz's aide north, Hemingway keyed his mike.

"Iron Balls, Jai-Lai Uno."

"I have you Jai-Lai Uno," came the reply from Captain Barragan.

"How many minutes are you from our objective?" asked Hemingway.

"About 15," replied Barragan.

How in the hell did you do that? wondered Hemingway. Travelling at half the speed of the Harrier flight, the Cobra should have been at least 45 minutes behind.

By the extended silence, Barragan guessed what his boss was thinking and added: "My tour guide suggested we take the scenic route."

Colonel Valdes, anxious to reach Camp Cienfuegos, had persuaded the Cobra pilot to fly a straight line over land and sea.

Hemingway released an exasperated exhale. "Iron Balls, I have a driver in need of assistance on emergency frequency."

"Roger, Jai-Lai."

"When you locate him," said Hemingway, "tie him to a skid."

"Will do."

The instructions told Barragan to raise the downed Harrier on its pilot's pocket emergency-radio; and, after finding him, to strap the pilot onto the landing gear of the Cobra.

"Let me speak with your passenger now," requested Hemingway.

"This is Antonio," announced Colonel Valdes.

It was unnecessary to recap what had happened over the Caribbean. The two men in the Cobra had certainly overheard the transmissions during the dogfight.

"Antonio, I need instructions to your home."

"It's a few minutes east of bay center," replied Valdes. "My family is expecting you."

Hemingway rejoined his flight and instructed them to follow his lead. As he headed inland, Hemingway took the Harriers down to 100 feet, staying east of the 20-mile-wide bay on which the port of Cienfuegos was situated.

Knowing a Sea Stallion helicopter would be required to recover the downed Harrier, Hemingway shifted frequencies to contact the USS Tarawa. As he did so, he debated how best to ask the task force commander for more fuel.

"Pitstop, Jai-Lai."

"Go, Jai-Lai." The response was instant.

"We are taking safe haven. Request CH-53 Stallion to bring fuel and pick up downed aircraft."

There was a short pause before a more mature voice replaced the radio technician on the Tarawa.

"Jai-Lai, this is Pitstop CO."

Upon Hemingway repeating his request, he heard: "Wait one."

There was a longer pause, and Hemingway scanned the skies. How soon would the Cuban MiGs return? he mused. After losing one-tenth of its entire MiG complement in one showing, he thought the Cuban Air Force might not be in a hurry to lose more.

"Jai-Lai, Pitstop CO. Give me your fuel status."

Hemingway considered how to phrase his reply. The Cubans had inherited one of the most sophisticated listening stations in the world at Lourdes, hardly a 100 miles distant across the island. Were they listening?

He ran a fuel check. After relaying it to the Tarawa, its task force CO gave him an instant response.

"Send three Jai-Lai with sufficient fuel to Pitstop immediately!"

Hemingway didn't like the order. It would split up his flight, removing the Harriers which could best counter another MiG attack.

"Negative!" protested Hemingway. "If bandits return, that leaves a hundred million dollars worth of aircraft with near-empty fuel-tanks. We'll be sitting ducks!"

"I will repeat order once," growled the task force CO. "Aircraft with adequate fuel will head for Pitshop immediately!"

Goddamit! thought Hemingway, this is lunacy. Another bonehead in the chain of command at the wrong time and the wrong place.

"We will follow *our* orders!" offered the task force CO.

So, the bonehead's higher up, decided Hemingway, and he wondered exactly how high? Norfolk....the Pentagon? Could it be the White House? Whoever it was, decided Hemingway, he would have his own say....someday.

"Roger," said Hemingway disgustedly.

"Stallion with fuel on deck and preparing to lift," responded the task force CO.

When his Harrier pilots also objected to the order, Hemingway cut them short, telling the three returning pilots to lodge their protests on board the Tarawa in as specific terms as they desired.

Hemingway raised the Tarawa CO again. "If Stallion is still aboard, suggest loading up some Stingers. We may need them while refueling."

"First Stallion is airborne," replied the CO. "We'll launch another."

"Roger....out," said Hemingway.

Below and to his port, he made out the distinctive outline of a military base. The tan-colored brick buildings of Camp Cienfuegos and its network of roads were arranged in consistent north-south patterns.

As Hemingway and his two remaining AV-8Bs came over the grassed parade ground of the base, he saw a substantial crowd gathered along its southern perimeter. General Diaz and his staff had listened over Cuban military bands as the dogfight with the MiGs transpired. The army men agreed that the Harriers had done an excellent job of announcing themselves.

Few of the soldiers this far north on the island had ever seen an AV-8B, and Hemingway regretted his fuel situation. Like all Marine Harrier drivers, he enjoyed showing off.

This time, each of the Harriers simply swooped down like a hawk and rolled some 60 to 70 yards after touchdown before coming to a stop.

For the gathered crowd, the pilots would have preferred their grandstand approach---first, a high-speed pass....come back and slow to a perfect standstill just past the center of field....then fly backward to field center...and rotate in place 90 degrees to face their audience. The Harriers might creep forward, letting the roar of their straining engines intimidate the crowd. A final dip of the AV-8B's nose in a polite bow was usually sufficient to set any audience roaring its approval. Marine AV-8Bs were the stars of any air show.

As Hemingway popped his canopy, he saw a wave of soldiers running at him from the edge of the parade ground. Within seconds, he was surrounded by the cheering men, the nearest straining to shake his hand.

They were even more delighted when Hemingway stood in his cockpit and returned their greetings in Spanish.

A jeep blared its horn to clear a path to the Harrier. In its front seat, an officer with gold epaulets on his shoulders stood and gave Hemingway a sharp salute as his jeep came alongside the Harrier's nose. When the jeep halted, the officer extended his hand to Hemingway.

"I am General Diaz," he announced. "Welcome to Camp Cienfuegos!"

"Buenos dias, general. I am Colonel Hemingway, United States Marine Corps."

"Hemingway?" repeated Diaz.

The American nodded. "Yes, sir."

The general's smile widened. "Are you related to Papa?"

"Who?"

"Ernesto," explained Diaz, "the author."

The Nobel-laureate author was greatly revered in Cuba, where he'd written the work that led to his prize. Hemingway's home on the island---a national shrine and major tourist attraction---was maintained just as it was when he had last lived there.

"Not that I know of," responded the pilot.

Diaz studied the Marine a moment. "You have his square jaw and bright eyes," observed Diaz. "You must be related."

With that, General Diaz enthusiastically announced the name of the American pilot to all within hearing.

"Papa! Papa! Papa!" was immediately called out by the milling men. Many pushed closer to touch the aircraft.

Hemingway shouted a question to General Diaz. "What type of aviation fuel do you have?"

"We have fuel for light planes and helicopters," answered Diaz.

"Do your helicopters have turbine engines?"

Diaz shook his head in the negative.

Hemingway frowned disappointment.

"I have fuel arriving in an hour," he told Diaz. "Can you push my planes into hiding until then?"

"Where?" asked the general.

As he'd flown over the military base, Hemingway had noted where his Harriers could be best hidden from a surprise MiG attack. He pointed toward the remaining brick walls of some smoldering barracks---the target of an earlier raid.

"Next to those buildings," said Hemingway. "I doubt if they'll get hit again."

The Cuban general shouted orders to the assembled men, then jumped out of his jeep and climbed up the handholds to Hemingway's cockpit.

Coming even with the American pilot, General Diaz told him: "I always wanted to ride one of these helicopter planes."

Pulling himself behind the cockpit and straddling the top of the plane as if he were riding a horse, General Diaz pointed his men toward the ruined barracks. Dozens of soldiers scurried to get behind the wings and started pushing.

Diaz patted the fuselage affectionately. "This is a fine plane!" he shouted. "I listened to what you did."

Hemingway gave him a quizzical look.

"My radios monitored the MiG pilots," explained Diaz, "as they tried to shoot you down."

"What'd they say?" asked Hemingway.

Diaz laughed. "Strong language. They kept overflying your planes."

Hemingway grinned back. "A Harrier's hard to catch."

Diaz patted the fuselage again. "Since you have come to join my army, I think I shall make you a general."

Hemingway, for a moment, pondered a general's star. He seriously doubted he'd be even a colonel much longer in the American military.

Diaz made a show of unpinning one of the double-stars on his collars. He slid forward on the fuselage and, reaching over the popped canopy, handed the stars to the American.

The soldiers walking the aircraft immediately responded with: "General Papa! General Papa!"

Though the unusual acclaim embarrassed Hemingway, it also warmed him. For a moment, he considered whether to share with the Cubans that he was now an ace....and decided against the idea. Their friendly welcome had been reassuring, and he didn't wish to risk offending them.

When Hemingway could make himself heard, he shouted to Diaz:

"I regret that I shall have to leave as soon as my fuel arrives by helicopter."

The face of Diaz registered shock. "But you have just arrived!"

Hemingway locked eyes with Diaz a moment, then dropped his gaze. How do I explain this? he asked himself. Hemingway shook his head and simply said: "I don't have permission to be here."

"How can that be?" asked Diaz. "You are here."

Hemingway grimaced. In case his words were repeated by the general, it would be better to tell the truth.

"My planes were on a training flight," he began, "when we were attacked by the MiGs. This caused my aircraft to run out of fuel."

A deep frown creased the face of the Cuban general....and he viewed Hemingway with suspicion. "Colonel Valdes told me that your planes were coming to protect my base."

Hemingway maintained steady eye contact this time. "Sir, that was my intention when I left Guantanamo."

Diaz raised both hands in a querying gesture. "So....what happened?"

"Someone"---Hemingway glanced skyward---"above me countermanded my flight."

The general narrowed his eyes. "Who ordered this *training flight* from Guantanamo?"

Hemingway hesitated. "I did, hoping permission to help you would come in flight."

Finally understanding, the Cuban general gave a low whistle.

"My friend"---Diaz made a sly grin---"I believe you have a very large problem waiting for you back at Guantanamo."

Hemingway replied. "I know."

"And I have a larger problem here," continued Diaz.

Hemingway nodded. They both knew that, in the next few hours, the remaining aircraft of the Cuban air force would pulverize the general's armor.

The Harrier pilot offered the general's stars back to Diaz.

After thinking a moment, Diaz shook his head. "No. Please keep the stars as a gift. I appreciate what you have attempted."

The two men rode the Harrier without speaking further as it turned into a deadend street bordered by blackened buildings.

Hemingway turned to Diaz. "I have a disabled Harrier in a field south of here. If you can have it brought here, it may help you."

"What good is a crippled plane?" asked Diaz.

Hemingway pointed back to where he'd just landed. "Put it in the middle of your parade ground. If returning MiGs see it, they may think there are other Harriers protecting your base."

Diaz's demeanor brightened.

"I'm sure those MiG pilots," Hemingway added, "know how fast a Harrier can get airborne."

"How fast is that?" Diaz asked for himself.

"With a warm engine"---Hemingway had a gleam in his eye---"five to six seconds."

"Where is this plane?" demanded Diaz.

After Hemingway gave hurried directions, Diaz ordered his soldiers to stop pushing the Harrier. Motioning his jeep over, he used a field radio to send a tank-carrier for the downed aircraft and then summoned a helicopter.

Diaz faced Hemingway. "You must come with me in my helicopter to find this plane."

Hemingway checked his watch. "In a few minutes, your Colonel Valdes should arrive here in a Marine helicopter. It will also carry the crippled Harrier's pilot---who will be a better guide back to his plane."

Diaz nodded. "Excellent!"

The general's helicopter landed at the other end of the deadend street, flushing a small cloud of ash and debris into the air. The two other Harriers were positioned on adjacent streets among blackened barracks. To further disguise the aircraft, Diaz ordered large tarps. When they arrived, Hemingway cautioned the soldiers to tie quick-release knots so the tarps could be instantly pulled away.

Hemingway told Diaz: "I would like to be notified if your radios hear anything over frequencies used by the Cuban Air Force. The more warning we have of MiGs showing up, the better we'll be able to counter them."

"I have already issued orders to be notified myself," replied Diaz. "But what can you do if your planes are low on fuel?"

As Hemingway considered the question, Diaz said: "Why don't you siphon the fuel from the two other planes into yours so at least one of your aircraft can fight?"

Hemingway replied with an admiring grin. "I'll need a two-inch hose."

"We use this method all the time," said Diaz, who obtained a hose from a nearby jeep. Empty gas cans arrived faster than the tarps. The switching was near completion when Captain Barragan came overhead in his Cobra.

When Barragan saw his downdraft throwing up too much debris, he moved down the street away from the Harrier. As he eased the Cobra to the street near Diaz's helicopter, both Hemingway and Diaz ran toward him.

As his rotor blade wound down, Barragan received instructions from Hemingway. As soon as the crippled Harrier's pilot was unstrapped from the Cobra skid, he took the seat of Colonel Valdes and Barragan lifted off again....with the Cuban helicopter close behind.

When the sound of the departing Cobra permitted him to speak, General Diaz told Hemingway: "I shall stay beside you with my radio."

Hemingway, feeling his football injury, roughly massaged his shoulder. The muscles had tightened, and he worked his upper arm in circles for a minute before remounting his Harrier.

Plaza De La Revolucion

When he spotted Castro's helicopter, the agitation-propaganda director of the mass rally did a fast radio-check with each team captain of the Young Communist cadets.

The moment Fidel Castro appeared at the raised podium on the Jose Marti memorial, 26,000 teenage voices greeted him with:

"VIVA CUBA! VIVA CUBA!"

By the third repetition, others in the Plaza joined in. A million voices visibly swelled the chest of the Cuban president.

After precisely a dozen repetitions, the Young Communists fell silent. And without their cue, the crowd began to quiet.

Castro waited until the chant had completely faded before leaning into his microphone to shout:

"Viva Companeros!"

At this prompt, the voices of the Pioneer children were joined by the Young Communists in the Plaza.

"VIVA FI-DEL! VIVA FI-DEL!"

This chant was as routine as the previous one, and had been for three-and-a-half decades.

From the podium, he strained forward, hearing a faint yet distinctly different chant between his.

"VIVA FI-DEL!"

"Viva Che!"

"VIVA FI-DEL!"

"Viva Che!"

"VIVA FI-DEL!"

"Viva Che!"

Forewarned, the Pioneers, Young Communists, CDR officials, Rapid-Action-Brigade members, and other supporters of the Castro regime automatically increased their own volume to drown out the rebellious counter-phrase.

"VIVA FI-DEL! VIVA FI-DEL! VIVA FI-DEL!"

But after two minutes, when the Communist voices began to fade, Castro once again heard the weaker:

"Viva Che! Viva Che!"

Fricke, sitting on the edge of the pool, glanced over his shoulder at the students atop the dolphin fountain. The four boys were shouting "Viva Che!" at the top of their lungs, and the girl with them was filming the crowd with her videocamera.

The agit-prop director of the rally hastily revived his contingents.

"VIVA FI-DEL!" resumed....once more overpowering the "Che" outcry.

At the dolphin fountain, a squad of Young Communist cadets hopped over the edge of the pool and into the murky water. Approaching the students atop the fountain, they demanded a halt to their dissident words.

Ignoring the warning, the students continued chanting.

"Viva Che! Viva Che!"

When the cadets attempted to climb onto the fountain platform, the students pushed them back into the water. One cadet, grabbing the foot of a student, managed to yank him off the fountain. The cadets quickly pounced on their captive.

Other dissidents in the Plaza who did not fall quiet when confronted by RAB and CDR members received similar rough treatment.

After a second dozen chants of "VIVA FI-DEL," the agit-prop director let the chant halt.

"Viva Che!" re-emerged, this time stronger.

At the fountain, the Young Communists were trying to push their beaten captive under the shallow water.

When the other male students atop the fountain jumped down to rescue their drowning companion, the girl continued to record the battling students with her videocamera.

As the agit-prop director frantically signalled again to his contingents, Fidel Castro began to notice the first commotions in the Plaza where dissenters were being beaten.

The sight of the melees gave Fidel an uneasy feeling, a sense of sadness and disappointment. Never before had it been necessary to suppress vocal opponents at one of his rallies. And it brought to mind the beatings he himself had suffered from Batista henchman at protests which he'd organized during his university days. The bruises had only served to stiffen his resolve.

It was Castro's second disappointment in the last quarter-hour. As his helicopter approached the Plaza, he'd received the first word that a flight of his MiGs had intercepted an unknown number of hostile aircraft off his southern coast. His Air Force commanders were unable, or unwilling he suspected, to furnish sufficient details of the engagement yet. Castro had enough experience as a military leader to know what the vagueness of his commanders meant. When clarification came, it would not be favorable.

"VIVA FI-DEL! VIVA FI-DEL!" began to dominate the Plaza again, this time at a more rapid pace, in order to prevent Che's chant in between.

Satisfied that his own chant had discouraged the other one, Castro hurried off the podium to yell instructions into the ear of his agit-prop director. Then, stepping back onto the podium, he waited for his personal chant to end.

When it abruptly halted, Castro immediately bellowed into his microphone:

"VIVA CHE!"

His amplified voice resounded across the Plaza, shocking his people into silence.

Again, he called out the tribute to Che....and again.

At the sound of Castro's repeated shouts, the embattled youths under the dolphin fountain stopped fighting. After their initial surprise, the Young Communists---hearing and seeing Castro lead the Che chant---came out of the pool. Their enthusiasm nearly matched that of the university students in repeating the newly-sanctioned cheer.

Elsewhere in the Plaza, other confrontations also halted due to Castro's initiative in usurping the dissident chant. Soon, everyone in the Plaza joined Castro.

As "VIVA CHE!" continued, Fricke noticed the students had rejoined the dolphins at the top of the fountain.

They and other student demonstrators in the Plaza---realizing they'd been co-opted by Castro---finally let the Che chant die.

As it ended, Vilma Espin joined her brother-in-law on the podium. Fidel stepped back to give her the microphones.

Vilma began the first verse of the Cuban national anthem and was joined by 130,000 voices from her Federation of Women.

When Maria and Diego stood to sing, Lou and Camille also came to their feet. Most of the people about them sang with the Federation of Women. At the anthem's end, Vilma Espin disappeared from view, leaving the Cuban president alone on the podium.

Before he could speak, a chorus of voices at mid-Plaza cried out:

"Cuban Food For Cubans!"

The rushed words had an air of uncertainty. Throughout the Plaza, other students raggedly repeated the slogan. For several seconds, the hundreds of voices sounded meager compared to the hundred-thousands of before.

Gradually, the crowd picked up the chant. The words were well chosen, as they gave voice to a strong sentiment of the people. Most Cubans resented the bland diet to which they were restricted while the best foods grown in Cuba were exported or offered to tourists. Angry voices soon caused the new slogan to reverberate throughout the Plaza.

"CUBAN FOOD FOR CUBANS!"

Lou glanced over his shoulder at the students atop the fountain. At the final *CUBANS*, the students raised a collective fist to the sky.

Maria's booming voice drew his attention next. Holding her baby in one arm, she had come to her feet and now blared out:

"CUBAN FOOD FOR CUBANS!"

To Maria's front, Lou noticed the tall CDR matron---with whom Maria had exchanged words earlier---spin around.

Maria shouted into her face. "CUBAN FOOD FOR---"

It happened too fast for Lou to react.

The taller woman shoved the young mother, causing Maria and her baby to flip backwards over the edge of the pool. Both disappeared under the stagnant water.

The child's head broke the surface first, held up in the hands of its still submerged mother. As the father jumped into the pool to help, Lou reached out to steady the squalling child.

Maria rose sputtering out the water, her blonde hair plastered across her face and shoulders. The red sash had sagged to her waist, and sunlight glistened off her wetted chest.

Maria pushed the child into its father's arms and, hurtling the pool's edge, screamed at the CDR woman.

"Pig-bitch!"

Maria's open hand was a blur as it loudly smacked into the other woman's face.

The blow staggered the CDR matron, who swung back and missed.

Lou, as did the other men nearby, delighted at the spectacle of the half-naked blonde fighting the mini-skirted matron.

Maria, winding up for another swing, forced Lou to duck.

The matron caught the blow on her shoulder.

Head down, Maria wildly began to pummel her opponent's body with her fists.

In defense, the taller woman reached out and grabbed a handful of blonde hair to hold Maria off.

As the two women circled, Lou noted the purple mini-skirt had popped its button and pin. Only the bulk of the woman's hips now held her skirt up.

The CDR woman, tiring of the punishment delivered by her quicker opponent, stopped trying to circle away from the furious fists and started to kick. As her shoes found their mark, Maria slowed her charge.

The matron, using both hands to grab the blonde hair, pushed Maria's head down so she couldn't see the kicks coming.

Unable to shake loose, Maria scratched at the arms of the older woman.

The raking of her arms only made the CDR matron kick harder.

At a hard strike to her shin, Maria threw a hand out and caught the hem of her opponent's mini-skirt. She yanked at the skirt, throwing the taller woman off-balance, forcing her to release one of her hands from the blonde hair.

Maria began to use her shoes also.

The scrapping women kicked at one another in rapid succession, one holding hair, the other holding a skirt.

Maria connected to her opponent's ankle, and the CDR woman yelped in pain. Feeling her hair come completely free, Maria gave the purple mini-skirt a strong yank as she straightened up.

A spirited cheer arose from the men around the fountain. The seam under the faulty zipper had given way.

Maria danced away from the other woman, holding aloft the purple mini-skirt.

With her hands, the CDR woman attempted to shield her tattered underpants, but her hands were too small for the task. They could not hide a checkerboard of fatty flesh poking through numerous holes in the black lace panties.

On any other island of the Caribbean, the frayed undergarment would have been discarded long ago.

Maria, seeing her embarrassed opponent at the edge of the pool, charged. Sinking her shoulder into the side of the matron, Maria bowled her into the water. And, with satisfaction, Maria tumbled after her.

As both women splashed into the water, Lou noticed the girl atop the fountain with the video-camera was filming the fight.

Maria stood up in the water first. Clasping her hands on high like a victorious athlete, Maria pumped them and shrieked:

"CUBAN FOOD FOR CUBANS!"

With few exceptions, the applauding people around the fountain joined their bare-chested cheerleader in the slogan.

With each pump of her arms, their enthusiasm grew. Even Maria's husband had to admire the natural beauty of his wife as her elegant bosom bobbed upward with each flex of her arms.

"CUBAN FOOD FOR CUBANS!"

When the CDR woman sat upright in the water, Diego Roca tossed her the purple mini-skirt. The matron, busily wiping her eyes, didn't notice when the skirt landed nearby.

Maria, still leading the chant, grabbed the mini-skirt and flung it over the heads of her onlookers. As the people applauded anew, Maria paused to draw her red band about her bosom and stepped out the pool.

Gawking in admiration at Maria, Lou thought the wet elastic band clung to her jutting bosom in a manner even more appealing than when her chest had been bare.

"CUBAN FOOD FOR CUBANS!"

At the opposite side of the pool, the CDR woman made her way out of the water and slunk off.

When Castro first heard the "food" slogan repeated in the Plaza, he angrily turned his back on the new words of dissent. Summoning his State Security chief, Castro demanded of him:

"Remove those people from my Plaza! They will not disrupt my rally!"

161

But even as his State Security jefe scurried off, Castro heard the food slogan picked up by more and more of his people. Realizing it would be impossible to haul off all those who now repeated the slogan, Castro called for the agit-prop director of the rally--- the man with whom he'd drawn up the precise schedule of its events.

The harassed man mounted the backsteps of the podium with eyes full of apprehension. In his hand, he held a green leaflet.

"What can we say now?" yelled Castro to his agitation-propaganda jefe.

With a shrug, the man replied: "Let us repeat the revolutionary anthem."

"No!" snapped Fidel. "That would be ridiculous. I need new and better words....to smother what they shout."

Fidel Castro, a man who controlled people by knowing when to apply either a grand charisma or an utter ruthlessness, was confounded. Until the previous evening, his people had never openly challenged him.

Knowledgeable critics of the dogmatic Cuban president often faulted him for his lack of ingenuity. Improvising for the unpredictable had never been his forte.

"Try 'Viva Fidel' again," suggested his agit-prop director.

"Fool!" exclaimed Castro. "Do you forget what happened the last time we used that?"

The downcast man remained silent.

"Think of something!" demanded Castro.

The agit-prop jefe turned the green leaflet over in his hand. When an assistant had first given it to him, he'd hesitated to reveal its existence to the Cuban president. Desperate now, he offered it.

Castro grabbed the leaflet and reached in a pocket for his glasses. Examining it, he spouted out:

"Who gave you this? Where did it come from?"

"It was found in the Plaza just before you arrived. Running youths threw it to the people."

Castro reread it....and closed his eyes to think. Behind him, the maddening chant continued to build.

"CUBAN FOOD FOR CUBANS!"

Castro called for his brother. Raul came with Vilma, and the three conferred out of sight on the podium.

Throughout the Plaza, many of the people were also confused.

For 35 years, their *directed* responses at mass rallies were Fidel Castro's idea of direct democracy. When he had reneged on his 1957 promise to hold free national elections, he told the people they "voted each day." And by signifying their approval at his mass rallies, Castro maintained, they had no need for formal elections.

Cynical Cubans, on the other hand, referred to the large gatherings as Fidel's *rent-a-crowds*.

Accustomed to participating in choreographed assemblies, many of the people in the Plaza were uncertain which chants were official and which were not. The RAB henchmen who'd confiscated the green leaflets were now roughing up anyone who joined in the chants, heightening the tension in the Plaza.

At the rear of the Plaza, behind the dolphin fountain, were the six Havana University students who had distributed the green leaflets. They were now coordinating the dissident chanting. That they were related by blood was considered a vital safeguard. At the first notice of the rally, the six students had stuffed litter containers throughout the Plaza with the pre-printed leaflets. Later, when the crowd had built, the leaflets were retrieved and given to other students for distribution.

At the front of the Plaza, Castro asked his brother: "Are my Special Forces in position?"

Raul nodded confirmation. The elite military unit waited in trucks two blocks north of the Plaza.

"How many?" asked Fidel.

"Three thousand."

"Where are the rest?"

"One thousand protect the radio stations in Havana. Another thousand are at the TV station."

A momentary alarm froze the face of Castro. "What do you have in front of me then?"

"State Security"---Raul confidently smiled---"with 600 automatic rifles loaded with rubber bullets."

The alarm on Fidel's face frightened Raul. Pointing to the crowd, Raul encouragingly asked: "Is it not time to use the knives?"

Fidel glanced over his shoulder at the chanting people. Yes, he thought, the troublemakers must be silenced. When his face came around to his brother again, Fidel nodded approval.

Raul returned a satisfied grin.

With that, Fidel pivoted to mount the podium. There was no alternative.

He came to the lectern and stood tall before his protesting people so they could all see that he had returned. Fidel then began to shout into his microphone....in unison with his people.

"CUBAN FOOD FOR CUBANS!   CUBAN FOOD FOR CUBANS!"

For the second time, his Communist loyalists---hearing the amplified voice of their leader---paused in their attacks.

Fidel, throwing up his arms in rhythm with the words, shouted at the top of his lungs. He intended to excite his people to a fever pitch in order to exhaust them.

"CUBAN FOOD FOR CUBANS!   CUBAN FOOD FOR CUBANS!" resounded from the loudspeakers across the great square.

As Castro continued leading the chant, the crowd's collective rage gave him pause to think. In their voices, he could sense an accumulated frustration and pent-up anger of 35 years. A man less certain of himself might have been cowed by the mass outburst of hostile emotion, but the Cuban president was invigorated, even inspired by the challenge of his people.   His first reaction to an insurmountable problem was never despair.   Problems were only opportunities to create new solutions, he endlessly told his ministers.

And it is only food, Castro told himself. How can they care so much for food? It made little sense to him.

"CUBAN FOOD FOR CUBANS!"

As he strained his voice with the crowd, Castro thought of the night before. Every food store in Havana had been picked clean. Restaurants were stripped of their food stocks. Even the hotels catering to foreigners had been ransacked. Other consumer stores in Havana---due to the shoddiness of products on their relatively barren shelves---had been left untouched.

"CUBAN FOOD FOR CUBANS!"

Fast thinking on Vilma Espin's part had saved the food warehouses within Havana. State Security men had been dispatched to guard their entrances, until army units arrived to cordon off the buildings.

"CUBAN FOOD FOR CUBANS!"

However, no one on the ruling triumvirate had thought to black-out communications soon enough. For a short time, the food riots in Havana were reported on Cuban TV and radio, encouraging similar riots throughout the island. And the damned TV Marti in Miami had continued to rebroadcast the initial Cuban transmissions even after the communications black-out....until Vilma had suggested the cutting off of all electricity on the island nation.

"CUBAN FOOD FOR CUBANS!"

When will you crazy people quit? silently asked Castro, still chanting with them. Already, they'd repeated the food slogan at least 50 times.

He recalled the last time a chant had received such spontaneous repetition at one of his rallies. It was many years earlier....the culmination of his triumphant march to Havana in January of 1959. The chant had been his name.

"CUBAN FOOD FOR CUBANS!" Castro felt his voice becoming hoarse.

He had decided what he must say when the crowd quieted, though it sorely vexed him.

Remembering to choose his words carefully, the Cuban president cynically grinned. In the autocracy of Cuba, it had never been necessary to follow up on promises.

"CUBAN FOOD FOR CUBANS!"

Finally, Castro fell silent at his microphone.

He gave a benevolent smile to his people. Early in his reign, Castro had studied a hour-long tape of the Pope addressing a stadium of the faithful in Mexico City. The second time he reviewed the tape, he'd turned off the sound and simply watched the gestures of the religious leader. The Pope's powerful presence was most evident in his knowing facial expressions. And, for long hours, the new Cuban president had practiced the same body language before a mirror.

"CUBAN FOOD FOR CUBANS!"

Between the chants of his people, Castro began to shout into his microphone the word:

"YES!"

It did not occur to Fidel that---in this, his acquiescence---it would be the first time in 35 years that his people were truly exercising his version of democracy.

"CUBAN FOOD FOR CUBANS!"

"YES!"

"CUBAN FOOD FOR CUBANS!"

"YES!"

Those nearest the podium broke out in applause at Castro's new response. And, gradually, the chanting switched to wider applause throughout the Plaza.

You're mine now, thought Castro. *Once, again.*

Camp Cienfuegos

"Jai-Lai, Stallion One."

The metallic voice crackling over Hemingway's earphones gave him a start. He keyed his mike to respond to the pilots of the CH-53E helicopter.

"Go ahead, Stallion One."

"Jai-Lai, we're inbound. Approaching Cienfuegos Bay. We'll need vectors."

"Stay 15 clicks inside eastern edge of bay, Stallion One. You'll fly right into me."

At the announcement of the pending arrival from the Tarawa task force, Hemingway had mixed emotions. Within a short time, the fuel brought by the helicopter would have him out of harm's way. His Harriers could be back aboard American territory---the deck of the USS Tarawa---inside of 40 minutes.

Hemingway also knew he'd be ordered to Admiral Country as soon as his aircraft touched down on the Tarawa, and he wondered where the task force commander would begin his chewing out. For taking the initiative to run a "training flight"....the loss of the Harrier pilot and aircraft....or the unauthorized landing on Cuban territory?

After the Admiral's tongue-lashing and debriefing, Hemingway knew a general court-martial would follow, and he debated what could be offered in his defense. A training flight was within his authority, but its timing was certainly questionable. While the aerial engagement had been initiated by the MiGs, it wouldn't have occurred without the training flight. As for landing on Cuban territory, that too was an unforeseen result of his initiative.

Deciding the best policy was to mutely wait out the wrath of his superiors, Hemingway felt some anger of his own as he pondered the identity of the bonehead who'd cut his flight in half. That decision is worthy of a court-martial too, he told himself.

The thunderous whop-whop of a Sea Stallion built in his ears. The fat fuselage of the CH-53E passed directly overhead, shading Hemingway's cockpit. It was a lengthy shadow, as a Sea Stallion was the largest helicopter in the Western Hemisphere at 91 feet. Its pilot was hugging the ground to minimize observers from above.

Hemingway, squinting through debris the Stallion's downdraft flushed from the street and adjacent, burnt-out buildings, promptly shut down his engine. Swirling ash and dust reduced his visibility to less than 15 feet.

"Jai-Lai, Stallion One."

"Go," muttered Hemingway, irritated at the Stallion pilot's choice of flightpath.

"Setting down," began the helicopter pilot, "four-hundred yards to your northwest, in open field."

Hemingway leaned out of his cockpit and shouted to General Diaz.

"It's landing on your parade ground!"

When Diaz's jeep and several others disappeared down the street, Hemingway closed his canopy most of the way to halt the ash buildup in his cockpit, then keyed his mike.

"Stallion One, unload fuel containers onto jeeps."

"Roger," replied the CH-53E pilot.

As Hemingway waited, the dirt, leaves, and other debris in the air began to settle. Fine ash continued to obscure his vision beyond 60 feet.

"Jai-Lai, Stallion One. Most of your fuel is off-loaded. Where's this Harrier that needs an external?"

Hemingway hesitated. "It may be coming to you, Stallion One."

"Clarify, Jai-Lai."

Hemingway decided to switch frequencies and check with Captain Barragan to see if the Cubans had placed the crippled Harrier on a tank-trailer yet.

"Wait one, Stal---"

"Let's get outta here!" came from the CH-53E pilot.

"What is it?" yelled Hemingway.

When the CH-53E pilot didn't reply, Hemingway crunched his fist into his knee.

No, thought Hemingway. Not now!

Though he couldn't see the object that had taken the Stallion pilot's attention, Hemingway could hear it. The scream of a diving MiG was joined by the chatter of its 23mm cannon.

For a moment, Hemingway put himself in the place of the Sea Stallion crew. On the ground, they were an easy target for a MiG. In the air, they could dodge and weave to protect themselves from the shells of a fighter jet.

Unless, winced Hemingway, *the MiGs came back prepared for me.* And he was certain they had.

"Stallion One! Do you see Atolls?" demanded Hemingway.

The two CH-53E pilots were too busy yelling between themselves to hear the Harrier pilot's query.

Hemingway raised his voice. "Do the MiGs have Atolls?"

Still no answer.

"Stallion One, get out of your aircraft!" he yelled. "Get out of your aircraft!"

Hemingway was almost positive the MiG-23s had returned with Atoll medium-range missiles. It was their best offensive weapon against an enemy aircraft found at altitude. Even at lower levels---if the missile could distinguish its target from ground clutter---a lucky lock-on could take his Harrier.

What Hemingway had encouraged the Stallion pilots to do was what most Marine aviators were least likely to do. But, abandoning their helicopter offered the best odds of survival.

Hearing and feeling the concussion of nearby explosions, Hemingway looked skyward. Overhead, more blue sky was showing through the ash-grey haze, and he realized the outline of his aircraft was no longer hidden from a close flyby.

Though the remaining ash in the air might hinder his engine performance, Hemingway hit his start button and heard the low whining noise behind his seat begin. The whine retarded for a half-second, then detonated in a deafening roar with the firing of the Harrier's engine.

For the next 60 seconds---as he brought up his engine---Hemingway alternated between checking the sky over his aircraft and the instruments on his control panels. Attaching the oxygen mask to his flight helmet, Hemingway strained to see in front of his aircraft. He needed 200 feet for a rolling takeoff and estimated his line of clear sight down the street was now at 150 feet. For a moment, he considered a vertical takeoff, then discarded the notion....the fuel expended would be too precious.

Praying his aircraft would deliver on a compromise, Hemingway adjusted his exhaust nozzles to 10 degrees off the horizontal, applied his brakes, and brought his throttle to 55 percent. He glanced at his gauges, simultaneously releasing the brakes and jamming his throttle to full power.

The Harrier snapped forward.

On a normal rolling takeoff, he would watch his speed dial during the 1.6 seconds it took his engine to come to full power. And at 40 mph, push his exhaust nozzles to 60 degrees for instant liftoff after 200 feet.

Now....watching his speed dial was a luxury Hemingway could not afford. Instead, he concentrated on the haze before his accelerating Harrier.

When the jeep of General Diaz suddenly materialized, racing directly toward him from the opposite direction, Hemingway's aircraft was moving at 25 mph, having travelled little more than the first 100 feet.

Hemingway instantly pushed his nozzles to 80 degrees.

He felt a bump and saw his nose dip dangerously as the Harrier leapt off the ground. Hemingway knew his aircraft had hit something, but he was airborne, climbing fast, and concerned elsewhere.

Below him, the jeep driver could no longer hold his steering wheel. The windshield frame---hit by the Harrier's nosewheel---had flipped into his arms, snapping the bones. As the aircraft passed overhead, the heat-flash of its exhaust nozzles singed the shoulders of the driver.

General Diaz, seeing the onrushing plane at the last moment, had doubled his body behind the dash. His back was equally burnt by the aircraft's exhaust.

At 100 feet elevation, Hemingway viewed the source of the explosions he'd heard earlier. The two other Harriers---now flaming wrecks---had been spotted and strafed. Silently thanking the Sea Stallion drivers for creating the smokescreen of ash over him, Hemingway prudently descended to 20 feet off the deck. As an added precaution, he remained over grass to minimize his profile as he moved toward the parade ground.

Coming to the edge of the field, Hemingway frowned at the decision of the Sea Stallion pilots. They had elected to ride it out. Their helicopter was erratically flying the perimeter of the parade ground.

The CH-53E reminded Hemingway of an injured bird, able to fly but not effectively. A MiG swooped down on the Stallion, throwing up dirt as its 23mm rounds peppered the ground. Hemingway couldn't determine whether the helicopter had been seriously damaged, but he knew it was taking hits.

Another MiG came in view, headed for the Sea Stallion.

The diving aircraft was a MiG-29 Fulcrum, one of the newer fighters given to the Cubans as a parting gift by the Russians in 1991. In addition to having a look-down/shoot-down radar capability equal to the Harrier, the Fulcrum possessed a 45 percent better turning rate than the Floggers which the Jai-Lai flight had fought earlier. Hemingway could see that the MiG-29 was armed with air-to-air missiles similar to his Sidewinders.

As he pushed his aircraft higher and armed his AIM-9s, he shouted: "Stallion One! Get out of that crate!"

Again, his entreaty was ignored. The helicopter continued to circle.

Assuming a hover at 100 feet, Hemingway manipulated the air vents at his wingtips and the ends of his fuselage to orient himself to the departing MiG.

"Kiss it goodbye," Hemingway told his counterpart at the steady aural tone of a Sidewinder's lock-on. He squeezed it off.

The 86-pound missile dropped from his wing-tip smoking and free-fell 50 feet before rocketing forward. Hemingway watched the white-hot flames exit its 5-inch wide tail as the Sidewinder sped out from beneath him, homing in on the MiG-29's exhaust.

Remembering his exposed position, Hemingway eased the power of his engine to lower himself back nearer the grass background.

The Fulcrum was still climbing at 1,800 feet when it got a kick in the ass. At the jolt, the MiG pilot---for a split-second---thought his engine had mistakenly gone to afterburner. When the front half of his fuselage started to cartwheel in the air, the Cuban pilot reached between his legs for his ejection handle.

The spectacular orange/white fireball made by the rear half of the Fulcrum was readily seen by the other seven MiG pilots over Camp Cienfuegos. Their attention had been drawn by the surprised exclamation of the downed pilot.

To assess the situation, their flight commander ordered his MiGs higher and out-of-range of whatever had fired upon them. Somewhere down below, he knew there was a deadly adversary, and until the challenger was spotted, it would be foolish to risk losing more planes.

Hemingway touched down on the grass as the MiGs got smaller in the sky. He keyed his mike.

"Stallion One, Jai-Lai! Do you read me?"

"I read you, Jai-Lai!" responded one of the CH-53 pilots.

Hemingway could see them still curving around the parade ground in an unsteady fashion.

"Stallion One, I've just punched the number of that last MiG. While the rest of them are thinking it over, you probably have half-a-minute to get out of your *flying coffin!*"

Watching the airborne Stallion, Hemingway added: "You can always get another helicopter, but you can't fly dead!"

Harshly reminded of their mortality, the CH-53E pilots came to a hover. Hemingway could almost sense the reluctance of the pilots to abandon their ship as it gradually settled to the ground.

The first of the three-man crew beat a hasty retreat from the rear cargo hatch when the wheels made contact. After five seconds, Hemingway started a silent count. It was another fifteen seconds before the two other crew members appeared. One of the pilots had the other slung over his shoulder as they moved away from their doomed machine.

Hemingway scanned the sky overhead. At 4,500 feet, he counted seven MiGs circling, trying to spot him.

Glancing around, Hemingway was thankful his grey/tan/green paint job blended so well with grass, but he needed more protection than that. Staying with the green background as much as possible, he slowly taxied his aircraft back to the deadend street. At least there, he would be protected from strafing on three sides.

Plaza De La Revolucion

"Companeros!"

This time, the crowd gave only a lukewarm response to their President's salutation. They quickly became silent....anxious to hear what he would say next.

With his chin high, Castro brought himself ramrod erect before the lectern. The black beard of the guerrilla fighter was now a dirty grey, yet still a vital part of his intended image. He was convinced it gave him the air of a philosopher, in addition to serving as a symbol of his continuing Revolution.

Castro began in a quieted voice, as was his custom.

"I have heard my people speak." He paused, then dramatically waved an arm across his front. "Your wishes will be honored."

There was the beginning of applause, which abruptly died.

So, thought Castro, you are doubtful.

"I will ask the minister of agriculture," he continued, "if we can increase the monthly one-pound chicken ration to one-and-a-half pounds."

The crowd applauded a bit stronger this time at the specific words of their president.

Castro inwardly smiled. I have no problem giving you more, he mused. You could even have two pounds. I will simply divert chicken from the state restaurants. Of course, the price of rationed chicken will go up, but I need not tell you that now.

An outcry came from the middle of the crowd.

"Lobster and shrimp!"

Other students in the Plaza began to repeat the demand.

Within seconds, the first student who had shouted it felt a hot pain in his right thigh. As he looked down and saw warm blood soaking through his trousers, a gloved fist caught his jaw and collapsed him senseless to the ground.

The shorter member of the RAB trio---giving those nearby a threatening glance---adjusted the glove over his brass knuckles, then followed his two partners as they dragged their victim out of the crowd.

"Lobster and shrimp!" shouted Castro loud and clear over his microphone. He did not intend to give the new chant a chance to build as the others had.

"Someone has called for lobster and shrimp," continued Castro. "Yes, I will see if this is possible."

Even as Fidel spoke the words, he doubted them.

Cuba's coastal waters yielded a generous supply of the two seafoods, yet the ration stores sold neither. Only a few exorbitant nightclubs and hotels---catering exclusively to wealthy foreigners and the Cuban elite--- served this seafood in Cuba. Ninety-seven percent of the fishing fleet's catch was exported for sorely-needed hard currency.

"I will ask the ministry of agriculture if res-taurants can begin serving lobster and shrimp," Castro told his people.

There was extended applause at the new concession.

By the dolphin fountain, Maria twisted around to Lou and bitterly spoke.

"At the State-run restaurants, the prices are *five times or more* than the rationed prices for the same food. Fidel will probably charge us more for this lobster than he does the fat tourists!"

When the applause subsided, Castro decided to offer his audience some hard choices. It was a favorite tactic.

"I must ask a question of you," he told them. "But first, let me explain."

Fidel paused to stare down into his lectern, then brought his hand to his beard as if in deep thought. His face came up with a solemn expression.

"It has been necessary to trade Cuban lobster and shrimp to other countries in exchange for hard currency."

Castro gripped his lectern and leaned forward.

"Why do we need this hard currency?" he posed. "We need it to buy the imported beans for our coffee. We need it to pay for our imported rice....and other important foods."

There was a grumbling in the crowd. What he'd said was partially true, and they knew it. The entire nation was addicted to coffee, and no meal was considered complete to a Cuban unless it contained a portion of polished white rice.

"Fidel does not tell all the truth!" snapped Maria to the Americans beside her. "If our farmers had free markets, they could grow enough rice so imports would not be necessary."

Lou debated whether to tell Maria that Castro's rice statement was patently false in another way. Since the mid-1980s, Cuba had bartered for all of its imported rice---trading nickel and manganese to China. The hard currency went elsewhere.

"And coffee, too!" Maria angrily added. "My father is a farmer, and he is forced to sell everything to the State....at fixed prices which are too low to permit increasing his crops."

The Cuban president continued.

"Come, let us vote. When I raise my left arm, tell me how much you want lobster and shrimp. Then, with my other arm....tell me if you prefer coffee and rice."

Raising his left arm, Castro blandly announced: "Lobster and shrimp."

There was a moderate acclamation for several seconds....as Castro expected.

"Now, coffee and rice!" shouted Castro, throwing his right arm high in the air.

General applause lasted for close to a minute.

Castro resisted a grin, and, in a magnanimous tone, he told his people: "We shall see what can be done. Rice and coffee, of course, must remain available to everyone. And for those few who require lobster or shrimp, perhaps the restaurants can fill that need."

When lackluster applause greeted this announcement, Castro decided it was time to lecture his people. In the next month, it'd be essential they understood why increases in these rations would be meager.

After decades of his broken promises and shifting the blame for economic failures to others, the Cuban president had learned it also was wise to prepare the people for belt-tightening in advance. Let them think it was their fault....due to their own appetites....their own shortcomings.

At the dolphin fountain, Lou and Camille were taken aback by the sight of two university students rushing past, carrying another student whose chest was covered in blood. The injured youth's head hung away from his body.

Castro raised his voice, feigning a controlled fury. "We would have more food if the farmers were more productive! And if the officials improved their planning.   But there are lazy farmers and inept officials....and I am trying to ferret them out!"

He went on in a softer voice. "We Cubans must always dream of a better future. When we work hard, our dreams can---"

A strong voice near the front of the crowd cut him off:

"No more dreams!"

Disbelieving the defiant remark, Castro scrutinized the throng before him....waiting....daring the bold voice to repeat itself. When he spotted a brief commotion to his right front, Castro knew the bold voice would not be raised again.

The brave man who had cried out was being dragged away by his feet. He made no protest and bled lightly.   The knife---expertly inserted---had penetrated the heart.

Castro, deciding not to repeat *dream* lest it remind another fool to speak out, continued speaking as if there'd been no interruption.

"When I was a boy," he recalled, "half the people on this island were peasants living in squatter shacks around the cities and even worse in the countryside. Only four percent ate any meat at all.

Eggs were consumed by only two percent. Milk was received by---"

"Eleven percent," said Maria at the edge of the dolphin fountain. "We have heard these statistics a thousand times!" she sighed.

Around her, people nodded agreement.

"The peasants in the fields," continued Castro, "made up one-third of the population then. All the farmland was controlled by rich Cubans and Yanquis. Because sugar was so profitable, that is all these wealthy landowners would grow.   Therefore, the peasant farmworkers were needed only at harvest-time. At the most, they worked five to six weeks. The rest of the year, they were lucky to find work."

The Cuban president paused---as he always did in his speeches at this point---to ask:

"When their money ran out, do you know what the peasant families ate?"

Again, Castro paused before giving the answer. This time, he was not fast enough.

"Sopa de gallo!" came up from the Plaza. "Sopa de gallo!" was shouted contemptuously from all corners.

Never before had anyone interrupted his little story. Castro instinctively wanted to lash out at the disrespect. But he could not. To display his temper in the Plaza would imply he was out of control, and he would not permit that impression.

"What's sopa de gallo?" asked Lou of Camille.

"The words translate to rooster soup."   She shrugged. "I've never had any."

Diego Roca offered: "It is a mixture of water and brown sugar."

Maria leaned forward to speak to the Americans. "Now, instead, we have ketchup with bread for supper several times a week."

"Which is worse?" she acidly added.

At the lectern, Castro was wondering how wise it had been to permit his people to vote earlier. Had that emboldened them? He took a deep breath and resumed.

"In the mountains of the Sierra Maestra, I ate many bowls of sopa de gallo. And was glad to have it. But now, that is no longer necessary. Today, all Cubans share the food resources of our country. Our rationbooks guarantee it! And prices---"

Maria loudly intoned: "---are kept low so everyone can buy food."

Around the fountain, several other Cubans---tiring of the lecture---also finished the sentence they'd heard their Maximum Leader repeat several times a year for more than three decades.

Maria bent forward to speak to Camille. "Do you know what my family ate for dinner last night?"

From Maria's angry tone, Camille hesitated to ask.

"It has been three weeks since we've had any meat," said Maria, "so I breaded grapefruit, put it on the fry pan, and we pretended it was steak!"

Behind the dolphin fountain, someone with an electronic megaphone blared out:

"FREE ELECTIONS! FREE ELECTIONS!"

The students atop the fountain picked up the slogan, and it spread rapidly throughout the rear of the Plaza as if it were organized and preplanned.

When Maria came to her feet, adding her piercing voice, Lou considered covering his ears.

"FREE ELECTIONS! FREE ELECTIONS!"

At the Jose Marti platform, the agit-prop director of the rally was standing directly behind the podium, waiting for Castro to call him.

Hearing the new slogan, the Cuban president faltered back a step from the lectern. His mind wildly raced. He wanted to join in the chant, to assume it himself and then kill it as he had done before. But that was not possible this time. He would never risk the rejection of his people by an open ballot. And even worse, his ears told him that already too many people were repeating the chant at the back of the Plaza. Too many for his henchmen to halt.

The Cuban president glanced around the podium, searching for an idea. Seeing his agit-prop jefe, Castro glowered at the man. He knew his jefe could offer no solutions. The unimaginative man was typical of Fidel's other ministers and underlings. Unquestioned loyalty, quick to execute orders, and little else.

I will ignore it, Fidel told himself. He almost smiled at the thought. This was a final solution when nothing else worked....a solution which he'd been forced to use with increasing frequency in the 1990s.

Disregarding the growing chant, he continued his lecture.

"Our medical research programs are reaping vast rewards. The sales of Cuban medical products in Latin America, Europe, Africa, and Asia are mult-iplying each---"

Finding himself exaggerating, Fidel went on, unable to resist presenting the brightest picture possible.

"---generating more income every month. Soon we will have enough hard-currency to purchase all of our consumer---"

At the dolphin fountain, the Young Communist cadets returned to harass the university students, bringing help this time. A trio of RAB thugs, stepping into the pool with the cadets, unsheathed their machetes.

The female student with the videocamera hastily slid off the fountain bowl and left the pool. After concealing herself among the onlookers, she proceeded to film the scene.

The four students on the bowl, watching the intruders with apprehension, continued to shout:

"FREE ELECTIONS! FREE ELECTIONS!"

The Young Communist cadets again tried to scale the fountain, but were kicked back by the students. One of the RAB men then approached the bowl and began to swipe at the feet of the students with his machete. When the students shifted to the other side, another RAB thug approached as well to swing his machete.

Watching the students hop about the fountain bowl, Lou was reminded of children jumping rope. The Cuban flag fluttered from its pole above the dolphins, giving the scene an almost a festive appearance.

A shrill scream jolted the image in his mind.

The CIA man wanted to look away, but he could not. A machete had caught the ankle of one of the students. The force of the blow swept the student off his feet, and Lou watched him tumble from the fountain, grasping his ankle.

The three other students climbed higher onto the dolphins to escape the machetes, enabling the Young Communist cadets to scramble onto the bowl. One by one, the cadets tore at the students, heaving them off the fountain.

In the water, the RAB men surrounded each student before he could regain his feet. Using the hilts of their machetes, they hammered at the heads and shoulders of the students.

People around the pool began to hoot at the savagery, trying to shame the RAB thugs into halting their beatings.

Maria, baby in arm, jumped into the water. Screeching at the brutal men, she grabbed an arm of the student whose ankle had been split and dragged him away.

Other women, following her example, entered the water to rescue the remaining students.

The RAB men kicked at the limp bodies as they were pulled away. Then, sheathing their weapons, the henchmen congratulated each other on their quick work and climbed out of the water with the Young Communists.

At the edge of the pool, Maria handed her baby to Camille before helping her husband lift out the student she'd rescued.

As the student coughed water out of his lungs, blood flowed from ugly gashes on his head and the wound at his ankle.

"Alex, give me your shirt!" demanded Maria.

Before her husband could strip it off, a man shoved the purple mini-skirt into Maria's hands.

Using her teeth, she bit into the flimsy material and ripped it two. She gave half to Alex and used the other half as a compress at the boy's ankle.

Behind Maria, the worried voice of a girl asked: "Fernando, are you alright?"

The slumped student raised his eyes and nodded to the girl with the videocamera.

"He should go to a doctor," Maria told the girl. "Do you have friends who can take him?"

"Yes," said the girl, pivoting away to find them.

"No, Kristine!" called out Fernando. "Do not leave. Keep taking pictures."

The girl shook her head. "After you're taken care of!"

She was gone before he could say more.

Ripping off a strip of purple cloth, Maria bound the boy's ankle.

"Thank you," Fernando managed to tell her between pained gasps.

Maria tore another strip and used it to wipe the blood from his face. When she'd finished, he asked of her:

"Please help me to my feet."

"Are you sure?" said Maria.

"No, I'm not," he candidly replied. "But help me anyway. If I can walk, then I'll find a doctor myself. My friends must stay here....in the Plaza."

Maria stared a the boy a moment. "My husband and I will take you to a doctor," she offered.

"No." Fernando made a tight smile. "I saw you fight the CDR woman. You are needed here, too."

The boy used his arms to push himself up. Maria and her husband helped him to his feet. After steadying himself, Fernando looked to Maria.

"When Kristine returns, tell her I am okay." Keeping his injured leg stiff, Fernando shuffled off.

Lou's attention returned to Castro. Camille had given the baby back to Maria and begun to translate again....until Lou bent over to whisper into her ear. "You don't have to interpret anymore."

"Why not?" she asked in a normal voice.

He bent over again. "I understand what he's saying."

"What?" she exclaimed.

Glimpsing at No-Chin, Lou put a finger to his lips.

Camille lowered her voice. "Then why'd you ask me to come with you?"

Lou considered the question a moment and decided the truth---that her presence helped guarantee his own security---might not go over that well.

"I didn't want anyone to know I understood Spanish," he whispered back.

Camille glared at him. "I want to go back to the embassy! Right now!"

Lou glanced around uncertainly and spoke from the side of his mouth. "I have to observe this."

"Well, I don't!" Camille came to her feet. "Goodbye!"

Lou shot a hand out and caught her wrist. "You're better off staying here with me. Remember last night?"

Camille stopped pulling away.

"We're way in the back of this crowd," he reassured her. "Any commotion that happens will be up near the front."

Seeing the fire in her eyes, Lou shrugged. "We're so far from the obelisk that we can barely see Castro."

Camille irately pointed at the dolphin fountain. "What do you call what just happened right there?"

Kristine appeared before them and asked of Maria: "Where is Fernando?"

"He was able to walk," replied Maria, indicating the direction he'd taken.

The girl nodded in relief. "It's just as well. I couldn't find my friends," she said dejectedly. "My name is Kristine. May I stay with you?"

"Of course," Maria told her.

Lou looked up at Camille who was still standing. "We're safe here," he told her. "Sit down."

She reluctantly sat again and returned her attention to the amplified words of Castro.

"---is one-twelfth the size of Cuba. Yet, Puerto Rico receives more than one billion dollars a year in tourist revenue---three times more than we do. Six years ago, Cuba earned $250 million from tourism. That figure has now grown to $350 million. In five more years---at our current rate of growth---Cuba will surpass Puerto Rico in tourist revenues."

Castro paused, expecting an accolade from the crowd for the predicted accomplishment. When none was forthcoming, he went on.

"The money we earn from tourism is used to purchase machinery for our factories and oil for our refineries. This is why dollar-shops are located in our hotels....to get more hard-currency from the tourists. It was wrong to pillage these---"

Maria loudly injected. "It is also wrong that foreigners in Cuba eat better than we."

"---and the luxury items sold in dollar-shops are not necessary in Cuban society. We have no use for such luxuries. All Cubans live in decent houses or apartments. No Cuban pays more than 10 percent of their income for rent. No other country in this hemisphere can boast of such a standard. And what other country in the Americas has full employment? Only Cuba!"

"Hah!" exclaimed Maria. "After eight years, Alex and I are still on a waiting list for an apartment. And the best jobs are held by bloated bureau-crats....few of whom work more than two or three hours a day."

Castro was warming to his subject. He could expound endlessly on what his Revolution had done for his subjects.

"Before the Revolution, a third of all Cubans could neither read nor write. Only one in ten children finished the eighth grade. College was only for the wealthy. Now, 95 percent of Cubans are literate. And all children finish eighth grade. Any Cuban may attend the universities. How much does this cost? Nothing! Nowhere else in the Americas---"

Maria threw up her hands. "What good are our educations....if there are no real jobs available once we graduate? And if our universities are so wonderful, why is it so many foreign technicians are required to run our factories?"

"---completely free health care. Before the Revolution, there were few doctors outside Havana. That has all changed. All Cubans receive the same care. The prices of drugs are kept low so---"

"That is a another joke!" Maria snickered. "The doctors are poorly trained and have filthy offices. Drugs they prescribe may or may not be available. If they are, it often takes weeks to find them."

As the Cuban president went through his oft-repeated routine, one of his last quarrels with Che Guevara came to mind. It had been over food. Che maintained the rationing of food at artificially low prices created a dangerous precedent. It generated complacency. Che pointed out that the last Roman emperors and French kings had tried to placate their citizenry by the same method....and failed. The people would neither value nor respect that which was free, or nearly free, argued Che. And they would riot if it was withdrawn in a time of poor harvests and scarcity. Fidel had vehemently disagreed.

Castro went on. "Cubans can buy food at lower prices than in any other Latin country. In most of Central and South America, a significant percentage of the population must steal for their food or they will starve."

Taking a full breath, Castro exclaimed: *"And there is no malnutrition in Cuba! Not even the Yanquis can boast of that accomplishment!"*

There was little applause at Castro's exclamation.

Maria bitterly shook her head. "Everyone knows it was malnutrition that caused the eye infections of 35,000 Cubans in 1993!"

✈ ✈ ✈

Camp Cienfuegos

Hemingway, taxiing his Harrier to the deadend street again, found it no longer shrouded in a mist of ash.

As he entered the light haze still remaining over the street, he popped his canopy for better vision overhead and glanced at his fuel gauge.

"Damn," he muttered. His fuel registered only 500 pounds....one-eighth full.

At mid-block, he passed General Diaz's jeep. The vehicle's front bumper was up against the brick wall of a burnt-out barracks, and a group of men were gathered around it.

Hemingway recognized General Diaz, standing shirtless among them. A few of the men eyed the Harrier pilot in a hostile manner as he taxied by. Hemingway caught a glimpse of the general's beet-red back.

At the deadend, Hemingway turned his aircraft around. As he eased back on the throttle, his ears identified the sharp stutter of an airborne cannon kicking out shells.

To his direct-front, 150 yards out, Hemingway looked up into the fire-spouting nose of a MiG-29. As its cannon-fire chopped a steady path down the street, the Fulcrum floated lower like a great silver bird seeking its prey.

Hemingway instinctively strained his body backward into his seat. He started to close his eyes, to block out what would come next. From the oncoming path of the shells, Hemingway could tell the MiG was properly aligned with the Harrier. He considered throwing full power to his engines, to pop off the ground and throw off the MiG's aim. But there was no time for that.

For an instant---through the canopy of the oncoming MiG---Hemingway thought he saw a broad grin on the face of the Cuban pilot.

As the Fulcrum loomed larger, its cannon rocked Hemingway in his cockpit. Sensing shells making contact on his left, he swung his head to his port wing, expecting an explosion of a fuel compartment.

Instead, as the MiG screamed by, Hemingway watched the tip of the port wing collapse.

"Son-of-a-bitch!" he swore as his wingtip crunched into the street.

The shells of the Fulcrum had shot off the wing's wheel assembly.

Proudly, the MiG pilot reported his handiwork. He and a second pilot were ordered to finish off the Harrier, while a third MiG swooped down to dispatch the abandoned Sea Stallion.

Hemingway realized the MiGs would now swarm over him, giving him scant seconds to make his own life-or-death decision. Instinct told him to use the precious seconds to unhook his helmet and unharness his body from the Harrier's seat. If he could clear himself from the aircraft in time, he might survive. The thought of Sandi and the child he had yet to father flashed through his mind.

Yanking the communication line off his helmet, Hemingway scanned the blue sky above his aircraft and reached to unsnap his seat harnesses.

His fingers froze on a metal clip-release.

The two Cuban pilots---no longer concerned for their safety---approached the lame Harrier at a reduced speed that would ensure the accuracy of their cannon-fire.

Hemingway spotted the lead plane at 1,100 yards descending as if preparing to make a landing. The second MiG was only 200 yards behind the first.

It was a toss-up. Hemingway calculated he had 10 to 11 seconds. Barely time to clear his aircraft.

As the silver profiles of the MiGs leveled out for their run, he brought his engine to 55 percent and placed his exhaust nozzles at 50 degrees, thinking the last Sidewinder might buy some time.

Hemingway saw the red trails of tracers from the lead MiG pilot begin at 400 yards. When they started hitting at the other end of the street, General Diaz's entourage scattered into the smoking ruins beside his jeep.

After flipping the master-arm switch on his weapons control panel, Hemingway kept his eyes to the Fulcrums. He didn't bother checking the duct pressure at his air vents. There would be no time to make corrections. Shoving his nozzles vertical, Hemingway gave full throttle to his aircraft.

The Harrier jumped to rooftop level in two seconds as advertised, but Hemingway found his port wing dangerously overcompensating. It was 20 degrees above horizontal and drew his attention away from the MiGs.

With his aircraft critically unstable, Hemingway worked its nose up and looked back to the MiGs.

He was astonished to see the first MiG faltering itself. Its sputtering cannon was no longer firing with regularity, as if its pilot was uncertain whether to complete his run.

The first Cuban pilot stared incredulously at the tilted Harrier suspended in air 90 feet above the street. To his mind, it was impossible. No aircraft missing its wheel assembly could have the capability of getting airborne.

Without getting an aural, Hemingway squeezed off his Sidewinder. It hooked down before swooping up in a beeline at the oncoming MiG.

The threat of the missile shook the MiG pilot from his mental lapse. He banked hard to starboard, popping flares. The second MiG pilot peeled off in the opposite direction, and the Sidewinder neatly sailed between the two Fulcrums.

Without hesitation, Hemingway started settling his aircraft to the street, manipulating his exhaust nozzles in a struggle to maintain the Harrier's balance. In his concentration, he failed to see the Cobra attack helicopter barrelling across his front.

Iron Balls loosed a two-second burst of HEIT rounds at the nearest MiG.

"Turkey shoot," mouthed Iron Balls, as his high-explosive and incendiary rounds ripped into the fleeing MiG. With the MiG pilot flying slow and low, the Cobra driver couldn't have asked for a finer turkey. Seeing smoke billowing off the MiG's fuselage, Iron Balls didn't wait for the certain finale.

He curled his Cobra around to obtain an aural on the other MiG. Able to align his infra-red sight far quicker than any fixed-wing aircraft, Iron Balls got the desired tone and launched his Sidewinder.

"Get hot, sweetheart!" exclaimed Iron Balls, in his mind speaking to the MiG pilot.

Circling 6,000 feet above the action, the commander of the MiG flight had not spotted the Marine helicopter in the ground clutter....or the narrow 5-inch-wide Sidewinder. But, he did make out the trail of its rapidly-expanding exhaust, which built from the general direction of the crippled Harrier.

Hemingway's own missile---traveling in the opposite direction of the charging MiGs---hit the ground in a spectacular fireball.

Seconds later, the Cuban flight commander saw one of his MiGs go askew as Iron Balls' first MiG lost its pilot by ejection.

The disbelieving Cuban pilot had not been watching his tail; as moments before he'd seen the Harrier's missile harmlessly fly off in the opposite direction.

Now....from his parachute, he watched his aircraft create an even greater fireball than the Sidewinder on impact with the ground.

The second MiG pilot---at the terrible shriek of his flight commander in his earphones---jinked his plane left then right, trying to escape the second missile. He was too low to the ground to dive away from danger, and any attempt to climb would only slow his aircraft for the accelerating missile. Righting his Fulcrum, the pilot wisely reached between his legs and yanked the red-striped handle.

Seeing the second parachute blossom, the Cuban flight commander---convinced his pilots had been decoyed---ordered his remaining MiGs to an even higher altitude. At least, he told himself, I can report the destruction of two Harriers and the large helicopter on the parade ground.

As the Fulcrums circled Camp Cienfuegos, none of the Cuban pilots could spot a source of the killer missiles below....other than the lone Harrier.

Their flight commander was convinced several more Harriers lurked below, and he doubted if any of them would be foolish enough to come out of hiding and ascend for a dogfight. The Americans certainly knew the missiles of his Fulcrums would prove dominant in open airspace---just as the Cuban commander now knew better than to engage AV-8Bs near ground.

He ordered his surviving planes back to Santa Clara, where he would report Camp Cienfuegos was defended by an unknown but substantial number of well-armed aircraft.

Informally, the Cuban commander would report one more assessment. Now, he appreciated why Argentine pilots---after losing *27-to-0* in their encounters with the British Sea Harrier during the Falklands War---had labeled the bulldog-shaped aircraft the "Black Death."

Plaza De La Revolucion

"In Cuba," declared Castro with a flourish of upraised hands, "even your water is free!"

When that solicited little reaction from the throng in the Plaza de la Revolucion, Castro decided a popular food might.

"In Cuba," he began again, "the Coppelia parlors sell a scoop of ice cream for only 60 centavos. The gusanos in Miami pay ten times that!"

There was derisive laughter from the segment of the crowd which supported the Cuban president.

"What'd Castro say?" Lou asked of Camille. He'd been paying more attention to the nursing mother at his side than to the loudspeakers.

"Castro just referred to the Miami Cubans as worms," she explained, "who pay more for ice cream than---"

"But we stand in line," Maria loudly interrupted, "an hour or more for the ice cream....even at midnight!"

Her baby was noisily feeding, and as Maria bent forward to speak, Lou tried to keep his eyes from wandering back to her bosom.

"And often," Maria went on, "the ice cream is a gooey paste that has been oversweetened and makes our teeth ache. My parents are old and cannot stand in line for hours. Now, unless I can go with them, they do not get ice cream anymore."

When Maria briefly lowered both sides of the red elastic band to give her child a fresh breast, Lou felt Camille tug at his arm.

"Take me back to the embassy," she implored in an undertone.

"Why?" countered Lou. "Nothing's happening here. Castro's talking about ice cream."

Maria suddenly stood, Miguel's feet brushing Lou on the way up. When Lou looked at the young mother, he saw her face flushed in anger.

"No more lines!" Maria cried out. "No more lines!"

Those nearby, recognizing the voice of the feisty mother, readily joined in. No other feature of the Cuban economy was more symbolic of its failure than the frustrating and hated lines....for virtually everything. The new slogan spread rapidly.

"NO MORE LINES! NO MORE LINES!"

When Castro first noticed the chant, he couldn't quite make it out.

With each repetition, it advanced up the Plaza toward the Jose Marti platform.

"NO MORE LINES! NO MORE LINES!"

At the dolphin fountain, Lou had to place his mouth against Camille's ear to be heard.

"Look," he said, pointing to a group of Young Communist cadets who were chanting with the rest of the crowd. "I think Maria's struck a common chord."

The call of the people rolled in waves across the Plaza toward the Jose Marti monument.

"NO MORE LINES! NO MORE LINES!"

Standing in the shadow of the monument, Fidel Castro---unable to co-opt the slogan by joining it---pointed a finger at his agit-prop director and indicated that the man should come to his side.

"Start a new chant!" demanded Castro of the hapless man.

The agit-prop director asked: "But what?"

"Anything!" shrieked Castro, suggesting: "Viva Revolucion!"

The man hurried off the platform.

When the Cuban president turned back to his people, his legs began to shiver at their bold rebuke. It cannot end this way, Fidel told himself. To steady his body, he propped his forearms on the lectern.

"NO MORE LINES! NO MORE LINES!"

The collective reproach of the crowd continued to paralyze the body and mind of the Cuban president.   He felt like a child, caught in a lie that would not go away.

"NO MORE LINES! NO MORE LINES!"

The agit-prop director stood at Castro's side for several seconds before being noticed.   When Castro swung his head around, the man told him:

"My team captains no longer control the Pioneers and Young Communists."

"Why not?" bawled Castro.

The agit-prop director looked down at his feet. Castro's two hands gripped the man's shirt and jerked his head back up.

"Why not?" demanded Castro again. He barely heard his jefe's meekly spoken words.

"They are chanting."

"NO MORE LINES! NO MORE LINES!"

Castro shoved the useless man away.

As full realization of his dilemma finally set in, Castro turned toward his brother. When their eyes met, Fidel saw only fear on Raul's face. The beginning of panic, thought the older Castro, and he realized the need to display the exact opposite---an utter calmness to his people. He would be as a patient parent who waited out the tantrum of a child.

There were thousands of others in the Plaza de la Revolucion who felt equally threatened by the growing power of the repeating chant. With honed knives, machetes, and fists, the RAB thugs and CDR officials struck out at the voices which endangered their favored status in Cuban society.

"NO MORE LINES! NO MORE LINES!"

At the dolphin fountain, Maria's husband stood by her side. With each repetition of the chant, Alex thrust a fist high in the air.

A sharp pain across his rib cage caused Alex to drop his arm protectively. Checking his shirt, he found a line of blood building where a blade had sliced the cloth and raked his skin.

When Alex looked up, it was into the bloated face of a man wearing a RAB armband.

The thickset man waved a wide, double-bladed knife under Alex's chin and growled:

"Shut your mouth, gusano!"

Just behind the RAB thug, Alex saw a second hostile face, that of a younger man brandishing an upright machete.

Alex came back to the double-bladed knife before him.

Spotting blood on its tip, Alex sidestepped away from his wife, all the while keeping his eyes fixed on those of the man who'd cut him. When he was several yards from Maria, Alex brought his hands to his belt. Unhooking its thick-plated buckle, he yanked the belt off his waist.

At the challenge, the stocky man beckoned to Alex with his wide knife.

"Come to me, gusano! I'll carve you into little pieces to feed the pigeons."

Kristine, melting into the crowd a short distance, raised her videocamera.

Alex methodically wrapped a third of his belt around his right hand, leaving its buckle end free. The slanted hook of the buckle was a good half-inch long, and its tip had been sanded to a sharp point.

Maria called out: "No, Alex! There are two of them against you."

"And one needs a good whipping!" her husband called back.

The young mother pivoted to Lou. "Help him!"

The CIA man glanced at No-Chin. Lou thought he perceived a neutral expression on his State Security escort. Still, Lou hesitated. He had strict orders to observe only.

Diego Roca came to his feet and stepped forward. "I will stand by the machete," he announced.

Handing his hat to Camille, the elderly man took up a position beside of the man holding the machete. Diego looked to be twice as old as the RAB man, but his impressive display of macho was given respect and the machete was lowered.

"Thank you, old man" responded Alex.

The knife-wielding thug, taking advantage of Alex's inattention, lunged forward and took a swipe.

Though Alex recoiled, the knife grazed his forearm, laying open the flesh. Alex's other arm lashed the belt buckle at the RAB man's head.

Squatting low, the thug ducked under the belt and swiftly came upright.

Alex, assuming the thug would dip again, decided to aim lower and began another swing of the hook.

The thug went into another crouch, but it wasn't quite low enough. When the hook caught the back of his ear, he rotated his head to unsnag it.

Sensing contact, Alex yanked the belt like a fisherman setting a hook.

At the ripping of his ear, the RAB man straightened with a howl.

The hook, having caught the cartilage of his lower ear, had torn through the soft tissue. For a few seconds, a thin stream of blood spurted from the wound.

Moving his hand up to touch his stinging wound, the thug stared into his blood-splattered hand.

"You bastard!" snarled the man.

More wary now, he extended his knife before him like a scythe, waving it to and fro, forcing Alex to keep his distance.

Alex circled, waiting for his adversary to come in range again.

After several feints, the crouching RAB man thrust his knife like a sword and punctured Alex's hip.

With his rival committed and in range, Alex swung the hook with another overhand motion that would not be ducked.

Looking up from his crouch to track the flying buckle, the thug crooked his head away at the last moment, taking the hook where his neck met his shoulder.

Once more, Alex expertly yanked, and the hook ripped out a jagged wound that would heal poorly.

The RAB man, realizing his rival was well-experienced with the belt, came upright. He would take one step at a time, as he regretted not doing in the first place.

Concentrating on the hand which held the belt, he began to jab his knife at it, intending to keep the dangerous hook better occupied.

Alex circled away, winding more of the belt around his right hand for close-in work.

In a fast movement, the thug switched the jabs of the knife back to Alex's hip.

Thrown off-balance, Alex sidestepped away. The RAB man quickly followed, slashing at Alex's belt hand again, then back to the hip which could not escape as easily.

To protect his hip, Alex parried with his left arm and felt its flesh go hot with the bite of the knife. As he retreated, Alex was already swinging the buckle at his relentless foe. Though the buckle did not fly with its previous force, its aim was true.

The thug dodged too late.

At the sensation of the hook snagging his soft cheek, the man's eyes widened. He'd fought many belts, but never before had he been caught in the face. Instantly, he rotated his cheek in the direction of the coming yank.

Alex, having extended his arm to draw the hook across as much of the thug's face as possible, jerked hard to wrench the belt away.

The hook sliced through the tender flesh, emerging at the open lips of the startled man.

Seeing the work of his hook, Alex gave his opponent a satisfied grin. The devastating damage he'd inflicted was usually final.

A loose flap of raw cheek hung off the jaw of the thug, exposing all the teeth and gums on the left side of his face.

As blood gushed from the ghastly wound, the RAB man cautiously brought his free hand up to it.

Alex relaxed his stance. His opponent required medical attention quickly, if he did not wish to be horribly scarred.

The thug's hand halted before reaching his disfigured face. He'd felt a wetness on his shoulder and glanced at it. Blood spilling from his jaw had completely drenched his shoulder.

Squealing with rage, the maddened thug leapt forward, his knife aimed low.

Alex backstepped away, awkwardly swinging his buckle. It caught the charging man on the temple and drew more blood....but the enraged man was no longer concerned with pain.

The younger RAB thug---to help his partner---shoved the elderly Diego into Alex as he passed by.

His retreat slowed, Alex swung his belt, again hitting his opponent on the head. But there was no time to set the hook, and that would have been useless anyway.

The frenzied man kept coming, heedless of the buckle.

Alex had no choice but to reach out in an attempt to catch the knife.

The RAB man, seeing the searching hands, withdrew his knife and continued charging with lowered head and shoulders. When his head made contact with Alex's ribs, and only then, did he bring the hidden knife forward again.

With one hand, Alex caught the thrusting forearm of the thug.

As the two men struggled, Alex towered over the head-down RAB man.

Unable to get a good grip on the arm holding the knife, Alex attempted to shove his opponent away, but the crazed thug stayed with him. In frustration, Alex pounded the man's back with his buckle.

Though his vision was obscured by his own blood, the thug continued to blindly plow forward. The blows of the buckle only served to further infuriate him, and he now grasped the hilt of his knife with both hands. Withdrawing the knife a short distance, he loudly grunted in bringing the knife forward in an upward thrust.

Alex uttered an abrupt groan, which was heard by all nearby.

His voice was drowned by the scream of Maria as the RAB thug shoved the blade deeper with a twist.

A sickened expression clouded the face of Alex. He rose on his toes like a bullfighter over the horn of a bull, his arms trying to lift himself off the knife.

Maria, rushing in, tore at the eyes of the thug with the nails of her free hand.

At her sudden attack, the thug withdrew from Alex and swung the bloody knife blindly about him, catching Maria's upper arm.

Her wound was only superficial, and she started at him again.

Lou, seeing the woman endangering both herself and her baby, reached out to pull her away. Alex had collapsed to the ground.

For cutting a woman holding a baby, another man kicked the RAB thug in the groin, collapsing him in a heap. A second kick to the back of his head rendered him unconscious.

The elderly Diego, with bare hands, held onto the machete blade of the younger RAB thug, shouting threats into the man's face. Others moved in to help Diego disarm the man.

Wrenching herself free from Lou's grasp, Maria dropped to the ground beside her husband. The baby dangled from one arm as she tried to hold Alex's head up.

Camille knelt beside Maria and eased the dangling baby into her own arms, while Kristine moved out of the crowd with her camera to film the fallen man.

Seeing a widening pool of blood collecting under Alex, Lou knelt beside Camille. The dull eyes of the wounded man gazed into the stricken face of his wife.

Holding her husband's head with one arm, Maria yanked off her red elastic band and made a compress of it over his oozing wound.

"Water," begged Alex. "Water."

Maria yelled over her shoulder. "Bring water!"

Lou thought to tell her that stomach wounds always caused a terrible thirst, but giving water to such a person was dangerous. It would further spread contamination.

"Water!" Maria screamed again.

As Diego approached with water cupped in his hands, Lou remained silent. The water would be a small comfort. He'd seen the extent of the damage. With each labored breath, Alex pushed more of his life fluids from the wound. The twisting knife had gone too deep.

Diego knelt and eased a trickle of water into Alex's mouth. The face of the wounded man was already ashen from loss of blood.

"Keep....fighting," Alex wanly told his wife.

A smile wavered on his lips. "Keep...."

Lou felt a constriction of his face at sight of the expiring man's final breath.

Feeling her husband's head slump in her hands, Maria gasped. The eyes of her husband were open, but they no longer followed her.

Diego reached out his thick fingers and passed them over the inanimate eyes, bringing them gently closed.

At the realization of her husband's death, Maria lifted her face and wailed.

As she arched her body back, Diego gently removed the dead man from her lap.

Throwing her arms overhead, Maria released a long, piercing, agonized scream.

The grief-stricken woman would have fallen over backwards had Camille not caught her.

The chanting of the people in the plaza had begun to fade, permitting Maria's outcries to carry well above the din around the dolphin fountain.

Fidel Castro, relieved that the protest was finally ebbing, had decided what he would say if given the opportunity. Facts cannot be refuted, he told himself. Facts will bring sense to my people.

When only isolated chanting continued, the Cuban president was tempted to shout angrily at the unruly crowd....to invite them to leave Cuba....to join the gusanos in Miami. That will not do, he corrected himself. I must not inflame them further.

Castro leaned into his bank of microphones.

"We have lines," he calmly began, "because of the Yanquis trade embargo. Batista's government made Cuba dependent on the Yanquis for everything--- food, oil, tractors, clothing, everything. Rationing was necessary to ensure that our limited food supplies would not be hoarded by the rich. Rationing guaranteed---"

Castro recited facts and figures detailing how he had returned Cuba to self-sufficiency in most food items and articles of clothing. He did not mention anything of their poor quality and the severely limited choices.

As he spoke, Castro decided---this time---not to blame the bureaucracy for the chronic deficiencies which still necessitated the lines. For 35 years, he'd used the bureaucrats as safety valves. They were his goats. It was too close to a lie, and he did not wish to encourage another censuring chant.

Having shrieked herself to exhaustion, Maria dropped her chin upon her chest. When her eyes finally came open, they stared blankly before her for a moment. She calmly bent down to her husband. Kissing his cool lips, she came up with a frozen expression.

"Let's move him to the pool edge," suggested Lou. He and No-Chin assisted Diego in carrying the body to the side of the pool.

Camille, still holding the baby, watched Maria as the young mother put a hand out to push herself to a standing position. When her hand slipped in the pool of her husband's blood, Maria threw out her other hand to catch herself.

Maria raised her moist palms, both wet with blood. Staring at her reddened palms for a moment, she brought them to the top of her chest and drew them down across her bare skin again and again, anointing her bosom with the last warmth she would receive from her husband.

Diego, who'd returned to help Camille with Maria, gently brought the young mother to her feet and led her to the pool's edge to sit. Camille remained alongside with the baby.

The distraught mother rested on the pool's rim, stiff-shouldered and unmindful of anything around her. Camille and Diego sat on either side of her.

Saying nothing, Maria shifted around to place both feet in the water.

When she stood and began walking toward the fountain bowl, Diego entered the water to follow alongside. At the bowl, she turned to him and said: "I need the flag."

Diego looked at the dolphin to which the flag was attached and shook his head. "I cannot climb up there".

"Then help me," she ordered.

He boosted her atop the bowl. The attention of those around the fountain was drawn to the blood-stained, half-nude woman as she toiled to untie the flag from its perch beside the dolphin.

When Maria managed to release the flag's staff, she raised the flag high over her head. As it fluttered in the breeze, Diego could see tears streaming down her face.

Maria gazed across the Plaza to the Jose Marti monument. She attempted to speak, but no words would issue from her constricted throat. Swallowing several times, she tried again. Words were spoken, but too low to be heard by Diego.

The young mother violently shook her head, throwing her long hair from side to side. Where it touched her blood-smeared skin, the blonde hair became streaked in red.

From a distance, the bright blood on her chest gave the impression that she had been grievously injured.

Diego finally heard her voice, but he did not dare repeat the words she had spoken.

A few years earlier---during a televised boxing match---Diego had heard the same words.

A young man, who had positioned himself where his image would be televised between rounds, had shouted out the words. Immediately, uniformed police appeared from every direction and beat him into silence.

The brutality of the police had been excessive and disturbing to Diego, who'd watched from only two rows behind the disturbance. As the unconscious young man was hauled off, one of the policemen had winked at Diego and said:

"He's just a crazy person."

Gaining her full voice, Maria shook the Cuban flag as she repeated:

"Down with Castro! Down with Castro!"

Camp Cienfuegos

After clipping the wings of the two Fulcrums, Captain "Iron Balls" Barragan prudently assumed a hover near the ground. Rotating his Cobra in place slowly, he and his passenger checked the sky for more targets.

When he saw the MiG formation headed northeast toward Santa Clara, Barragan gradually climbed to 500 feet to confirm their departure.

With the MiGs out of sight, he descended to the deadend street that held Hemingway's aircraft.

Barragan found the cockpit of the tilted Harrier unoccupied and spotted Hemingway at the jeep of General Diaz. The other two Harrier pilots and crew of the downed Sea Stallion were also at the jeep.

Since Hemingway had been too busy earlier jockeying his aircraft back to the ground, he had not observed the double-shot of his Cobra driver. The other pilots were filling him in. An aide to the Cuban general was flicking water on Diaz's bare back to cool his scorched skin.

After scanning the sky one more time, Barragan touched down at mid-block and slowed his rotor. The men at the jeep moved as one toward the Cobra.

Hemingway was the first to shake his captain's hand.

"Great shooting, Iron Balls!" he exclaimed.

"Nothing to it, Gorilla."

It was the first time Barragan had directly addressed the other pilot by his *call sign.* Hemingway grinned approval of the familiarity. The Cobra driver had saved his Harrier....and maybe his life, too.

"How many of these bandits," began Barragan, "have you tagged so far?"

Hemingway paused to count. "Four."

Barragan raised an eyebrow. "Not bad for a man your age."

Iron Balls thoughtfully added: "Sir."

"I don't mind having you youngsters around," grinned Hemingway benevolently, "if you can shoot straight."

Iron Balls scrutinized the skies again, and Hemingway joined him in searching for the MiGs.

"Looks like they ran home to mama," offered Iron Balls.

"You better hope so," said Hemingway. "We've got nothing to welcome them back. We're both Winchester."

The curt comment meant they were both out of missiles.

"I need fuel, too," said Iron Balls.

Hemingway jerked his thumb over his shoulder toward several jeeps loaded with fuel containers from the Sea Stallion. "They've got plenty over there. Shut down your engines and load up."

As they refueled the Cobra, Hemingway instructed Barragan: "If the MiGs return and you have time, I want you to stir up a dustcloud over my aircraft."

Barragan nodded and, looking over Hemingway's shoulder down the street, he said: "Good thing *that* Harrier didn't arrive any earlier."

A Cuban tank-trailer carrying the AV-8B crippled in the dogfight at sea had pulled up at the other end of the street.

Hemingway pivoted to study the aircraft, which was tied down with numerous ropes to the flatbed trailer.

"What happened to the four Sidewinders on its rails?" inquired Hemingway.

"The Cubans were having trouble getting the aircraft onto the trailer," explained Barragan, "so I thought it best to detach the hardware first."

"Where are they now?" demanded Hemingway.

"We loaded them on a jeep." As Barragan made his reply, the jeep with four Sidewinders came in sight behind the tank-trailer.

"Let's put two of them on your Cobra," said Hemingway, "and one on my starboard wing. We'll have to leave the other one here."

Both men turned their heads to the distinctive whop-whop of a Marine Sea Stallion. It was the second CH-53E, which had been dispatched with Stingers. As it landed down the street from the tank-trailer, Hemingway climbed into the Cobra to communicate with it on Barragan's radio.

"Stallion Two, Jai-Lai. You get lost?"

"No, Jai-Lai. We've been monitoring local transmissions....and decided to hang around the beach until matters cooled down."

"Smart move," replied Hemingway.

"Jai-Lai, we'd like immediate egress."

Urgency in the voice of the CH-53E pilot was due to the smoking remains of the first Sea Stallion which he'd spotted on the parade ground while coming in.

"Fine," replied Hemingway. "How many Stingers you bring?"

"Twenty."

"Let's get them offloaded," said Hemingway. After a pause, he added: "Can you take the Harrier on the truck home?"

"My orders are to get out of here," replied the Stallion pilot, "as fast as I came in."

The CH-53E pilot added: "Those are orders from the Tarawa, based on the burning Stallion on the parade ground."

While the two plane-less Harrier pilots and the first CH-53E crew helped offload the Stingers onto jeeps, Barragan and Hemingway worked on hooking up the three Sidewinders.

As the Sea Stallion lumbered away with the other Americans, Hemingway and Barragan were attaching the second Sidewinder to the Cobra.

General Diaz joined them and addressed Hemingway. "I have ordered my people to repair your wheel."

Hemingway gave the general a hard squint.

"We will fix the holes in your canopy, too," said Diaz with a confident smile.

"How will you fix the wheel?" asked Hemingway skeptically.

"It will be welded on like new," Diaz replied. "You can watch."

Hemingway decided not to discourage the general's initiative. His last flying effort had been tricky, and he didn't relish another one without all his wheels. Later, his crew back at Gitmo could always fix "the repairs."

"Go ahead," nodded the Harrier pilot.

"Excellent," responded Diaz. "My men are working already!"

Hemingway turned back to Barragan. "I'll have some of the general's men help me put my Sidewinder on. I want you upstairs covering me."

As General Diaz and Hemingway returned to the AV-8B, the pilot saw that the Cubans had his aircraft propped up level. A mobile generator was humming, providing electricity to the welder.

Hemingway glanced at the general's back, on which an aide continued to sprinkle water. The third-degree burn was ugly, but not serious.

"How's your back?" asked Hemingway.

Diaz grimaced at being reminded of his pain. "It stings like a bad sunburn."

Recalling the burns he'd suffered in Saudi Arabia, Hemingway thought to tell Diaz how mind-numbing his own burns had been. Two jeeps pulled up behind them, tires screeching.

Diaz announced: "Here are the MiG pilots you shot down."

Each jeep was crammed with soldiers, packed around a man in a flightsuit. The two pilots were brought before the general.

"You are Cubans like us!" bellowed Diaz into their faces. "Why do you bomb my soldiers?"

The older pilot looked to the other, then came back to Diaz.

"We have no choice," he revealed. "State Security holds our families hostage."

Diaz lowered his voice back to normal. "State Security?"

The MiG pilot nodded. "Last night, my wife and children were seized to guarantee that I follow orders."

The second pilot spoke up. "The same happened to the families of all married pilots. The bachelors are not permitted to fly."

"Where are your families held?" asked Diaz.

"We were told at State Security headquarters in Santa Clara," offered the second pilot.

Diaz paused to think.

"How does State Security know where you drop your bombs?" he inquired.

"Our flight commanders," answered the first pilot, "are loyal Communists."

Diaz lifted his chin and, sneering in contempt, he thought, too many of my own senior officers are no different. Mediocre in the field, but competent in the party. With promotions to field ranks now strictly controlled by the civilians in Havana, this is the result. Cubans bombing Cubans.

Signalling for Colonel Valdes, General Diaz whispered instructions to his chief-of-staff. If State Security could detain good Cubans, he could round up a few bad ones. There would be no disloyal officers on his staff when Valdes returned.

General Diaz took Hemingway by the arm and walked him a short distance away, nearer his aircraft.

"After we fix your plane," began Diaz, "will you accompany my soldiers to Santa Clara so I can rescue the families of the pilots?"

Hemingway looked over to his aircraft. Now that it was level again, the Harrier had regained its appearance as a fully capable war machine. He had a good idea what the Cuban general was asking of him....and he had a better idea what would happen to him back at Guantanamo if he acceded to the request.

"I need your plane"---Diaz looked above for the Cobra---"and your helicopter if I am to march on Santa Clara."

Hemingway remained silent.

"I also have helicopters," said Diaz, "but they have no missiles. If they were protected from the

MiGs, I could rescue the pilot's families and turn the pilots to my side."

Hemingway glanced at the two MiG drivers. From their forthright manner, he assumed they told the truth. But to help Diaz would be suicide, he told himself, and I've toed the edge enough for one day. My Harrier and one Cobra are a poor match for a determined attack by additional MiGs.

General Diaz tried a different tack. "Why did your helicopter pilot call you 'Gorilla' when he landed?"

Hemingway was surprised at the question. "It's an old nickname."

"Ernesto, the author, stood like a gorilla," said Diaz. "And he fought like one. Did you know that he outfitted his fishing yacht with machine guns during World War II?"

Hemingway shook his head in the negative.

"Yes!" said Diaz. "And he cruised Cuban waters looking for German submarines. There was a spirited man!"

Diaz gently shook the American's arm. "You have gone this far, Papa. If you will assist in bringing the pilots of Santa Clara to my side, I won't need your help any more."

The Harrier pilot studied Diaz a long moment before speaking.

"I can't do it, General."

"Why not?" persisted Diaz.

"Number one, I have only 4 missiles left."

Diaz grinned broadly. "But you have many more."

Diaz pointed to the jeeps stacked with Stingers at the head of the street. "That should be more than sufficient."

The American shook his head discouragingly. "General, I can't interfere in a Cuban problem anymore."

Hands on his hips, Diaz looked at Hemingway in amazement.

"You Americans are *always* mixed up in Cuban affairs! Teddy Roosevelt helped liberate Cuba from the Spanish....Eisenhower announced an arms embargo which helped overthrow Batista....Kennedy invaded the Bay of Pigs....Carter opened up Mariel."

Hemingway was thinking.

I've seen enough death and destruction, he told himself. My next year will be filled with investigations....and a court-martial. I don't want anything else to happen for which I'm responsible. Hemingway leveled his brow to Diaz.

"I've done enough, General."

The face of the Cuban general gradually mellowed, and he stepped over to place his hands on the American's shoulders.

"Yes," said Diaz calmly. "You are right."

He pointed to the shade of the nearest building. "Let's rest over there."

The two men walked into the shade and sat down.

"I will send for refreshments," said Diaz.

Plaza De La Revolucion

The words of Maria astounded the persons around the dolphin fountain who could hear her voice.

"Down with Castro! Down with Castro!"

Frightened, Diego backed away from the fountain as Maria repeated her forbidden phrase. He glanced left and right, expecting a horde of RAB henchmen to climb into the water.

The men and women about the pool listened in awe....afraid as Diego to utter the heretic words.

As Maria shouted, she waved the Cuban flag to draw attention.

Diego, sensing guilt even in permitting himself to hear her words, continued to move away.

At the opposite side of the pool, Diego spotted a trio of red armbanded men shoving their way to the pool's edge. The RAB thugs began to argue among themselves. One of them, a bald man with a thick mustache, appeared anxious to stop Maria, while his partners preferred to watch the half-nude woman shouting trance-like atop the fountain. All three had machetes tucked their belts.

As Diego quickly climbed out of the water, a short, chubby grandmother with two small children stepped into the pool near the RAB men. After draping a heavy purse about her neck, she lifted her grandchildren into the water also.

"Leave the poor woman alone!" the grandmother shouted at the RAB trio. "You've already killed her husband!"

Maria, oblivious to all about her, continued to shake the Cuban flag and call out:

"Down with Castro! Down with Castro!"

Keeping his eye on Maria, the bald man entered the water.

"Leave her alone!" repeated the grandmother at the man. "She's gone hysterical with grief!"

The bald man---his attention still riveted on Maria---walked through the old woman. When he stumbled over her and fell into the water, he took the woman and her grandchildren with him.

To those watching, it appeared he had deliberately bowled over the grandmother. Several women sprang into the pool to help her.

The RAB man came out of the water, wiping at his eyes. One of the enraged women grabbed the back of his collar from behind and pulled, while two others hit and scratched at his face.

Lou felt a hand on his shoulder and saw that it was Kristine. The university student balanced her camera on his shoulder to film the scene. Lou resumed watching the women, keeping an eye on the two remaining RAB men who were still observing the melee from outside the pool.

To Lou's surprise, the two RAB men abruptly disappeared from view. Four students, approaching from behind, had repeated a maneuver that was working quite effectively elsewhere with the armed men.

In unison, each student had grabbed an ankle and yanked hard to the rear. The upended men, caught completely offguard, were easily disarmed.

More women had joined the fray in the water; and the bald man, unable to concentrate on any single opponent, flailed out at all of them.

After shunting her grandchildren aside, the chubby grandmother returned to the contest. Unhitching her heavy purse from around her neck, she positioned herself to the man's side and swung. The first try bounced harmlessly off his shoulder, but the second one caught him square in the face.

Stunned, the bald man brought his hands up to his mashed nose.

Again, the chubby grandmother wound up, and this time brought her waterlogged purse around with both hands at waist level. It sailed evenly into his gut, doubling him over.

As the thug sank to his knees in the water, his hands came down to his stomach, revealing a bloody nose.

Lou grinned at the sight of the grandmother continuing to wallop the man with her purse. Now, each time she rocked the man in the water, the spectators around the fountain rewarded her with a resounding:

"Ole!"

When the chubby woman paused to catch her breath, three women grabbed the thug from behind and ducked him backwards into the water.

His legs kicked in the air as he floundered. By twisting about, he managed to bring his head above water, but as he gulped air, more women rushed in and shoved him under again. They piled onto the man, keeping him submerged.

"No!" yelled the grandmother. "Don't drown him!"

The women brought the man's head up for a few seconds, then plunged it back underneath the stagnant water. The turmoil in the pool had stirred up the thick algae which coated its bottom, and a green slime now floated atop its surface.

Looking up to the half-nude Maria, the grandmother turned back to her cohorts and yelled:

"Remove his clothes!"

With relish, the women in the water set upon the half-drowned man. To raucous cheers of the other females around the pool, his clothes were torn off and ripped to shreds. His machete was handed to a student in their cheering section.

Reaching under her shirt, the grandmother unsnapped her bra and yanked it through an open arm of the shirt. When she proceeded to tie the sputtering man's hands behind his back, another woman also removed her bra to bind the man's feet.

One at a time, the two other RAB men were thrown to the horde of women in the pool. Neither chose to put up any resistance.

A few students near Lou picked up the groggy RAB thug who'd knifed Alex and tossed him into the water as well. He was tied to one of the other men.

Empowered by their success, the women multiplied Maria's chant.

"DOWN WITH CASTRO! DOWN WITH CASTRO!"

Their strident voices acted as a magnet in drawing more RAB thugs and CDR members to the dolphin fountain. As the armbanded men arrived, they received the same reception as the first trio. Within minutes, a score of disrobed and bound men reclined in the slimy water. The men who verbally protested their treatment in the pool were silenced by underwater views of their companions.

The pool was soon guarded by a ring of university students armed with the knives and machetes of their wet victims.

A student leader climbed into the water and waded to the fountain bowl where he called to Maria. When she ignored him, he climbed onto the bowl and spoke to her.

Keeping the flag, Maria promptly slid off the fountain and went to her frantically crying child. The chant for the downfall of the Cuban president continued without her prompting.

"DOWN WITH CASTRO! DOWN WITH CASTRO!"

With genuine relief, Camille returned the crying Miguel to his mother.

Maria, holding the flag upright, sat down and put the baby to her breast. When Miguel's cries instantly subsided, the student leader told Maria:

"Wait here! I'll be back!"

The elderly Diego sat beside Maria and put his hand on the flag's staff to hold it for her, but she would not release the staff.

With the videocamera, Kristine moved in for a closeup and was taken aback by Maria's expression. The jaw of the nursing mother was tightly set with clenched teeth. Her eyes flared straight ahead, frozen in fury.

Camille yanked on Lou's shirt. "Let's leave now." she implored. "Before anything else happens!"

"DOWN WITH CASTRO! DOWN WITH CASTRO!"

The CIA man frowned at her request. The situation was just getting interesting, though he realized it had been a serious error in asking Camille to accompany him to the Plaza. For a moment, Lou debated whether No-Chin could be bribed to escort her back to the embassy.

The State Security agent slouched a short distance away on the pool's edge, keeping his back to the water, lest he be recognized by any of the captured Communists.

"Now!" Camille emphasized again.

Lou saw the student leader returning....with a phalanx of students behind him. Each of the young men was armed with confiscated knives or machetes.

"My name is Carlos," the leader told Maria. "We are ready for you."

Maria handed Carlos the flag. Getting to her feet, she pulled Miguel off her breast and pushed him back in Camille's arms.

The American woman stared aghast at the child. Miguel's face and clothes were now blotched with blood from his mother's bosom. And the baby began to howl at his rudely-interrupted feeding.

Camille started to hand Miguel back, but his mother was being assisted onto the shoulders of two crouching students. Each of the two students steadied one of Maria's knees on his shoulder. With the help of other hands, Maria came to a standing position on their shoulders.

When the two students under Maria came upright, the sight of the crimson-breasted blonde standing above the crowd---waving the Cuban flag--- doubled the chant she'd begun.

"DOWN WITH CASTRO! DOWN WITH CASTRO!"

Maria twisted her head around and searched the crowd. Spotting Camille's alarmed face, she shouted: "Bring my baby!"

Camille shook her head to protest, but Maria had turned away and the students were moving toward the front of the Plaza.

"DOWN WITH CASTRO! DOWN WITH CASTRO!"

Camille pivoted to Lou. "Damn you!" she shrieked. "What should I do now?"

He studied the bawling baby, then looked to its mother. The blood-streaked blonde hair streaming down Maria's back looked aflame in the bright sunshine.

"Wait here for her," he offered.

Camille, seeing the child's mother a good 30 feet away already, whipped her head back to Lou.

"What if Maria doesn't return?"

Lou creased his brow. He had no answer to the question.

"I don't want to be stuck with this baby!" Camille blared.

Hearing the woman's wrath, Miguel escalated his own protests. Camille wrinkled her nose and drew her head away from the baby.

"Oh, no!" she exclaimed in disgust.

"What's the matter?" asked Lou.

"He just filled his diapers!"

Lou pointed to the pool. "Change him in there."

"I've never changed a baby in my life!" she shouted in frustration.

"Just take the diapers off and clean him in the pool," suggested Lou.

She unpinned the soiled diapers and handed them to Lou. "Here, buster. You clean them."

Reluctantly accepting the fouled cloth, Lou first watched Camille gingerly dip Miguel's bottom in the water several times. Lou noticed the bound men propped nearby in the pool were looking askance at the additional pollution being added to their water.

Broadly grinning at them, Lou vigorously shook Miguel's stools off the diaper and into the water. As he rinsed the daipers, the captive men skittered away like crabs.

As Camille pinned the diaper back on, she told Lou: "I'm taking this baby back to its mother."

"I'd still wait here," replied Lou.

"I don't want to be stuck with this child anymore!" she lividly exclaimed.

After having repeatedly told Camille it was safe to remain in the Plaza, Lou now hesitated to take the opposite tack. He knew the danger of being caught in unruly crowds. It was best to stay on the fringes, in the rear, where they were.

Diego broke into the conversation, speaking to Camille. "I will help you take the baby to its mother."

Camille and Diego immediately set off through the crowd. As Lou followed, he saw Maria at least 150 feet away, still standing above the heads of the people, the flag fluttering in the growing breeze. Low clouds overhead had begun to partially shade portions of the great Plaza.

Lou glanced over his shoulder. No-Chin was right behind him, looking equally concerned.

The Cuban president, pausing mid-sentence, strained his ears to make out the faint chant from the back of the Plaza de la Revolucion.

Though his throat felt raspy, Castro spoke louder, continuing to laud the genuine accomplishments of his rule. When he paused again, he found that the simplicity of the heretical chant in the rear of the Plaza was now unmistakable.

Castro swung around, looking for his agit-prop jefe. The man was nowhere in sight, having slunk off after his last experience at the podium.

"DOWN WITH CASTRO! DOWN WITH CASTRO!"

Seeing the anxiety on his brother's face, Raul Castro rushed to the lectern.

"I need a counter-chant!" Fidel screamed at him.

"Which one?" asked Raul.

The right hand of the Cuban president went to his hip. The pistol was not there. On this day he wore the whipcord formal uniform of his office, instead of the more comfortable fatigues by which he was known.

Raul shouted. "Let us try 'Viva Fidel' again."

Fidel rapidly nodded. "Yes! Yes!"

His brother ran off the podium.

"DOWN WITH CASTRO! DOWN WITH CASTRO!"

216

Coming back to his microphone, Fidel Castro felt anger well up within him. Pointing a hand to the rear of the plaza, he screeched at the top of his lungs.

"Gusanos! It is gusanos I hear back there!"

Referring to those who were disloyal to his regime as worms had always brought laughter from his audiences, but this time Castro heard only the continuing condemnation of his people.

Castro consciously built the rage within him. It was a tool which he had used to perfection all his life. When reason could not prevail, intimidation would. Bringing himself to his full height, Castro hovered over his microphone like a vulture.

"It is time," he shrieked, "to rid Cuba of traitors! *There is no room on our island for gusanos."*

"DOWN WITH CASTRO! DOWN WITH CASTRO!"

A solution which Castro had planned to deliver near the end of the rally came to mind. Whenever dissenters became too vocal in his country, they could always be exported. Even en masse, as were 120,000 at Mariel in 1980.

"This time when the gusanos leave," shouted Castro, "we will send them to *Puerto Rico!"*

Castro gave the crowd an evil grin.

"In Puerto Rico," he went on, "the gusanos can join the one-third of the population who are *constantly unemployed!"*

The slight exaggeration gave Castro a pang of conscience. A true fact came to mind.

"The Yanquis make beggars of the Puerto Ricans! Fully half of them are on welfare and receive food stamps...and these gusanos will be beggars, too!

Castro raised his strained voice even higher.

"In Puerto Rico, the gusanos will not receive *free medical care* as they do in Cuba! *Nor free education! Nor free utilities! Nor free vacations!* If the gusanos are lucky enough to get a job, they must pay taxes. And rents will take more than half---"

"DOWN WITH CASTRO! DOWN WITH CASTRO!"

He pounded on his lectern in frustration. "All gusanos can leave Cuba *tomorrow!* I will give you free transportation to Puerto---"

"VIVA FIDEL! VIVA FIDEL!" interrupted him, and Castro stopped trying to speak over the new words. He straightened with a broad smile at the lectern, believing his just-stated promise had turned the crowd around.

Now....they love me once more. he told himself.

The organized voices of State Security, CDR officials, and other Communists at the front of the Plaza effectively drowned out the heretical chant.

Joyously, the Cuban president joined in with his supporters.

"VIVA FIDEL! VIVA FIDEL!"

After a minute, his faltering voice forced Castro to discontinue shouting. He tried to swallow in order to relieve the rawness of his throat. When this did not help, he gulped down a glass of water. The ice water, though it soothed his abused throat tissues for a moment, aggravated them even more. Accustomed to giving five to seven hour speeches, Castro had never before experienced such soreness. But before, it had not been necessary to shout down dissent.

Castro heard the opposing chants begin to alternate.

"VIVA FIDEL! DOWN WITH CASTRO! VIVA FIDEL!"

He stepped back from the lectern and, spotting Raul, motioned him over again.

The two brothers huddled.

"Who are these gusanos?" demanded Fidel.

"Students," replied Raul, "from the university."

"VIVA FIDEL! DOWN WITH CASTRO! VIVA FIDEL!"

"Why have you not stopped them?"

Raul flinched at the unfair accusation. "I gave orders to the RAB contingents as you instructed."

"What of State Security?" inquired Fidel.

"They remain at the Plaza front." replied Raul.

As Castro thought it over, he listened to the differing chants vying for dominance. The Communist voices still surpassed those of the students, but barely.

"That is not just students!" decided Castro.

"Shall I bring the Special Forces trucks closer to us?" asked Raul.

Castro nodded agreement.

Camille and Diego were falling further behind in their effort to catch up with Maria and return her baby. Too many people were joining Maria's banner as the students pushed forward.

The press of the throng reminded Lou of the previous night when Che's image had incited the people. Deciding to help Camille return the baby and then quickly get back to safety at the rear of the Plaza, Lou brusquely elbowed his way through the tightening throng. Reaching Camille, he took her hand to pull her forward.

The Cuban president, forced to shout his every word to make himself heard, continued to berate the protestors. His normally high-pitched voice had deepened with its growing hoarseness. Drinking water no longer helped.

"I would speak to the students among you!" Castro called out. "I have fought for your causes before you. In my youth, being a student on the campus of Havana University was extremely dangerous. To survive, it was necessary to carry a pistol at all times. Now, the university is a safer place to receive an education. Any Cuban can attend....and no one needs to carry a gun."

The opposing chants continued to alternate in their contest for supremacy.

"VIVA FIDEL! DOWN WITH CASTRO! VIVA FIDEL!"

Castro paused. Out in the Plaza, he could see plainly many scuffles in progress, much more than the few of before.

I am addressing a mob, he told himself, not a rally. He debated how to calm the mob....how to halt the fighting. Castro remembered the severe beatings he'd received from police on two occasions as a student at Havana University.

The Cuban president started to speak, and found himself only able to utter short phrases.

"I myself....led many protest marches. And I was willing....to face many dangers. As a student....I was knocked totally unconscious....by Batista's---"

Castro felt his voice fade.

As he drank the last of his water to try again, Castro spotted a Cuban flag approaching through the crowd at the middle of the Plaza. His ears told him that the flag was the focal point of the protestors. Sensing its threat, Castro stepped back from the lectern and motioned Raul over once more. Vilma Espin came with him.

"DOWN WITH CASTRO! VIVA FIDEL! DOWN WITH CASTRO!"

Taking Raul's arm, Fidel pointed to the Cuban flag and spoke in a rasp. "Silence that group with the flag!"

Brandishing machetes, the student vanguard leading Maria encountered little opposition as they spearheaded a path toward the Jose Marti platform. Their group numbered several thousand, though only a few hundred in front were armed. When RAB henchmen and CDR officials appeared before them, the students found the Communists usually chose to step aside in the face of overwhelming odds. Those who didn't back off were quickly surrounded and subdued.

Lou had managed to bring Camille within 50 feet of the baby's mother. Closer was impossible, as too many men and women had joined the march of the students. Most of them were also struggling to get nearer to Maria and her flag.

"DOWN WITH CASTRO! VIVA FIDEL! DOWN WITH CASTRO!"

The flag was sufficiently close now that Castro could discern clearly who held it aloft. And he stared in awe. He had viewed such grandeur once before.

The vision of the blonde woman standing over the sea of people, wearing only white shorts, and waving the red, blue and white Cuban flag reminded

Castro of the greater-than-lifesize Delacroix he'd admired years earlier at the Louvre.

The Paris painting---named "La Liberte"---depicted a bare-breasted woman holding the French flag on high and leading her countrymen over the barricades.

At the splendid sight in his own Plaza, Fidel Castro felt an urge to hasten from the lectern and congratulate the woman.

I must tell her of her magnificence! Castro told himself. The blonde with the banner also resembled the one woman he'd married. Mirta, a sensuously pretty dark blonde, had been described by many of his friends during and after their five-year marriage as a saint---for patiently accepting a husband who was frequently gone and paid no bills.

At that moment, a generous spirit welled up in the heart of the Cuban president, and he knew how he would placate these students.

Preceding dictators of Cuba---honoring an old Latin American custom---had always permitted free expression on the campus of Havana University. Police were banned from the campus. Having benefited by this token of democracy when a student, Castro knew its threat and had canceled it soon after taking power himself.

Now, he decided, I will restore freedom of speech on their campus. And with proper guidance from the Young Communists, mused Castro, it could even prove useful. Of course, student leaders who were persistent trouble-makers would be quietly exiled. To Miami. Better yet, thought Castro, to Puerto Rico.

He leaned into his microphones. "Brave young men of---"

The Cuban president moved his lips, but his vocal cords no longer functioned. His voice had died.

Finding himself speechless, Castro gradually straightened. Before him, the blonde woman bearing the Cuban flag was closer. He gazed reverently at the radiance of her figure.

Maria, her forward progress slowed due to the denseness of the crowd, spotted a contingent of brown-uniformed State Security police using rifle butts in an attempt to ram their way toward her.

The chant in the plaza had become only one.

"DOWN WITH CASTRO! DOWN WITH CASTRO!"

Between chants, Maria called for her baby.

The student leader, Carlos, spread her request among the surrounding students who called out for the baby.

When Miguel was found, a student took him from Camille and immediately held him aloft. The child was passed over heads until he reached his mother.

"I can't believe it!" said Lou to Camille in consternation.

"What?" she asked, unable to observe what he was viewing.

"The baby is actually nursing," said Lou, "right in the middle of all this!"

Lou raised Camille by the elbows to see for herself. As he lowered her again, Camille glanced behind them over the heads. The forward surge of the thick crowd would make it impossible to move back toward the dolphin fountain.

Feeling a tug at his shirt, Lou heard Kristine ask: "Can you lift me also to take pictures?"

He hoisted her up, positioning her buttocks in his gut to support her.

"They are hitting people with rifles!" called out Kristine, as she filmed.

The State Security column was making little progress though. When the packed throng was no longer able to part for the brown-shirted column, their commander had ordered his men to knock the people down and march over their bodies.

"DOWN WITH CASTRO! DOWN WITH CASTRO!"

The Cuban president leaned over his microphones once more to speak. Still, nothing would come forth.

Raul rushed to the lectern to ask what was wrong.

Indicating his mouth with a finger, Fidel shook his head in the negative.

Raul immediately stepped to the microphones with his brother.

Two hundred yards distant, he could see Maria standing over the crowd with the Cuban flag. The State Security unit was within 50 yards of the woman.

"DOWN WITH CASTRO! DOWN WITH CASTRO!"

Pointing at Maria, Raul screamed into the microphones:

"Shoot that woman!"

Fidel Castro violently yanked Raul away from the lectern, throwing his brother off his feet.

The Cuban president put his lips in direct contact with the largest of the microphones, desperately trying to countermand his brother's order.

Instead, he stood mute at the lectern. Nothing would issue from his mouth.

Castro started to shake his head vigorously from side-to-side to indicate his rejection of Raul's order. He then came around the lectern and, in full view of the crowd, began to criss-cross his arms in an attempt to cancel what his brother had ordered.

Those to whom he wished to send these signals now had their backs to the lectern.

Having clearly heard Raul Castro's command--- as had everyone else in the Plaza---the State Security commander ordered his men to fire on the woman bearing the flag.

Her raised figure made an easy target, but none of his men could bring themselves to shoot the woman. Miguel was still nursing at his mother's breast.

The State Security commander, armed with only a pistol, aimed over Maria's head and fired it. His sharp report was followed by a volley of the rifles.

Camp Cienfuegos

Hemingway and General Diaz left the shade every few minutes to inspect the progress of the welder working on the Harrier. The welder was a perfectionist and would not be hurried by the general as he restored the integrity of the two struts connecting the aircraft's wheel assembly to its port wing.

When the general's driver brought food, Hemingway washed his share down with a bottle of dark amber beer.

Upon the return of Colonel Valdes, the Cuban officer expressed an interest in learning how to fire the Stinger missiles brought by the Sea Stallion.

"Bring one to me," Hemingway told him.

"Bring two!" ordered General Diaz.

When the shoulder-launched missiles were delivered, Hemingway handed one to Diaz and the other to Valdes.

"This weighs 35 pounds," began Hemingway, "of which the missile is 30. The Stinger homes in on a heat source"---he touched the nose of the missile---"by a miniature infra-red device at the tip of its 3-pound explosive charge."

After being talked through the 18 steps necessary to fire the Stinger, Valdes took out a pen and paper, then asked Hemingway to repeat them. When Valdes completed a written list, he and the general grilled themselves on the firing sequence until they'd both memorized it.

"Have three Stingers placed in my jeep," Diaz then ordered an aide.

"I forgot to warn you," cautioned Hemingway, "that a hydrogen-chloride cloud is formed by the exhaust of the missile. Just before you pull the trigger mechanism, take a deep breath and close your eyes."

"How long do we hold our breaths?" inquired Valdes.

"The longer the better," said Hemingway.

Diaz ordered another aide to bring goggles.

Their attention was drawn to the Cobra which Hemingway had ordered into the air to watch for MiGs. Iron balls swooped down to street level and, getting Hemingway's attention, pointed to his ears to indicate his superior was wanted on the radio. When the Harrier pilot responded by running for his aircraft, Iron Balls again ascended to fly cover.

Inside his cockpit, Hemingway put on his flight helmet and connected his communication lines.

"This is Jai-Lai One," he announced.

"Jai-Lai, Pitstop." The gruff voice of the Tarawa task force commander sounded impatient. "Do you have a transportation problem?"

Hemingway hesitated. It was a not so subtle reminder that his presence on the Tarawa was expected immediately if not sooner. Deciding not to reveal the problem in case the Cuban Air Force was listening in, Hemingway replied: "Will be under way within quarter-hour."

"Confirm when you liftoff," replied the task force commander.

"Roger."

Hemingway paused, then keyed his mike again.

"Iron Balls, Jai-Lai."

"Go ahead, Jai-Lai."

"Come in and top off. We're making for Pitstop."

"Gotcha."

For a moment, Hemingway grinned at the thought that the Cuban Air Force could be listening in. Iron Ball's lack of protocol might convince them that the two Marine pilots were civilians.

Hemingway pushed himself out of his cockpit and stepped down the fuselage to the ground. Kneeling beside the welder under his port wing, he watched as supporting rings of solder were being applied to the top of each strut.

"Are you nearly finished?" asked Hemingway.

The welder lifted his visor. "Yes, but this needs 40 minutes to cool properly."

"I must leave before that."

"Then keep my sawhorse which supports your wing in position until you lift off," advised the Cuban.

The Cobra landed down the street, and the two American pilots helped each other fill their fuel tanks. This completed, Hemingway walked to the shade where General Diaz was demonstrating how to launch a Stinger to a group of his officers.

Hemingway noted that one of them wore a flightsuit, and he recognized the man as one of the MiG pilots who'd been shot down. When Diaz saw Hemingway staring hard at the man, the general laughed.

"I asked him if he would identify the aircraft of his flight commander for me," explained Diaz, "and he offered to shoot the plane down himself."

Hemingway offered his hand to the general. "Good luck, sir. I'm going now."

Diaz gazed at the hand a moment, then moved forward to engulf the Marine pilot in his arms. After a firm hug, Diaz stepped back.

"Thank you for coming to Cienfuegos, *General Hemingway!*" said Diaz.

Hemingway returned a half-smile. "I wish I could have stayed longer."

"We leave soon also," announced Diaz proudly. "I shall use your Stingers against the MiGs on my way to Santa Clara."

"I hope we meet again, sir," said Hemingway. "Perhaps....in Miami."

"Better in Havana," Diaz heartily laughed.

With that, the general snapped to attention and formally saluted Hemingway. The Marine returned an immaculate salute of his own.

Striding to his aircraft, Hemingway prepared for takeoff. He was tired and took his time bringing the Harrier up. After the initial whine was replaced by the roar of the engine, he methodically conducted his instrument check.

His hands automatically went through their own routine---connecting his oxygen supply, the G-suit pressure system for tight turns, his life vest and dinghy survival pack, plus five pairs of harnesses in case he needed to eject. His hands concluded their work by hooking the radio leads to his flight helmet.

226

All his instrument readings were normal, except one. The duct pressure at the vent of his port wingtip registered below the acceptable minimum. Though he didn't like expending the extra fuel, Hemingway knew he had to execute a vertical takeoff.

A glance down the street revealed Barragan in his Cobra. Hemingway keyed his mike.

"Iron Balls."

"Go."

"I've got low pressure at my port vent," Hemingway told Barragan. "Wait till I'm airborne before you lift off."

"Will do."

With his exhaust nozzles at the vertical, Hemingway pushed his throttle to full power.

Barragan watched the Harrier jump off the street. When the aircraft was at rooftop level, its port wing started to dip. Increasing power, Hemingway shifted his nozzles to 45 degrees and his forward movement righted the Harrier.

Hemingway keyed his mike. "Pitstop, Jai-Lai."

"Go Pitstop."

"On the way," announced Hemingway, adding: "Keeping Iron Balls company."

The last words would explain why the Harrier would arrive at the USS Tarawa in an hour instead of the expected 30 minutes. The top speed of the Cobra would slow the AV-8B to approximately half its cruising speed. And Hemingway wanted company in case his aircraft had sustained additional damage which was not yet evident.

"Iron Balls, Jai-Lai."

"Gotcha."

"We'll stay at this altitude." The Harrier was 200 feet off the deck. Hemingway added: "Go combat spread."

Barragan picked up his port side at 75 feet.

In three minutes, the deep verdant green of the countryside below was replaced by the light green of Cuba's shallow coastal waters. Hemingway watched the color gradually turn blue as the two aircraft reached the open water of the Caribbean Sea. The azure blue was sprinkled by occasional and varied shades of green which revealed the presence of shoals and submerged sandbars.

His thoughts drifted to the comforts offered by the Tarawa. He was anxious to get out of his clammy flightsuit....to stand in the cool spray of a shower....to forget the godawful pickle that he'd gotten himself into by initiating a "training flight." Feeling drowsy, he decided it'd be a good idea to engage Iron Balls in conversation. At their low level, it was no time to doze off.

"Iron Balls, Jai-Lai."

"Righto," replied Barragan.

"Those were your first fixed-wing kills, weren't they?" asked Hemingway.

"Yep."

"Did you get any Iraqi helicopters in the Gulf?"

"Yep."

When Barragan didn't offer the number, Hemingway asked: "How many?"

"Four."

Damn, mused Hemingway, I didn't know that. It hadn't been in the younger man's personnel jacket. Iron Balls was an ace now, too.

"Congratulations," Hemingway offered.

He heard Barragan chuckle.

"The four in the Gulf were all on the ground," revealed Barragan. "How many you got now?"

"The last one made six," replied Hemingway.

After a short pause, Barragan said: "I'll have to buy you a case of beer."

"It's the other way around," countered Hemingway. "I'm the one who owes the case of beer. You saved my life."

"Nah," replied Barragan. "That's just a specialty of mine."

"Damn," Hemingway muttered under his breath. There's not one ounce of humbleness in Iron Balls, he mused. Hemingway didn't hold the thought long. Lack of humility was a common trait among Marine pilots.

"How old are you, Barragan?"

"Thirty-one."

"Been married?"

Barragan delayed his answer, wondering why the other man was getting personal.

"Nope."

"Why not?"

Barragan's answer came in a drawl. "Women are too much like whisky."

"How's that?"

"A steady diet of either will do you in," replied Barragan.

Hemingway thought the statement sounded odd coming from a man who devoted most of his leisure time to the opposite sex.

"Are you serious?" inquired Hemingway.

There was a weariness in Barragan's reply.

"Too many pretty women I've known come on kitten-soft....and turn snake-mean."

Hemingway studied the merit of the assertion. Thinking back over his own experiences with lookers, he had to agree. Generally, they had been more difficult to please. But, thinking of Sandi, he decided she was the exception that made the rule. For a lovely woman, she'd turned out to be unusually mellow. Maybe, it was simply a matter of searching for the exception, mused Hemingway, and he started to say as much.

"Don't give up on---"

Barragan cut him off. "Farewell party coming in at seven o'clock."

From the Cobra pilot's calm tone, the words didn't immediately register with Hemingway. Checking over his shoulder in the direction of the Cuban coast, he didn't see a thing.

"At two miles," added Barragan.

Again, Hemingway swung his head left. He scanned the sky and found what he was looking for at 2,000 feet. It looked like four tiny bugs on his canopy, except they were symmetrically arranged.

"Bring it up!" shouted Barragan, seeing the Harrier begin to drift lower as Hemingway stared into his rearview mirror. Barragan thought the other pilot was unintentionally losing elevation.

"No! Get on the deck!" retorted Hemingway.

If the MiGs were armed with missiles, moving closer to the water surface would make a lock-on harder for them to obtain. And Hemingway was near certain the MiGs would have missiles.

Both pilots came down to a scant 15 feet off the deck. The surface of the water was glassy, and Hemingway damned the smooth surface. He would have preferred choppy swells, that could interfere with an interceptor's radar.

"Lock-on!" called out Iron Balls.

A short glance told Hemingway the Cobra had popped up as soon as the MiG radar blasted Barragan's ears. The helicopter would need elevation, and fast, to lose the missile.

As the Cobra pilot fought for altitude in the few seconds still available, he veered west to better view the approaching missile.

Hemingway, deciding to get perpendicular to the oncoming MiGs, banked in the opposite direction, staying on the deck. The move would lessen his heat signature for the sensors on the MiGs. As he curved around in a tight circle, Hemingway could see Barragan climbing rapidly, close to 300 yards. The Cobra suddenly dipped, taking a steep dive.

Hemingway glanced right. He saw only two MiG-29s, each heading toward the Cobra helicopter from a mile out. Forgetting Barragan's problem, Hemingway hurriedly searched for the other MiG pair. He found them where he'd expected. The MiG pilots had circled around to get on his tail again.

Iron Balls was timing his dive to maximize the Cobra's speed when the missile arrived---near sea level.

Hemingway cut sharp right, heading east in the direction of the distant coast. The two MiGs banked to stay on track with the Harrier. The Cubans were at a bad angle to get a missile off, but in an excellent approach for their cannons.

Plunging down toward the blue water, Iron Balls edged his Cobra slightly to port to bring the missile left. When he judged the water was only 50 feet away, Iron Balls altered the angle of his helicopter to abruptly halt his dive, then cut sharp to starboard. The missile, trying to turn with the Cobra, skimmed over the glassy water.

Glancing behind him, Iron Balls gawked at the rooster tail thrown up in the water by the missile's exhaust as it unsuccessfully tried to turn with his Cobra. The sight reminded him of a fan created by a hard-cutting waterskier.

Hemingway, unable to escape his pursuers, aligned his Harrier at the charging MiGs.

The first MiG came in straight and slow, as a decoy. Its partner angled away a few seconds, to make his approach diagonal to the line of the Harrier's flight, thereby obtaining a broader profile of the AV-8B.

With two choices, Hemingway took the decoy. Getting an aural, he squeezed his wing arm firebutton. For a split second, he observed the Sidewinder as it jumped forward of his wing. Had he not been fatigued, Hemingway would have switched his attention more promptly to the other MiG.

Barragan, with the Cuban missile no longer tracking him, spotted his two MiGs now maintaining a respectful two-mile distance. Descending again, Barragan spun around to the Harrier.

For the second time that day, Hemingway felt an ill, sinking sensation as MiG shells bracketed his aircraft. After firing his Sidewinder, he had turned too late into the oncoming path of the second MiG. The distinct shudder of Hemingway's aircraft as high-caliber shells thudded into it was unmistakable.

Barragan, from three-quarters a mile, saw one of the silver MiGs splinter into pieces. It appeared as if the decoy MiG had flown into a giant shredder.

The other MiG crossed above Hemingway's Harrier at low altitude. Seeing flames billowing from the AV-8B's wing, Iron Balls frantically shouted:

"Eject! Eject!"

Hemingway, with his wing tanks full of fuel, didn't need the advice. He had already reached between his legs to grip the yellow banded loop and was giving it a sharp tug.

When Barragan saw the Harrier seat---riding up the rails---explode through the canopy, he rotated his helicopter in the direction of the escaping MiG. The Cuban pilot, in lining up for an accurate run, had slowed somewhat. Barragan got a near instant aural.

A Sidewinder sped off the Cobra's wingtip rail at the same moment Hemingway separated from his seat at the apex of its arching climb.

The Harrier pilot plummeted downward, his blossoming parachute whipping him taut 20 feet above the water. Two seconds later, Hemingway hit its surface.

Iron Balls looked back to the MiG in time to see his Sidewinder matching the final jinking of its pilot. Barragan knew the MiG pilot had only one logical choice.

The Cuban pilot punched his aircraft noseup a moment for altitude, signifying he'd made the choice.

Just before his Sidewinder plowed into the aircraft, Barragan watched the Cuban's seat rocket off the MiG. Returning his attention to Hemingway, Barragan saw that he had evidently ejected over a submerged sandbar. The downed pilot stood shoulder-deep in water, holding onto an inflated yellow dinghy. Satisfied that Hemingway had survived his ejection intact, Barragan pivoted north and searched the skies for the remaining MiG pair.

Spotting them, he made a beeline toward their position.

The Cuban pilots promptly responded to the Cobra's threat by spurting up to 5,000 feet where they could dive away from the helicopter's missiles.

Having bluffed the MiGs further away, Barragan turned back to Hemingway. He found the Harrier pilot struggling to pull himself into the yellow dinghy with only one arm. Barragan assumed the explosive ejection from the Harrier must have wrenched one of Hemingway's shoulders.

The Cobra pilot made wide circles around the dinghy, alternating his attention on the struggling man below him and the two MiGs above.

Each time Hemingway got his right arm inside the dinghy and tried to hoist himself inside, the raft rolled away. Seeing the problem, Barragan positioned his Cobra on the opposite side of the raft and used his downwash to push it toward the downed man.

This enabled Hemingway to get his head and right shoulder over the edge of the raft. As he began to bring himself facedown into the dinghy, Barragan pulled up abruptly.

Thirty yards on the other side of the yellow dinghy, he'd spotted a large fin breaking water. In the distance, other fins followed.

"Get in!" screamed Barragan.

Though Hemingway had no way of hearing him, Barragan again yelled:

"Get in!"

Hemingway was squirming his body, inches at a time, into the raft. Kicking with his feet, he managed to get the upper half of his body into the dinghy.

My fangs, thought Barragan. The turret directly below his gunship's nose held a 20mm Gatling cannon, and the ammo can under his cockpit held 750 HEIT rounds on a belt that was 50% high explosive, 30% incendiary, and 20% tracer. They had peppered a MiG. Why not a shark? thought Barragan.

He swung his Cobra around to the opposite side of the yellow dinghy. But the large fin was too close to Hemingway to risk a shot. Watching helplessly, Barragan saw the shark approach Hemingway's kicking boots.

Intending to alert Hemingway, the helicopter pilot squeezed off a short burst. At the report of the Cobra's cannon, Hemingway tightened his grip on the dinghy and paused in his efforts.

By the savage jerk of Hemingway's body, Barragan knew the shark had slashed at a leg. When both of Hemingway's boots appeared above water again, kicking wildly in a renewed effort to get aboard, Barragan breathed easier. One of the boots did appear slightly smaller.

Unable to stop the first shark, Barragan directed his Gatling at the others. He released a three-second burst, and his triple, rotating barrels spit out thick shells that tore through the predators.

Clear water around the raft became a foamy red as the uninjured sharks immediately turned to feast on the broken pieces of their brethren.

A burst of adrenalin pushed Hemingway entirely into his small raft.

"Alright!" shouted Iron Balls to himself.

He saw Hemingway roll onto his back and promptly raise up a bloody boot. Blood discolored Hemingway's hands as he attempted to remove his boot.

More sharks, attracted by the smell of fresh blood in the water, created a feeding frenzy that rocked the small dinghy, forcing Hemingway to forget his bleeding foot and hold onto opposite sides of the raft to keep from capsizing.

Barragan moved his Cobra away so its downwash would not cause additional instability to the dinghy. As he did so, the helicopter pilot checked the skies overhead. The MiGs were still circling, though lower than before. When Barragan looked to the raft again, he saw its occupant waving him in.

The turbulent water around Hemingway was awash in blood, foam, and sand thrown up by the crazed sharks. It was impossible to see in the water. Hemingway, in the center of it all, wanted out. The floor of his raft was splattered with blood that would eventually draw the sharks to him. Looking at the Cobra, Hemingway made more frantic hooking motions with his good arm.

Iron Balls knew what he had to do, but not how. Approaching the small dinghy with his powerful downwash would risk tipping the man into the mouths of the sharks.

Hemingway was now pointing in a southerly direction. When he saw Barragan's eyes on him,

Hemingway pushed at the side of his raft with his good arm in the same direction.

"Gotcha!" exclaimed Iron Balls.

The Cobra pilot promptly moved to the north of the raft and came in as low as he dared. His skids touched water as Barragan edged his helicopter nearer.

The raft began to move south from the force of his downwash, out of the feeding area.

Iron Balls gradually moved directly over the swirling predators as he pushed the raft further from them. When he had Hemingway a good 30 yards away, Barragan halted and moved his Cobra higher.

Now the tricky part, Barragan told himself, never having rescued a man from water without a rope or harness.

The effort to pick up Hemingway risked sinking the dinghy with the Cobra's downwash, but Barragan had no choice but to lower himself directly over the raft so his downwash would not push Hemingway out of reach of a skid. He popped his hatch in order to lean out and see better.

Barragan descended, keeping the Cobra aligned with the constantly shifting dinghy. At 15 feet from the water, the helicopter's propwash began to throw out spray from the perimeter of its 44-foot-wide rotor span. This created a salty drizzle overhead that partially obscured the vision of both men.

As the Cobra eased past 12 feet, Barragan prepared to pull up fast in case his wash started to upset the dinghy.

He estimated that Hemingway, with one outstretched arm, could reach up four feet.

When the Cobra dropped below 10 feet, Hemingway could only glance up every few seconds before having to wipe his eyes clear of the stinging water.

His last view of the Cobra's skid was at a three-foot distance. After that---in the maelstrom created by the helicopter's prop---Hemingway could only wave his arm blindly in search of the skid.

Seeing the flailing hand, Barragan shifted his gunship slightly to starboard.

His head down, Hemingway banged a wrist into the skid. Fighting pain in his left shoulder, he grabbed the skid first with his right hand, then the left.

Iron Balls immediately felt the pull on the helicopter. He tried to give himself only enough power to counter-balance it, as more might pull the skid out of Hemingway's wet hands.

For a split-second, the man in the dinghy opened his eyes to orient himself with the skid in his grip. His vision obliterated again, he threw a leg up and around the skid. With his last strength, Hemingway pulled his body off the raft and locked himself to the skid by wrapping his bloody boot around it also.

Plaza De La Revolucion

At the sound of the rifle volley, the front of the crowd recoiled as if lashed by a whip.

Stung by rubber bullets, they reacted at first as if hit by real bullets. Then, realizing the solid rubber slugs had caused only severe bruises, they frantically sought to avoid further pain by charging into the people behind them.

Further back, the discharge of the weapons was barely distinguishable over the chanting of the crowd.

"DOWN WITH CASTRO! DOWN WITH CASTRO!"

With the crack of the rifles, Maria had collapsed onto the shoulders of her bearers, gripping her baby in one arm and the Cuban flag in the other.

When she felt someone trying to shove the flag higher, Maria held on and struggled to come upright with its staff. In the buffeting of the crowd, she could only bring herself to a crouching position on the unsteady shoulders of the students.

With the first volley of the rifles, Lou dropped Kristine to her feet. She stood wedged between the CIA man and the elderly Diego, who was nearest the rifles. Camille was to Lou's side.

"DOWN WITH CASTRO! DOWN WITH CASTRO!"

The State Security commander at the front of the Plaza---still hearing the forbidden chant---again fired his pistol, signalling another volley from the rifles.

Many of those facing the rifles, with nowhere to escape, dropped to the ground, hugging the surface of the Plaza. Others in terror continued pressing to the rear.

With the second rifle volley, the panicking people forced Lou and those around him to shuffle backwards. When Lou stumbled, hands from behind gripped his shoulders to steady him.

"It is I," said No-Chin when Lou twisted his head around.

Getting sideways to the movement of the crowd, Lou brought his arms up above his shoulders to better balance himself and shouted to Camille.

"Turn and face to the rear!"

"I can barely stand!" replied Camille, ignoring his advice.

"Turn around!" Lou implored again. "Or you'll trip."

"DOWN WITH CASTRO! DOWN WITH CASTRO!"

Diego, having managed to come about, was trying to help Kristine also face in the direction of the crowd's movement.

"I can't turn!" yelled Camille. The tight pack of the people had trapped her arms to her sides.

Lou attempted to push the bodies from her, but it was impossible. As soon as one was shoved away, another took its place.

He tried to bring Camille around himself by twisting her shoulders. That too proved impossible. Another volley of rifle-fire came, causing a sudden surge of the crowd.

"DOWN WITH CASTRO! DOWN WITH CASTRO!"

Over the chanting, Lou began to hear shrieks from the terror-stricken. As he shuffled faster, a new surge caused Diego to stagger. Unable to regain his feet, Diego hooked his hands on Kristine's shoulders to pull himself up. When she faltered under his weight, Diego released his grip on her.

Lou, seeing the head of the elderly man slip lower, winced as Diego's face froze in his realization of the inevitable.

Diego locked eyes with the CIA man. In their silent communion, Lou saw a calming of the old man's face, as if he'd accepted his fate.

Diego's head gradually disappeared. When his fallen body slowed those directly behind him, Kristine was able to pivot all the way toward the rear.

The CIA man, thinking of the videocamera, shouted to Kristine.

"Hold onto my shirt!"

Lou felt his shirt immediately go taut.

As he kept sideways to the jostling crowd, Lou was now chest-to-chest with Camille. He hooked an arm around her head protectively to ward off the flailing elbows and arms.

"DOWN WITH CASTRO! DOWN WITH CASTRO!"

Another volley of the rifles jarred the massed bodies, causing No-Chin to lose his own footing. The Cuban immediately grabbed Lou's arm.

Bracing himself, Lou kept No-Chin upright until he'd regained his feet. Again, a volley caused the crowd to billow backwards. Lou heard Kristine's voice as she tugged his shirt.

"Help me!"

Lou, seeing Kristine down on one knee, grabbed her arm and pulled.

"Get up!" he urged.

"Someone's standing on my leg!" she cried out. A rotund man was behind the girl, struggling to stay upright himself.

Lou dragged Kristine along with the crowd as best he could, but his sweaty hand slipped along her arm and he knew his grip wouldn't last.

The deafening report of a gun near his ear rendered Lou senseless for a few seconds.

Craning away from the blast, Lou recognized a small pistol in No-Chin's hand. In the space created by the shock of the pistol's report, both Lou and Camille grabbed Kristine's hands, but they could not extract the girl from her trap.

"DOWN WITH CASTRO! DOWN WITH CASTRO!"

No-Chin brought his pistol down and aimed it directly into the round face of the man behind Kristine. The tip of the pistol was inches from the man's nose.

"Get off her!" demanded No-Chin.

The round face wobbled back-and-forth in protest. "It's not me!"

"Help her up then!" commanded No-Chin. The pistol adjusted to a point between the man's eyes.

The fat man cautiously bent lower. As he reached an arm down, a volley of the rifles sent another shock wave through the crowd, pitching him forward and over Kristine.

Crouching, Lou grappled with the man's body and rolled it off Kristine. From above, he heard No-Chin's pistol fire again.

Both Lou and Camille gripped Kristine by the armpits and wrenched her forward. When she came free, Lou lifted the girl to her knees.

As Kristine brought the videocamera to her chest, Lou felt a light body folding itself over his back. He violently shook his shoulders and saw a young boy flip off him and onto Camille.

"DOWN WITH CASTRO! DOWN WITH CASTRO!"

Another volley of rifles.

Lou, facing into the oncoming wall of people from a crouch, had the sense that an ocean wave was about to break over him.

As people struggled by on both sides, he attempted to keep them from stumbling over Kristine and Camille.

When Lou shoved a woman away, a bulky man carrying a child tripped over the woman, then landed on Camille. Grappling with the man, Lou rolled him partially off Camille.

All Lou and Camille could see about them was a frantic rush of legs and torsos scrambling to get by. Those still on their feet, in desperation, now stepped on the fallen with impunity.

No-Chin emptied his pistol in the air, attempting to discourage the human stampede. Kristine had managed to crawl beside Lou, while Camille still knelt on his other side. No-Chin stood behind the three.

The wall of bodies kept coming.

"Lie on your sides!" No-Chin shouted down to them, *"or your chests will be crushed!"*

"Do as he says!" commanded Lou to Camille. "Lie on your side."

When Camille hesitated, Lou forcibly pushed her to the stone surface of the Plaza and stretched himself alongside her. With Camille's head and shoulders protected by his own torso, Lou pulled her tight into the curl of his body, then braced an arm alongside her exposed ribs.

Kristine hastily snuggled up to Lou's other side, huddling as close as possible, her belly to his back.

Bodies piling over them began to block out the light.

The chanting of the crowd became fainter and was replaced by the cries of the fallen. Initially, the voices heard by Lou were mostly children.

He found the whimpering of a young boy particularly pitiful. It was nearby, and Lou thought it might be the child he'd tossed off his back. Each time he heard the whimpers, they sounded weaker. Lou wished he hadn't thrown off the boy so violently.

Cross-wise above Lou, a woman trying to squirm out of the pile, drove the heel of her shoe into his neck. Lou twisted away, letting the heel slip off.

"Ow!" exclaimed Camille.

"You alright?" inquired Lou, realizing the heel had scraped her head.

She gave a delayed yes.

Weight from the building bodies jammed Lou's hipbone into the stone surface of the Plaza. He foolishly wiggled his body, thinking to relieve the steadily accumulating pressure, but his futile effort only served to further concentrate the weight on his hip.

When it became obvious he was wedged in place, Lou damned the advice of No-Chin, though he could think of no better position. At the bottom of the mound of packed bodies, it was almost dark. All Lou recognized before his eyes was a long bare arm, of uncertain gender.

The black void was filled with more moans and now the crying of both children and adults. A few feet above him, Lou could hear the coughing of a baby.

"I can't breathe," gasped Camille.

For a few seconds, Lou debated what she meant. Was her chest being crushed? Or was she simply protesting the thick, fetid air they were inhaling? The arm he'd placed alongside her ribs was going numb.

"Yes, you can," he told her.

"There's no...." Her voice trailed off.

After a few minutes, the groans around them became shorter. A girl close by cried out for her mother, while an older woman kept repeating:

"Sweet Jesus.... Sweet Jesus.... Sweet Jesus...."

As the weight above grew more unbearable, Lou grunted at an elbow burrowing into his ribs.

The rifles of State Security came nearer. With each volley, the trampled bodies built over Lou and the air became even more difficult to breathe.

When the firing of the weapons passed directly overhead, the terrible pressure from above no longer worsened.

Lou tried to budge and could rotate only his right ankle a few inches. His arm along Camille's side was completely numb.

Labored breathing dominated the human sounds about him now. Above him, Lou thought the breathing resembled an anxious gasping born of fright. At the bottom of the heaped bodies where he was, Lou heard only the deep wheezing of lungs desperate for more air.

"Sweet Jesus" continued, and the young girl still called for its mother, but Lou no longer heard the whimpering boy.

Fidel Castro---still unable to talk---mutely watched his rally disintegrate. After the crowd was forced away from the Jose Marti platform and the chanting began to subside, Castro decided it was best to let State Security continue to clear the Plaza. He did not wish to hear a resumption of the chant calling for his downfall.

How could this have come to be? Fidel asked of himself. His mind wanted to reject the scene unfolding before his eyes, and he wondered whether the recurring nightmare---the jaws of the rabid dog at his throat---was coming true?

"I have been more than fair to you," he silently told his fleeing people. "When you would not work within my socialist state, I let you go."

And this was partially true. When imprisonment, brainwashing, and work farms failed to convert dissidents, his regime had encouraged their emigration....providing those leaving were older than 45 and signed all possessions over to the state.

"I've been kind to you," Fidel silently told the throng in the Plaza. "I even let you leave Cuba for free."

This too was once true. The 120,000 who'd left in a massive two-week boatlift to Miami in 1980 had paid no fee. Of course, Castro had also managed to empty his prisons of hardcore criminals and export them with the political troublemakers.

"Why did I not repeat the Mariel success again in the early 1990s?" Castro asked of himself. "Why did I, instead, follow the advice of Raul and Vilma?"

The two other members of Cuba's triumvirate had encouraged him to lower the legal emigration age to 20 and charge each person leaving the island a fee of $800---to be raised by their foreign relatives. Raul argued it would be an excellent means to export dissent and also raise hard currency. Vilma had finally swayed her brother-in-law by playing on his ego, for she knew Fidel didn't wish to experience the international embarrassment of losing so many of his people in another massive migration.

The sale of his citizens had been lucrative, but it was too slow. A bottleneck soon arose in the form of quotas and paperwork from countries to which Cubans wished to emigrate. And many citizens who wanted to leave had no foreign relatives available to pay the ransom.

"Raul and Vilma took advantage of me," Fidel told himself knowingly. "They took advantage of my eternal optimism."

Lately, Fidel had openly acknowledged to his inner circle the peril of his eternal optimism. His positive attitude had caused him to misjudge Glasnost. The cutoff of Moscow's aid had come much faster than he'd expected, devastating the Cuban economy. Fidel had found it difficult to fix the blame elsewhere for Cuba's unpreparedness when the ensuing shortages crippled many of his factories.

"Is there still time to exile the protestors?" Fidel asked of himself. Viewing the horde in the Plaza, he suspected it would be necessary to release far more than 120,000 this time.

Fidel studied the scattered clumps of bodies which remained motionless after the State Security line passed over them. They are smart to remain still, Fidel thought. So would I. He knew the rubber bullets left a long and painful bruise, often ripping the skin when the face or hands were hit.

Between the clusters of fallen people were single bodies---stretched out in positions that suggested they were swimming, except the bodies were stationary.

When his State Security had cleared half the Plaza, Castro thought it strange that there was still little or no movement among the stacked bodies. To him, the scattered mounds resembled a vast herd of sleeping cattle, such as he'd seen on his father's ranch in the evenings. Then, thinking of the blonde woman with the flag, Fidel swung around, looking for Raul.

His brother stood off to the side of the podium, also concentrating on the retreating crowd. Fidel went to him and, taking a pen from an inner pocket, wrote a message on Raul's palm.

Stop the guns.

Fidel pointed toward the line of State Security still firing into the crowd. Raul got the point and hurried down the steps of the Jose Marti monument to halt the rifle-fire.

Someone squirming above Lou pushed his arm away from Camille's ribs, and she began to moan with each exhale.

"How you doing, babe?" asked Lou.

She coughed before feebly telling him: "I'm suffocating."

Lou, sorry for asking the question, decided to try distracting her.

"Where do you take your vacations?" he inquired.

When Camille didn't immediately reply, he repeated his question.

"Why are you asking something like that now?" Camille asked back.

"We've got to talk," said Lou. "It'll help us."

After a long moment, she weakly answered his question. "I stay here in Cuba."

"In Cuba?" puzzled Lou. "Where do you go?"

"Varadero"---Camille paused to groan---"with the Shakespeare Surfing Society."

"The what?"

"A bunch of friends from the diplomatic community and a few Cubans. We'll spend a week at the beaches, reading a comedy each day."

Reading Shakespeare didn't sound too exciting, but Lou kept on the subject.

"Why's it called a surfing society then?"

"Midway in the play," explained Camille, her voice losing some of its feebleness, "we break to go wind-surfing and then have a potluck feast."

I could get into that part, thought Lou. "You do this every day of your vacation?"

"Sure. We take turns being director."

Lou was running out of questions on the subject. "So....which comedies did you read last time?"

Camille thought for a moment. "It was a three-day weekend. *Harvey* and *Man of La Mancha* and *The Importance of Being Earnest.*"

"Those aren't Shakespeare," responded Lou.

"We don't do his comedies very often," she answered, "or we'd run out of them."

"Sounds like a weird way to spend a vacation," said Lou.

"Actually," Camille countered, "we have a great time. Here in Havana the days can get pretty dreary, especially when the water and electricity are going out all the time."

"Doesn't that happen up at Varadero, too?" inquired Lou.

"No," said Camille. "Castro can't afford to let it happen up there. The resort hotels along the beaches are full of foreign tourists."

"Interesting," commented Lou.

While he considered what subject to bring up next, Camille began to groan again with each exhale.

"I was thinking," Lou began. "When we get out of this, I'd like to take you to Cozumel."

Camille moaned.

"Have you ever been there?" he asked.

When she still didn't reply, Lou spoke in an encouraging tone.

"Come on, babe. We have to keep talking!"

She groaned again.

"Have you ever been to Cozumel?' he tried again.

"No," she finally managed.

"Do you like to skindive?" he inquired.

"I don't know. Haven't tried it.'

Lou grunted himself. Someone above had shifted, adding more weight on him and grinding the point of his hip even harder into the surface of the Plaza. Lou tried to keep the pain out of his voice.

"They say the only place with better diving than Cozumel," he offered, "is the Great Barrier Reef off Australia."

Camille released a lighter moan.

"Would you like to go to Cozumel with me?" he asked once more, being direct this time.

Waiting in silence for her reply, Lou only heard a quickened breathing from Camille.

God, it's hot in here, thought Lou. We're baking alive in this pile.

Camille began to pant.

The crushing weight over them was worsened by the unreleased body heat of the crammed people. As the temperature in the pile soared, perspiration pouring off those above cascaded onto Lou's face.

He wrenched himself in disgust as the sweat of others washed over him, but his movement only served to mash his hipbone worse into the stone of the Plaza.

"I feel faint," groaned Camille between pants.

Lou spoke with a strained edge he couldn't help.

"I've always thought....the perfect honeymoon would be to spend a month....visiting the top skindiving spots in the world."

Camille continued panting.

"Come on, honey," he encouraged her. "Respond."

"I can't," she muttered.

"You just did," Lou told her, and he continued.

"Skindiving at Cozumel is like visiting another planet. You float over transparent turquoise water, swimming among coral and tropical fish."

"That's nice," said Camille, adding a sigh.

"The water's clear for hundreds of feet," he went on. "You can't believe the riot of color."

"Riot...." repeated Camille.

Regretting his choice of words, Lou quickly asked: "Where would you go on your honeymoon?"

"Honeymoon?" she mumbled.

Lou paused.

"Sweetheart," he began in a frustrated tone, "did you ever notice how you answer all my important questions with a question of your own?"

"That's an important question?" she irritably retorted.

Good, mused Lou. Keep talking, babe.

"See," emphasized Lou. "You just did it again---another question."

A brief silence.

"So, where would you like to go on your honeymoon?" he tried again.

"Why ask---"

The ugly snap of a thigh bone cut Camille short. It resembled the crack of a thick, brittle branch, but both she and Lou knew better. It had come from only two or three feet away.

Lou thought it strange that no outcry came with the break of the bone. When the reason for the lack of sound occurred to him, he didn't share it with

Camille. The owner of the thigh bone was probably unconscious....or worse.

Deciding he might as well encourage her questions, Lou ventured: "Pretend it's our honeymoon in Cozumel."

"What?" she burst out in an almost normal voice.

"I'm just curious," Lou told her. "Where would you like to go?"

"I've never given honeymoons any thought," said Camille.

"Where's your favorite country?" he asked.

"Here," she told him. "Cuba."

Lou was amazed. In their predicament, he couldn't believe she could voice that. During his stay in Havana, he'd found the atmosphere and living conditions little better than what existed in Haiti, the poorest country in the Caribbean. Though the Cubans were not unfriendly, there was a pervasive fear of speaking with foreigners, especially in the open where they might be observed. Nowhere else on the American continents did such fear exist. In his mind, living in such a place would be intolerable.

He released a heavy sigh of his own. "At least, we both like to wind-surf."

Getting little mileage on the honeymoon subject, he started a new one.

"What are your dreams?"

Camille gave it some consideration before answering with another question.

"Why are you interested?"

Lou paused. "I'm becoming enamored with you."

"What enamors you?" She spoke with little feeling.

"I like your challenge?"

"Challenge?" she repeated.

"The two-year challenge," Lou explained. "Once you thaw out, I think you'll make one helluva woman."

Camille wasn't sure she liked the compliment.

"So, what are your dreams?" he tried again.

"To be alone," she admitted.

"I can understand that," said Lou. "Where would you like to be alone?"

Camille thought for only a moment. "On a sailboat."

"What would you do on a sailboat?"

"Feel the cool breeze," she told him. "Trail my hand in the water."

"Would you like company?"

"For what?"

For krissakes, thought Lou, it's impossible to have a conversation with this woman.

"Well," he began, "someone to prepare your meals, someone to handle the rudder, someone to raise the sails."

"One other person....maybe," she grudgingly stated.

They were quiet for a while before Camille spoke.

"You mentioned a riot."

Lou waited.

Camille pointedly asked him: "Did you have anything to do with that hologram of Che last night?"

Lou thought to deny it, but he didn't want to be untruthful to her. He answered by remaining silent, letting Camille assume his involvement.

There was disappointment in her voice when she spoke next.

"Then, you're responsible for this."

Thinking of the injured people around him, Lou could find no ready response to her accusation. Yes, I am responsible, he admitted to himself. It had to be done. Wait a minute, he told himself. I didn't fire those guns. I didn't cause the stampede. It's not my fault. Castro must have ordered it. Lou kept the thought. Still, he could find no response for Camille. It wasn't something she would understand, he tried to tell himself. Yet, he knew she did, as otherwise she would not have asked the question that silenced him.

He did not speak until Camille had begun to moan again several minutes later. No longer hearing the firing of the State Security rifles, he said:

"They've stopped."

Camille made no reply.

"Do you hear the rifles?" he asked her.

"No." Her tone was disgruntled.

"Good," said Lou. "That means we'll be free soon."

A crashing thunder shook the ground.

No! thought Lou. Why should Castro shell the Plaza? It isn't necessary. His people are fleeing already. Why slaughter them?

Again, the thunder pounded the Plaza de la Revolucion.

The effect was ten-fold on those pressed to the reverberating stone bed of the great Plaza.

Lou, clenching his jaws to stop the rattling of his teeth, waited for the next crash.

Pure terror had silenced everyone around them.

Waiting for their moment of death, thought Lou. Camille and Kristine seemed to huddle closer.

Beach Near Cienfuegos

Captain Barragan, watching Hemingway cling to the skid of his Cobra, cautiously moved to 10 feet above the water. Satisfied the other pilot had a good grip, Barragan checked the cloudless skies.

The two MiGs still described a wide arc more than a mile above.

Keeping the Cobra close to the water in case Hemingway lost his grip, Iron Balls headed for the Cuban coast. Every few seconds, he popped his head out the cockpit to check that his passenger was still secure.

At the beach, Barragan slipped in a grove of tall palms to screen his helicopter from the pair of MiGs. Hovering close to the ground, he permitted Hemingway to ease himself from the skid.

With the injured man safely on the ground where he could tend his wound, Barragan sped back over water to relocate the MiGs. The Cuban pilots had come closer. Barragan angled up the beach as if patrolling, staying close to the palms.

After reversing his direction, Barragan saw Hemingway in a sitting position. He had unzipped his flightsuit to remove his green t-shirt and appeared to be wrapping it around his foot.

Iron Balls accelerated his gunship out to sea again, directly at the MiGs. The feint was enough to cause them to move back to a more respectful distance.

Barragan headed into the palm grove and touched down. Concerned about being strafed, he kept his engines at full power and waited for Hemingway to re-enter the gunship.

Awkwardly coming to his feet, Hemingway hobbled under the Cobra's rotor. When Barragan saw the bloody t-shirt around the foot, he jumped out to assist Hemingway into the front cockpit. After strapping the injured man in, Barragan handed Hemingway a flight helmet.

The Cobra flew out of the grove, hugging the palms along the shoreline. Barragan searched for the MiGs, but they were nowhere in sight.

Swinging north toward Camp Cienfuegos, Barragan spoke into his mike. "Ace, this is Iron Balls."

There was no reply from the front cockpit.

"Ace, how do you hear?" Barragan tried again.

"Yah," came a subdued reply.

"What's with the foot?"

A pause, then Hemingway said: "Three toes."

Barragan thought to ask which toes but---feeling his own tingling---decided he didn't want to know.

"I'll find a hospital," offered Barragan.

Neither man spoke again until they arrived at Camp Cienfuegos. Coming over the parade ground, they found a half-dozen assault helicopters arranged along its northern perimeter. At the southern edge, a column of trucks and jeeps were formed, extending a half-mile down a street. Mixed through the column were flatbed trailers carrying tanks. One of the trailers had an AV-8B aboard. Men were working at its tail.

Barragan did a 360 pedal turn---checking for unfriendly aircraft---and set down beside the trailer holding the Marine Harrier.

As Barragan threw open his canopy door, General Diaz's jeep drew up under his rotor.

The Cobra pilot shouted: "I need a doctor!"

Diaz took one look at Hemingway's tightened face and motioned for the Cobra to follow him.

At the one-story base hospital, Barragan and Diaz assisted Hemingway out of the Cobra. The makeshift bandage was dripping blood.

The injured pilot was seated on an examining table, his back against a wall. Both General Diaz and Barragan---anxious to know the extent of the wound---stood over Hemingway as the soggy t-shirt was unwrapped from his foot.

At first sight of the shark's bite, Barragan averted his eyes. The front of Hemingway's foot was a pulpy mass, barely recognizable. Caked blood had mixed with the flesh. Barragan couldn't tell whether "three toes" were missing or if that was the number of toes remaining.

"I must use alcohol to clean this," the physician told Hemingway. "Do you wish a painkiller?"

The frowning pilot studied his foot. His initial gnawing pain had progressed to a throbbing that was only slightly less excruciating.

"Try without it," muttered Hemingway.

Handing the pilot several wooden throat swabs, the physician instructed him to place the soft wood between his teeth.

As the physician applied an alcohol-soaked gauze to where the big toe should have been, Hemingway ground his teeth into the swabs.

Watching the coagulated blood come off, Barragan became fascinated by the clean cut of the shark. Only the suggestion of a stub remained where the big toe had been. The physician neatly halted its bleeding by capping the stub with a small compress.

Stubs of the two adjacent toes received similar treatment. As the physician dressed the wounds, General Diaz spoke to Barragan.

"Captain, we have confirmed that the families of Cuban pilots are being held at the State Security headquarters in Santa Clara. My helicopter rescue force leaves in 20 minutes. I would like to ride in your Cobra."

Grinning at the suggestion, Barragan looked to Hemingway for the go-ahead.

"Santa Clara is 40 miles away," said Diaz, facing Hemingway. "You are welcome to come also."

The physician was dressing the third toe, which had lost only the top knuckle to the shark.

Diaz spoke to Hemingway again. "You have seen that I am taking your Harrier with me."

Hemingway didn't feel like protesting. He only gave Diaz a tired look.

"My men have repaired the rudder and reconnected its hydraulic lines," said Diaz.

When the physician finished, the Harrier pilot scowled at his foot. The brief conversation had distracted him from the pain. With the wounds raw again, the throbbing returned.

"I wouldn't mind riding shotgun," posed Iron Balls.

Hemingway's scowl went from his foot to the face of the Cobra pilot. "We can't interfere anymore."

Iron Balls returned the steady gaze of his superior officer, switched to Diaz, and came back to Hemingway.

"I'm defecting," announced Barragan with a broad grin.

Hemingway stiffened, again forgetting his pain.

"You're joking," he said.

"No," corrected Iron Balls. "I'm defecting."

Hemingway paused. He wanted to shout down the contrary pilot, but he didn't have the energy. Instead, he quietly said:

"You can't do that?"

The Cobra pilot's grin was gone. His eyes narrowed knowingly. "I got a license."

At the dry comment, Hemingway exhaled noisily. Some three weeks earlier---during the last chewing-out he'd given the young pilot back at Guantanamo---he had cautioned Barragan that too many winners of the Medal of Honor considered it a license for behavior that eventually curtailed their promotions and career.

Hemingway spoke without conviction. "We have to return to Gitmo."

"With due respect, sir," began Barragan, "I've been in that prison long enough. It's a lousy place for a bachelor."

Hemingway contemplated Iron Balls a moment, then dropped his chin. He agreed. The desksitters in Washington had made a mistake sending the troublesome young captain to such an isolated base. But then, remembering the Cobra pilot had saved his life twice in the last hour-and-a-half, Hemingway was damned glad they had.

"I speak fluent Spanish," continued Iron Balls, "and I'm sure the general here can get me a Cuban uniform that fits. No one will know I'm American."

Hemingway thought to remind Barragan of the court-martial charges he'd certainly face, but thinking of his own forthcoming judicial proceeding, he discarded that idea.

"Cut me some slack, Gorilla," cajoled Barragan. "You just got number seven. I only need two more MiGs for my Ph.d."

General Diaz checked his watch. "We must leave now!"

"If you go," Hemingway told his pilot, "bring your Cobra back in one piece."

"Yes, sir!" Iron Balls threw a salute as he pivoted out of the room.

After hastily hooking up the spare Sidewinder to his gunship, Barragan put the shirt of the general's driver over the top of his flightsuit.

"How does the radio in your helicopter work?" asked General Diaz.

After installing Diaz in the front cockpit, Barragan demonstrated the Cobra's communication. When it was adjusted to his tank column and helicopters, Diaz told Barragan: "Your Stingers are distributed along my column. They will protect the Harrier."

Iron Balls stood beside the pod which held his remaining two Sidewinders. He glanced at the empty pod on his other wing and came back to Diaz.

"General, I wouldn't mind having a few of those Stingers myself."

Diaz gave him a quizzical look. "Where would you put them?"

"They could be tied under my wings." Iron Balls cupped a hand around the nearest Sidewinder and stroked its smooth surface. "Once these babies are gone, I haven't got much to throw at those MiGs. We could try launching a Stinger alongside your hatch."

A grin grew on the face of Diaz and he delivered an order over the Cobra's radio. A jeep in his column raced up to surrender its Stingers. After they were tied under the Cobra's short wings, Iron Balls took off.

Following the directions of Diaz, he flew down to the end of the column then turned around. As they passed the Harrier, Iron Balls spotted a man on crutches exiting a jeep beside the aircraft.

"That's Colonel Hemingway!" exclaimed Barragan.

He put his gunship in a hover, and they watched several men assist Hemingway onto the trailer, then into the cockpit of the Harrier. When Hemingway had put on his flight helmet, Diaz said:

"Let me talk with him."

Iron Balls switched frequencies. "Jai-Lai, Iron Balls."

When no reply came, Barragan started to repeat himself, then realized why it was useless.

"He can't hear us," Barragan explained to Diaz. "The UHF/VHF antennas were shot off his tail-fin."

Setting his helicopter down, Barragan climbed onto the Harrier's platform with the Cuban general.

"Where are you going?" called out Diaz, thinking the injured pilot intended to take his Harrier back to the USS Tarawa.

Hemingway spoke in an exhausted voice. "With this column...to protect my aircraft."

Diaz pointed to the Harrier wing. "But you have no missiles."

"My cannon's loaded," stated Hemingway, giving his voice a hard edge. "Tell your men to slash the ropes securing me to the trailer if we get company."

Observing the fatigued appearance of the Harrier pilot, Barragan told him: "Colonel, you don't look so hot."

"I'll rest on the way to Santa Clara," responded Hemingway.

Iron Balls said no more. He was glad to have the firepower of the other aircraft, and even more pleased to have his superior officer in on his caper.

Once back in the Cobra's cockpit, Diaz selected his unit's frequency and announced in a clear voice: "This is Stinger One."

He paused, giving his unit commanders time to acknowledge him.

"Move it out!"

Iron Balls pushed his Cobra into the air as the Cuban gunships rose from the other side of the parade ground.

"Follow behind my helicopters," instructed Diaz. "We will be in Santa Clara in 20 minutes."

As Iron Balls took up position, one of the Cuban gunships peeled off and returned to the slower truck column.

"Where's he going?" asked Iron Balls.

"To accompany the tanks," answered Diaz. "He has one of the MiG pilots you shot down. If MiGs show up, he'll attempt to communicate with the pilots....to ask them not to attack."

Good idea, thought Iron Balls.

"The other MiG pilot is in front of us," continued Diaz, "for the same purpose."

"So what's the plan?" inquired Barragan.

"A 36-man commando unit wearing civilian clothes," began Diaz, "is in Santa Clara already. After we isolate the State Security headquarters with our helicopters---to prevent escape or reinforcement--- my commandos will assault the building."

"Why the tanks?" queried Barragan.

"They will arrive 25 minutes after we do....and decide whatever is still unresolved."

"What if someone---spotting the helicopters or tanks---warns State Security?" inquired Barragan.

"The commandos have already cut the telephone lines on their way to Santa Clara," replied Diaz.

Covered your bases well, decided Barragan, and he asked no further questions. With renewed respect for Diaz, Iron Balls decided to fly his gunship a bit more conservatively. It wouldn't be a bad idea to preserve the leadership of the Cuban rebel force.

His radio came alive. "Jai-Lai One, Pitstop."

Damn....not now, thought Barragan. Do I answer, or leave it alone?

When the call from the Tarawa task force repeated, Barragan relented.

"Pitstop, this is Iron Balls."

A pause. "Iron Balls, where is Jai-Lai One?"

"Injured enroute. Flight delayed."

There was a longer pause as the Tarawa task force commander digested Barragan's deliberately brief explanation.

"Iron Balls, this is Pitstop. Do injuries permit egress?"

Barragan debated whether to reply in the negative. Later, he could always claim ignorance of Hemingway's condition. With reluctance, Barragan responded.

"Affirmative."

"Then, egress without delay!" demanded the task force commander.

Hesitating in his reply, Barragan was duly considering the practicalities of traversing hostile and shark-infested waters without another aircraft to back him up. A vision of the threshing sharks under his Cobra came to mind.

"Negative your last," Iron Balls replied. "Would prefer company over open water."

There was a short silence on the radio before the terse reply came.

"Your preferred company is on the way."

Plaza De La Revolucion

At the thunder resounding across the Plaza, Fidel Castro gazed skyward.

Light droplets of rain began to splatter on his face. For several seconds, they spit out of the thundercloud over the Plaza before building to thick, silvery needles that pricked his skin. The fast-moving cloud front blotted out the low-lying sun.

Castro returned his attention to the line of State Security units, who had now advanced well past the middle of the Plaza. Though their rifles were no longer firing, the massed people continued to flee.

In front of the Jose Marti platform, Castro spotted a few individuals beginning to crawl from the piles of bodies.

The deluge of water suddenly increased, hiding the distant line of State Security from his view.

He squinted into the tropical cloudburst as the stacks of bodies immediately before him faded in the falling torrent. When the rain finally drove down in sheets, reducing visibility to a mere 20 feet, Castro left the lectern.

As he stepped off the raised platform, he was met by Vilma Espin. Castro brushed by her, marching down the marble steps of the Jose Marti monument toward the Plaza, followed by a unit of his white-uniformed bodyguards.

Hurrying after him, Vilma called out: "Fidel, what are you doing?"

After making an unintelligible rasp, Castro did not attempt to speak further.

In the pouring rain, he continued down the steps. His contingent of bodyguards rushed ahead to form a moving perimeter around him.

Stopping at the first mound of bodies, Castro stooped to turn an older woman faceup. Vilma reached down to help. Together, they rolled the woman over.

As raindrops pelted her face, the woman's eyes opened to a narrow squint. One of her arms slowly came around to enfold her chest.

"Are you hurt?" asked Vilma, leaning close.

"My ribs." The woman clamped her eyes shut in pain. "It hurts to breathe."

As they eased her off the piled bodies, Vilma saw a thin pair of child's legs protruding from under a man's body whose arm displayed a RAB armband.

After setting the old woman down, Vilma pointed Castro's attention to the thin legs. The two of them pulled off the RAB man, who proved to be alive by coughing.

The child was lying face-down position and dressed like a boy. Vilma placed her palm on his shoulder and jiggled him. When the child didn't respond, Vilma turned him over. The eyes of the boy stared unblinking into the driving rain.

She guessed the child to be no more than six. His lower jaw was partially open, giving his face the appearance of crying.

Vilma placed her fingers along the carotid artery of his neck. After ten seconds, she shook her head at Fidel who stood over her.

"Dead," she pronounced.

Castro motioned the officer of his bodyguard to his side and whispered into the man's ear. The officer called several of his men to the mound, and they pulled it apart. From the tangled bodies, they removed three more corpses---those of a woman and two children.

Castro then marched through the clusters of the bodies until he was near the middle of the Plaza. At that point, he whispered instructions to the commander of his bodyguard, and the white-uniformed men began pulling apart the mounds in search of the blonde woman with the flag.

Seventy feet distant, No-Chin was assisting the injured off a cluster of trampled bodies. When he came to Lou, No-Chin helped the CIA man work his limbs to restore their mobility. After Lou had recovered the use of his arms, No-Chin switched his attention to the woman who had given him the Montecristos. As No-Chin worked on Camille's arms and legs, Lou pivoted in his sitting position to massage the limbs of Kristine.

When freed of the weight upon her, Kristine had kept her fetal position. Her eyes were open and her breathing normal, but she remained frozen in whatever position Lou placed her. When he could find no physical injury, Lou decided the girl had gone into shock. Kneeling over Kristine to shelter her body from the pounding rain, Lou spoke her name.

"Kristine?"

Her eyes blinked, but there was no other movement of her body.

"You're okay, now," said Lou.

An inch of rain had collected on the stone of the Plaza, and Lou raised her head and shoulders out of the water.

As he held Kristine, Lou noticed No-Chin was now trying to revive Diego, who was stretched out like a scarecrow on his back. Glancing over his shoulder, Lou was relieved to see Camille sitting up and rubbing her legs.

Spotting heavily-armed men in white uniforms through the driving rain, Lou recognized a familiar figure standing in their midst. Keeping Kristine's head in his arms, Lou eased the videocamera strap from her wrist.

Activating the camera, Lou zoomed in on the Cuban president.

His white-uniformed bodyguards were working on a large mound of bodies. Lou saw one of body-guards remove a Cuban flag from the mound and hand it to Castro, who promptly passed it on to Vilma Espin. Castro, having seen the person for whom he searched, moved in to help his guards.

Lou filmed Castro as he waved away the guards a moment later and picked a familiar-looking woman off the packed bodies by himself.

Castro carried his burden away from the stack, then knelt and propped the woman on his knee. Lou

261

recognized Maria through the viewfinder and saw that she had Miguel gripped tightly in her arms. The CIA man zoomed his camera to the maximum, filling his viewfinder with Maria.

As the rain scoured the dried blood from the young mother's skin and hair, Castro brushed the blonde strands from her face.

Maria's eyes were closed.

The gloom over the Plaza was momentarily lit up by a flash of lightning. Lou looked up in time to see an electrical bolt spike into the wet surface of the Plaza. Instantly, he felt a numbing electrical charge at his submerged knees. Directly overhead, the accompanying crack of thunder re-sounded like an artillery piece, its keen report momentarily obliterating thought in the minds of everyone near the front of the Plaza.

When Castro looked down again, Maria's eyes had come open. She was intently studying his bearded face.

Maria switched her attention to Miguel, speaking to the listless child and nuzzling her nose to his cheek. Thinking her child asleep, the young mother lowered him to her bare breast. As she huddled her arms around Miguel to warm him, Maria placed his lips to her nipple.

When this didn't bring her child alert, Maria brushed his cheeks with the nipple. It had always stimulated his lips before, even when Miguel was fast asleep.

For a second, Maria's alarmed face looked up into Castro's as if seeking help.

Then cradling her child, she forced his mouth open and pushed her nipple inside. Miguel still did not react.

Frantically, Maria began to blow puffs of air into Miguel's mouth.

When she tired, Maria glanced up in desperation at Castro again. As the mother tried to resuscitate her child, Castro motioned to Vilma, who bent down to hear his whisper.

"Bring me an ambulance."

Lightning struck the watery surface of the Plaza again, and Castro felt his skin crawl at the electricity entering his body.

As the small shock wore off, Castro sensed a new discomfort. His face felt as if it was being torn off.

Maria had his beard by a hand.

She pulled his chin down and screamed into his face.

"You killed my baby!"

She tugged harder, jostling Castro's military hat off his head.

"You killed Miguel! You killed Miguel!""

The hat floated upside down in the water, and rain swiftly drenched Castro's bobbing head as Maria continued to yank his beard with each accusation.

Castro had gripped her wrist to halt the painful tugs when the short butt of an Uzi passed in front of his eyes and clipped the temple of the overwrought woman.

Maria's head slumped to one side, and Miguel rolled out of her arms.

As Maria's hand loosened from his beard, Castro saw bright blood well up where the Uzi had split her skin. The blood from the wound flowed down her face and mixed with rain before spilling onto Castro's knee.

The face of Cuba's president came up in rage, then went back to the unconscious Maria. Reaching for his hat, he placed it under her head before gently setting Maria down. Laboriously, Castro came to his feet.

Grabbing the Uzi from the bodyguard who'd freed him from Maria's grasp, Castro rammed its stock into the man's surprised face.

The bodyguard staggered back, and Castro chopped at his head again, dropping him to the ground. For a brief moment, Castro trained the Uzi on the fallen man....before heaving the weapon away.

It had been his intention---after finding the blonde woman with the flag---to invite her to his offices in the adjacent Palacio de la Revolucion.

Castro wished to converse with the woman, to ask her in detail why she'd led the chant against him and to tell her how magnificent she had appeared.

Above all, the Cuban president wanted to win her over with his intellect and charm, as he had done with hundreds of other dissenters over the years. Castro was certain this woman would be no exception. He had looked forward to the experience, and now it had been denied him.

Castro returned to the unconscious Maria and, beckoning to the nearest bodyguard, he whispered to the man: "Bring the dead baby."

With that, Castro knelt to pick up Maria.

The rain halted, as abruptly as it had begun.

After he rose with Maria in his arms, Castro noticed Vilma Espin holding his hat.

"Where is the ambulance?" he demanded of her.

Vilma raised her hands in a futile gesture. "I've ordered an ambulance three times."

"Then send the first doctor you find to my offices," Castro told her.

He carried Maria across the Plaza toward the Palacio de la Revolucion. When the Cuban president and his entourage disappeared into the building, Lou tucked the videocamera within his shirt and looked to No-Chin. Feeling a hand picking at his shirt, Lou looked down and saw Kristine attempting to get at her videocamera.

Lou placed his hand on Kristine's and told her: "I can get this to Miami."

"Who are you?" she asked.

The CIA man considered his response. "I'm a reporter from Miami. By tomorrow, what is on your cassette can be beamed back to Cuba on TV Marti. Okay?"

Kristine studied Lou a long moment, then nodded agreement.

"How do you feel?" he asked her.

"Better."

"Can you walk?"

"I don't know," she replied.

Glancing about to assure no one was watching them, Lou removed the cassette from the video-camera.

"I should leave with the cassette now," said Lou, returning the camera to Kristine.

She nodded once more.

Lou stood and helped Kristine to her feet. After seeing that she could move her legs sufficiently to walk, he gave her a brief hug.

"Thank you," he said.

Kristine was staring wide-eyed over his shoulder.

Afraid of what was there, Lou cautiously pivoted to follow her gaze.

Though the sky had partially cleared overhead, a light rain still fell at the far end of the Plaza.

High above the fountain of dolphins, Lou's eyes were drawn to a giant colored arc formed by the refraction of the sun's rays in the thin drops of rain. A rich, wide band of orange light dominated its upper curve. Then came a vibrant yellow that gave way to a third band of crystalline mint-green. A thin band of blue followed; and, along the bottom of the rainbow a brilliant band of solid violet glowed as vividly as the hot orange on top.

Lou smirked at the disparity of the scene. All around him on the floor of the Plaza were the broken bodies of the injured and dead. The resplendent rainbow had no place among such tragedy.

"I can't believe it," Lou commented outloud. He had never been so close to a rainbow, nor seen one with such clarity and beauty. Or participated in such horror,

"It is a sign," said Kristine with reverence. "Of the future."

Silently, they watched the great rainbow.

When someone gripped his arm, Lou shivered at the unexpected touch. Turning his head, he saw it was Camille and he breathed easier.

"Can we go now?" she tiredly asked.

"Sure, babe," he told her.

Kristine reached out to touch Lou's arm, looking where the cassette drooped within the pocket of his shirt.

"Be careful," she said with a small smile.

Over her shoulder, Lou saw No-Chin propping Diego into a sitting position. The eyes of the old man were blinking. Lou stepped over to No-Chin and bent over to tell him:

"I will be at the embassy."

Over Central Cuba

Lush farmland swept below Iron Balls' cockpit as he trailed behind the Cuban helicopters. Their flight was in a contour-mode, skimming treetops and power lines. At the direction of General Diaz, Barragan had taken a 30-foot stepup behind the formation.

To their left, fields in cultivation extended to the horizon. A low-lying range of mountains---several miles to their right---paralleled their northeast line of flight.

"Where is Camilo Cienfuegos Airbase in relation to Santa Clara?" asked Barragan.

"Eight miles north of the city," answered Diaz.

"We could pay them a surprise visit," suggested Iron Balls, thinking to catch a few MiGs on the ground.

"It is heavily defended by---"

"Never mind!" interrupted Iron Balls. "Dead ahead!"

A mile to their direct front---at 800 feet---a formation of MiGs were coming at them. Iron Balls immediately veered a few degrees starboard, to clear the heat signatures of the Cuban helicopters from his sensors.

"Damn!" exclaimed Iron Balls, realizing his earlier error.

Because he'd obeyed Diaz's order to follow behind the formation of Cuban helicopters, his Cobra had certainly been spotted by the foraging MiGs. Barragan swore under his breath for not positioning himself at least a mile to the side of the highly-visible helicopter formation. A single helicopter moving near the ground would have been extremely difficult to see from above and almost impossible to detect with radar or infrared sensors.

A quick scan of the nearby terrain told Iron Balls there was no place to mask his position, and he brought his gunship tighter to the ground, still moving forward.

The MiGs were too thick to count. Iron Balls guessed at least twenty.

Without missiles to defend themselves against the MiGs, the Cuban helicopters had scattered like sparrows before a hawk. Only one of the five was still visible to Barragan.

Most of the MiG formation broke also, going after the dispersed helicopters. Barragan watched four of the MiGs continue their heading toward his Cobra.

"What are you doing?" Diaz yelled at Barragan.

Iron Balls was accelerating into the remaining four MiGs, obviously intending to run their gauntlet.

"Getting behind them" replied Iron Balls.

"Why?" demanded Diaz.

There was no time to explain that the maneuver would minimize exposure of the Cobra to the MiGs' superior firepower. Trying to run from the MiGs would simply give them a longer and better target.

In one-on-one mock dogfights with jet fighters, Iron Balls had found that a jet pilot had eight seconds, at best, to bring his nose to bear on a Cobra and open fire. After that, the advantage went to the more agile Cobra, for no fixed-wing aircraft could turn with a helicopter. In addition, the guidance system of a missile launched downward from a jet was often fooled by ground heat and clutter. On the other hand, a missile launched by a Cobra hugging the ground had a clear and cool sky from which to pick out its target.

Iron Balls was already veering to port in order to avoid a tracer-line of shells from the first MiG.

The first MiG's wingman then bore down on the Cobra, spitting out its own line of fire, forcing Iron Balls to lean in the other direction.

Easily avoiding the shells of the second MiG, Barragan sped toward the last pair of Cuban fighters.

The third jet loomed larger, coming in lower than the first two, making its tracers more difficult to track. As Barragan continued to weave and bob, he felt a bump beneath him. By the brief shudder of his gunship, he knew the Cobra taken a hit.

With another hungry MiG coming up, Iron Balls had no choice but to keep flying. The last MiG came in from a higher altitude. As the Cobra pilot raced to get under the hostile aircraft, he saw a missile launch from its wing.

Banking a few degrees left, Barragan waited for the missile to follow his lead. When he saw that it had, the Cobra pilot increased his speed in the same direction, giving the missile an opportunity to build momentum.

As he manipulated the cyclic-handgrip of his gunship, Barragan kept his eyes on the hostile missile, continuing to fly a near-collision course with it. He knew he had only a half-second margin of error if his maneuver was to work.

When Barragan judged the missile was fully committed, he banked 90-degrees sharp right, cutting directly across the missile's path and accelerating hard.

Barragan, watching the missile correct for the new direction of its target, cut his Cobra back toward the missile, forcing it to turn even sharper.

The tail of the missile wobbled as it curved with the Cobra, straining to turn with the helicopter. When Iron Balls was certain it was no longer tracking his Cobra, he made a quick stop and rotated his aircraft in search of his own prey.

As the Cobra rotated, Iron Balls eased higher to give his gunship sufficient clearance from the ground to launch a missile.

The wary pilot of the last MiG was ascending at a 45-degree angle in afterburner, anxious to remove himself from the contest.

Equally anxious to assist the Cuban pilot in his goal, Iron Balls lined up, got an aural, and launched his own missile. In that direction of the sky, the Sidewinder had no other target to choose from.

When his wingman warned him of the smoking Sidewinder, the MiG pilot leveled out and dove quickly. The AIM-9 missile followed suit, making its own parabola in the sky. Both plane and missile raced downward. Near ground level, the MiG banked left and cut away at treetop level, trying to lose the missile in the clutter.

The Sidewinder relentlessly followed the heat source of its victim, working as advertised. Though the MiG was far faster than the Cobra, its wide turning radius was no match for the Sidewinder and neither was its speed.

The first half of the contest had lasted seven seconds. Due to the higher speed of the MiG, the final half of the contest would last two seconds longer.

Certain of the conclusion, Iron Balls was already rotating his gunship in search of other MiGs. Coming around to the fleeing MiG again, he could see only the smoke and debris of an explosion.

"Numero quatro," commented Iron Balls.

"Do you mean you've shot down four planes today?" questioned Diaz.

Iron Balls hesitated, uncertain whether to gloat over shooting down Cubans before a Cuban.

"Something like that," Barragan finally offered. He added: "Do you see any hostile aircraft?"

"No," replied the general.

So, mused Iron Balls, we ran the gauntlet and survived.

"Keep your eyes peeled," said Iron Balls, "while I check out my snake."

Righting his Cobra, Barragan briefly flew level to confirm its aerodynamics. When his flight characteristics proved satisfactory, he glanced down the side of his fuselage. His port side looked fine, and he thought the armored portion of his fuselage might have deflected the blow. A glimpse to starboard proved otherwise.

"Jesus!" exclaimed Barragan, leaning over for a better look.

The Cobra's starboard skid dangled off the fuselage, completely severed from its forward stanchion. Barragan bit his lip.

Without the skid in place, he knew any attempt to land would risk the rotor blade digging into the ground and flipping the helicopter. And there was no safe way to exit the Cobra if he couldn't land.

"Look out!" shouted Diaz.

Iron Balls jerked his head up to a MiG dead ahead, its tracers ripping the terrain toward the Cobra.

The Cuban pilot had been playing a helicopter's card....by hugging the terrain to avoid detection in his approach.

Pulling his cyclic back hard, Iron Balls gained elevation in an effort to avoid the tracer track.

Getting insufficient response from his gunship, Iron Balls also banked to port to twist away from danger.

The roar of the MiG passing by blasted his ears.

Iron Balls was already rotating his Cobra and hitting the master-arm switch on his weapons panel.

The MiG pilot was obviously keeping his speed low to make a tight turn for another run.

"Taking candy from a baby," muttered Iron Balls to himself when the aural of a lock-on came. He held fire for several seconds until his Cobra had ascended enough to give his missile room to drop off.

"Magnifico!" exclaimed Diaz in exhilaration, as the Sidewinder sped off its pod.

The MiG suddenly straightened and went higher when another Cuban pilot far above detected the smoke of the Sidewinder's launch and shouted a warning. The desperate fighter pilot dove back toward the ground to gain speed. Obtaining only a small increase, he cut hard to port before again straining his aircraft for more altitude.

The MiG suddenly stalled in mid-air. In his panic, its pilot had flown out of his envelope. His aircraft appeared to be patiently waiting for the approaching Sidewinder.

"Pop goes the weasel!" drolly commented Iron Balls at the sight of the MiG pilot ejecting from his plane. It was becoming a common sight.

The pilot in his seat had not quite reached the zenith of his ejection arc when the exploding missile blew the MiG into the ground, causing Barragan to wonder whether its pilot might have elected to leave his aircraft too late.

Iron Balls grimaced at the answer. The Cuban pilot appeared to be hanging limply from his parachute during its brief descent.

Numero cinco, counted Iron Balls, this time silently.

He was an ace now, but the American felt little elation. The vision of the limp body had dampened his enthusiasm, and Barragan thought the MiGs had been too easy. Their pilots obviously had no training in fighting helicopters.

He recalled several briefings on the Cuban Air Force back at Gitmo. The Cubans had received their MiG-29 Fulcrums just as Glasnost brought Soviet military aid to an abrupt halt. The Soviets had not bothered to fully train the Cuban pilots, nor were they providing spare parts or technicians to properly maintain the MiGs.

As Barragan rotated his gunship in place to watch for more aircraft, the Cobra pilot was already debating whether to defend himself from further attacks by using his Gatling cannon in the air, or to land and use a Stinger.

"Hey, dummy," Barragan reminded himself outloud, "you can't land this crate anymore!"

Diaz, fascinated with the inferno created by the last MiG encounter, could give no warning of the next one.

Even if Iron Balls had looked directly over his gunship, he would not have spotted trouble coming either.

From high above, the Cuban flight commander had begun a steep dive. The older and more experienced man had positioned his diving MiG-29 in the background of the sun.

As the Fulcrum roared down on the Cobra, the Cuban pilot delayed his fire, not intending to reveal himself any sooner than necessary.

Barragan was making a full revolution of his gunship every 15 seconds. His first indication that he was under attack was the sight of a MiG's cannonfire churning up the ground nearby. Looking up, he followed its tracers directly into the sun.

Before he could react, Barragan felt shells from the MiG ripping into his fuselage, and his Cobra took on a life of its own.

Iron Balls fought to halt an undesired clockwise rotation of his gunship. The direction of movement told him hostile fire had damaged his tail rotor. Anti-torque provided by the tail rotor was no longer sufficient to neutralize the counter-clockwise force of the main rotor.

Every six seconds---too fast for sustained human equilibrium---the nose of the Cobra did a complete horizontal revolution. When Diaz realized the helicopter was out of control, he shouted:

"Get down! Land!"

"I can't!" yelled back Iron Balls. "We only have one skid!"

The gunship continued to revolve in place, regardless of Barragan's efforts. As he twirled, he also fought to keep the fuselage from rolling left.

Losing a skid and tail rotor simultaneously wasn't in the book, Iron Balls thought to himself as he moved his Cobra higher, looking for a soft landing site.

Iron Balls strongly doubted he could remain in control more than another 45 seconds. After that, dizziness induced by the spinning helicopter would impair his ability to execute even a controlled crash.

With his increased elevation, Barragan caught a glimpse of water. The next time around, he realized it was a small river. Manipulating all his controls, he angled the revolving gunship toward it.

He began to twist his head to the river---in the manner of a spinning ballerina---in order to maintain his own equilibrium.

"Open your hatch!" shouted Iron Balls, "and unbuckle your harness!"

General Diaz hesitated to follow the instructions as Iron Balls threw open his own hatch and added:

"We've gotta jump!"

When the Cobra had moved over the water, Diaz finally opened his cockpit door. The river was wider than the helicopter's 53-foot length, but shallow. As the Cobra spun over the water, Barragan guessed it to be only a few feet deep. He prayed the gravel underneath the clear water would be soft and thick.

"You first!" instructed Barragan. "Roll out in a ball!"

When Diaz hesitated, Barragan shouted: "It's going to get worse!"

After two more revolutions, the pilot glanced over the HUD. The front cockpit was empty, and he moved his helicopter upstream so it wouldn't come down on Diaz. Iron Balls took one look out his hatch and pushed away from his gunship....praying it would stay airborne until he was out from under it.

Hitting the water on his back, Iron Balls rolled himself rapidly downstream with the current to get outside the radius of the 22-foot rotor blades.

The helicopter gradually rolled left. With its fuselage listing at a 45-degree angle, the tips of the rotor blades made contact with the river first, swatting at its surface. Iron Balls, floating away at a safe distance, turned to watch as the tips of the slowing rotor blades skipped off the surface of the water, throwing spray onto the banks of the river.

Well, I'll be a sonuvabitch, Iron Balls told himself, realizing he could have ridden it in.

The slowing of the rotor blades by the water had permitted the Cobra---slightly inclined to port---to settle in an almost upright position. With only the bottom third of the fuselage under water, the rotor continued to spin.

As Iron Balls fought for footing in the fast-moving river, someone caught his body from behind. Gaining his knees, he saw that General Diaz had blocked his body.

Regaining his feet, Iron Balls shouted: "I've got to shut it down!"

After minor repairs, it might even fly again, thought Barragan as he struggled upstream. Diaz followed.

The stuttering boom of a MiG cannon halted them. A Fulcrum roared past, strafing the downed Cobra. Seeing no apparent damage, Iron Balls pushed ahead and leaned into his cockpit to kill the engines. That done, he set to work untangling the wire securing the nearest Stinger. Diaz joined him.

When the missile launcher came off, they both lugged it to a bank of the river. As Barragan activated the heatseeking sensor of the Stinger, he yelled to Diaz:

"Where's the MiG?"

Diaz pointed to it. The Cuban pilot was coming in at moderate speed.

As the Fulcrum came nearer, Iron Balls wondered whether he'd get credit for downing a plane from the ground.

Iron Balls focused on the Fulcrum, keeping it in the crosshairs of his firing-sight. The pounding of the MiG-29's cannon increased his concentration.

The aircraft was still 200 yards distant when orange flames unexpectantly flashed from its port wing. Barragan jerked his head away from the firing-sight of his launcher to get a better view. As the plane flew by, he watched the flames flow back along its fuselage in a swirl of black smoke.

Iron Balls brought the Stinger off his shoulder when he saw the MiG pilot select a new mode of flight. Sailing out of his cockpit, the Cuban did half a backflip before separating from his seat. His chute came open upstream over the river.

"Cripes!" exclaimed Barragan.

A MiG-23 Flogger roared overhead, drowning out his voice. Barely flinching at the close flyby, Barragan swung his Stinger onto his shoulder to aim at the new aircraft.

With the Flogger in his sights. Barragan began squeezing the grip of the Stinger's trigger mechanism when a blow to his arm jostled the missile off his shoulder, causing him to stumble.

Twisting around to his assailant, Barragan stared at General Diaz.

"What the---"

Diaz cut him off and pointed to the last plane which had overflown them. "That MiG shot the first one down!" he explained.

A lopsided grin colored Iron Balls' face.

"One of our captured pilots must have talked to him," said the general.

With that, Diaz withdrew the pistol from his holster.

The MiG-29 pilot who had just ejected was rolling in the water toward them, tangled in the shroud lines of his parachute. They dragged the Cuban pilot from the river, using his parachute lines to tie him, then turned their attention to the action overhead.

Far above, the flash of an explosion announced a missile hit, and another aircraft tumbled out of the sky. As they watched the MiGs dogfighting each other, Barragan observed: "It looks like the MiG-23s are battling the MiG-29s."

Diaz nodded. "That is because the best planes are assigned to the more ideologically-correct pilots."

"There must be a shortage of ideologically-correct pilots," observed Barragan. "I see at least twice as many Floggers up there as Fulcrums."

Diaz checked his watch. "I must talk to one of the pilots we captured back at Camp Cienfuegos."

Barragan helped Diaz back into the front cockpit of the Cobra and gave him communication.

Raising the Cuban helicopter with the captured pilot aboard, Diaz told him: "Inform the MiG-29s that my tanks have captured their families at the State Security building in Santa Clara. Order them to stop fighting! And send a helicopter to the river where the Cobra sits....to pick me up."

Signing off, Diaz commented to Barragan: "The tanks will arrive soon in Santa Clara and make what I have said come true."

As they waited on the river bank, Diaz spotted a damaged MiG trailing smoke and pointed it out.

"Which one is that?"

Iron Balls squinted at the aircraft. "A Fulcrum." After a minute of scanning the skies, he added: "I don't see anything but Floggers up there now."

Two Mi-2 Hoplite helicopters, flying nap-of-the-earth, rushed up on them. As Barragan and Diaz climbed aboard one, the general took the headset from the door gunner and spoke to the Hoplite's pilot.

"Inform the MiG-23s above that they are now members of the Cuban Free Air Force. Also tell them I am ordering my tanks to their airbase to make it safe for them to land."

Diaz then instructed his pilot to follow the main highway into Santa Clara with the other Cuban helicopters. Four minutes later, they spotted the tank column entering the outskirts of the city. Diaz instructed half of them to bypass the city and head for the airbase to the north.

At the center of Santa Clara, the Hoplites circled over the six-story State Security headquarters. It was several stories higher than nearby buildings. When fifty-caliber machineguns---concealed behind sandbags at the corners of its roof---opened up and dropped one of the thin-skinned Hoplites, the others scampered behind the protection of other buildings.

General Diaz landed on the street and ordered his commando team to delay their attack until the tanks arrived, then took off again, in search of the tank column. As their Hoplite skimmed the rooftops, Iron Balls shouted to Diaz:

"The Harrier can take out those machineguns!"

Diaz nodded acknowledgement.

Locating his tanks forging through the city, Diaz landed in a square they would pass through. The column was halted, given orders to surround the State Security headquarters, but to hold fire. Sending the tanks on ahead, Diaz and Barragan ran to the Harrier's trailer.

Hemingway appeared haggard, but some color had returned to his face. At his cockpit, Iron Balls called out:

"How's your foot?"

"Don't remind me," winced Hemingway. He asked: "Where's your gunship?"

"Caught a round in my tail," minimized Iron Balls, "and had to land in a small stream."

He hastily changed the subject. "Did you see the Floggers fighting the Fulcrums?"

Hemingway shook his head in the negative.

"The MiG-23s are on our side now!" said Barragan enthusiastically. "You should have---"

Diaz broke in with a question to Hemingway. "Can you fly this plane?"

The Harrier pilot stared deadpan at the general, not giving a reply, though he didn't relish flying in his weakened condition.

Diaz continued. "Machineguns on the roof of the State Security building have knocked out one of my helicopters."

Hemingway looked to Barragan. "See any SAMs?"

Barragan shook his head. "Just fifty-caliber guns at each corner of the roof."

Hemingway came back to Diaz. "Tell the driver of this trailer to place it at the center of the square. If this aircraft can fly, I'll raise my fist."

"State Security is a tall brown brick building," offered Barragan. "We'll lead you to it."

Hemingway took his time bringing up the AV-8B's turbofan. After two minutes of warmup, he double-checked the duct pressure at both ends of his fuselage and wingtips. Moving his nozzles to vertical, Hemingway considered his two alternatives.

Gradually coming off the bed of the trailer would give him the option of setting back down quickly in case his plane was not air worthy. On the other hand, if he used maximum thrust, it would jump the aircraft into the air and give him the maneuverability of horizontal flight which he knew the Harrier of capable of.

278

Deciding he was too exhausted to undergo the strain of fighting for stability at low altitude, Hemingway jammed his throttle to full power. In three seconds, the Harrier pushed over the rooftops surrounding the square. After determining his AV-8B responded adequately in hovers, Hemingway raised a closed fist to Diaz and closed his canopy.

The Harrier followed the Hoplite, going down to 30 feet off the deck. When the Hoplite paused behind another building and Barragan waved him on, Hemingway continued down the street toward the State Security headquarters.

Persons on the street and inside the buildings adjacent to the Harrier's path were stunned by the earsplitting howl of its turbofan engine. The deafening roar reverberated between the buildings, shattering windows; and its exhaust threw up a storm of debris---giving the effect of a cyclone passing through.

Coming upon the State Security building at second-floor level, Hemingway brought his aircraft up to the fifth floor level. As he adjusted his controls to a hover, he saw two heads pop over the edge of the roof to study him.

The two heads disappeared as quickly, then reappeared, struggling to prop a machine-gun over the edge of the roof and train it on the Harrier.

The armor of the AV-8B was strongest on its underside, and Hemingway had serious doubts that his Plexiglas canopy could withstand a hail of fifty-caliber bullets.

He rapidly angled his nose up 15 degrees, aiming just under the corner where the men were. A moment later, the Gatling gun mounted on his starboard underfuselage chattered into action.

Bricks scattered off the corner of the building, blown away by the delivery of 600 rounds a second from the Harrier's gun pod. Within a few seconds, the immense firepower chopped the corner off the building.

In the flying rubble and cloud of sand, Hemingway vaguely made out a machine gun and bodies flying backwards from the furious onslaught.

He shifted his aircraft around to the next corner, again staying below the roof.

In cutting off the second corner of the roof, his tracers ignited a fire. Using the cover provided by the smoke, Hemingway pushed his aircraft above the rim of the roof and saw several men running from the remaining corners of the building. They were headed toward the center of the roof, where a boxlike shelter displayed a wide open door.

Moments after Hemingway judged the last man had sufficient time to climb down into the building, he opened up on their boxlike access with his 25mm Gatling. The structure shattered into pieces, leaving a gaping hole from which more flames erupted.

Except for two deserted machine guns at the remaining corners, the roof was empty of targets. Feeling drained, Hemingway rotated his Harrier in search of a place to land.

As he moved over the rooftops, Hemingway didn't notice the MiG-23 swooping down toward the State Security building. When the Flogger passed him by, Hemingway saw the MiG dip its wings in the universal greeting of one pilot to another.

General Diaz, having watched the AV-8B's performance from a distance, now overflew the burning roof of the State Security building. He promptly canceled the attack of his commandos on the building and instructed them to keep it surrounded until the fire flushed the occupants outside.

When Diaz learned the Harrier had landed in a nearby square, his Hoplite rushed through the streets to it. Enroute, Diaz was informed that the tanks and troops he'd sent earlier to Camilo Cienfuegos Airbase were meeting no opposition. The MiG-23s were flying cover for his units.

By the time the Hoplite reached the Harrier, a large crowd had gathered around the strange flying aircraft.

Hemingway was still in his aircraft. He had removed his helmet and popped his canopy.

Pulling himself up to the cockpit, Iron Balls called out:

"Nice flying!"

Hemingway closed his tired eyes at the compliment, showing his exhaustion by the slump of his body.

"Get me out of here," he responded in a subdued tone. "My foot's making a mess."

Barragan leaned into the cockpit and saw the fresh blood pooled beneath the foot pedals.

"He's bleeding again!" shouted Barragan to Diaz, unfastening the harnesses securing Hemingway to his seat.

Diaz hoisted himself up the other side of the fuselage and helped pull the pilot from the plane.

"We will take him to the airbase," announced Diaz. "The Air Force has the best doctors in central Cuba."

As the Hoplite raced over the city, Diaz spoke with the MiG-23s overhead, requesting an escort. Successive pairs of MiG-23s began sweeping before the slower helicopter.

Acknowledging each pair by a wave of his arm through the Hoplite's open hatch, General Diaz shouted to Barragan:

"General Papa is being escorted by the Cuban Free Air Force!"

Swiss Embassy

Lou and Camille reached the Swiss embassy at the end of the Malecon 45 minutes after leaving the Plaza. In the last half-mile, Lou had leaned heavily on Camille's shoulder. The pain in his right hip hadn't become noticeable until they'd left the turmoil of the Plaza. With each step, the bruised joint of his hip grated.

Edward Bellin met them in the lobby. He pointed to Lou's limp and asked:

"What's wrong with the leg?"

"Got caught in a grinder."

"A what?"

"We were trampled in a stampede," explained Camille.

"I've heard about it," said Bellin. "The hospitals are loaded. Do you know how many were killed?"

Lou waited, then irritably inquired: "Are you planning to tell us....or asking a question?"

"I've heard more than 200 were killed," answered Bellin. "It must have been terrifying."

Lou withdrew the cassette from his shirt. "We've got it all on tape."

He handed the cassette to Bellin.

"I'm going to get cleaned up," said Camille, excusing herself.

As the two men headed for Bellin's office, Lou described what he'd seen after leaving the Plaza de la Revolucion. Students and other citizens were chasing down RAB thugs and CDR officials in the streets, beating and stripping them. The gutters were littered with red and yellow armbands discarded by their owners to avoid the angry mobs. Army units stationed around government buildings---either with orders to not interfere or content to remain bystanders---were making no attempt to restrain the street-fighting.

"Did you see any tanks?" asked Bellin.

"No."

"I understand they've moved onto the campus of Havana University," said Bellin.

"Tanks won't do Castro any good there," offered Lou. "The students are in the streets. I saw them chalking *'Down with Castro!'* on every building."

"Sounds like Romania all over again," commented Bellin.

Lou grinned. Along the Malecon, he'd also seen where someone scrawled: *"Better exploited under capitalism than starving under Castro."*

As the two men entered Bellin's office, Lou told him: "I'd like to make a duplicate of the cassette while you watch it....and get it to TV Marti in Miami as soon as possible."

Bellin thought a moment. "We could send a courier with a diplomatic pouch on the Miami flight tonight."

For years, the Castro government had permitted one clandestine flight daily between Havana and Miami. The aircraft---usually full of Cubans shuttling between families---arrived at Jose Marti airport south of Havana after midnight. The return flight usually left for Miami within the hour.

Lou shook his head. "I doubt they'll let any flights in or out of Marti tonight."

"How about using the night-train to Guantanamo?" offered Bellin.

"When does it arrive there?"

"It's a 14-hour trip." Bellin checked his watch. "It should arrive between 10 and 11 a.m. tomorrow."

"Would your courier have any problem?" asked Lou.

Bellin paused and nodded. "Considering what's happened, he might get searched."

"Let's make enough copies to try both plane and train," suggested Lou.

After Bellin inserted the cassette in a VCR, he connected a second VCR to record a copy. They silently watched the picture on the monitor.

Kristine, the university student, was obviously experienced with her camera. The picture began with the students climbing atop the dolphin fountain.

After panning the massive rally for a few seconds, she'd devoted several minutes to zooming in on the knives and machetes carried by RAB thugs around the fountain. Two armbanded Young Communist youths tussled with the female student distributing green leaflets.

Lou, recognizing himself in the picture sitting with his back to the camera, saw the RAB man who'd confiscated Camille's green leaflet.

As the footage displayed the Young Communists pulling the student off the dolphin fountain and pushing him underwater, Bellin muttered:

"Those bastards."

Lou turned the sound higher.

When Castro usurped the Che chant and the youths stopped fighting, Bellin pulled up a chair and sat directly in front of the monitor.

"This is amazing!" declared Bellin a minute later when the chant for food began. "We've got to get this to Washington, too!"

Lou nodded agreement.

Bellin came off his chair. "I'm going to get Jeremy Caldwell over here!"

As Bellin picked up a phone, Lou asked: "Who's that?"

"The British ambassador."

"While you're doing that," began Lou, "I'm going upstairs to make a report to Langley."

Twenty minutes later, Caldwell arrived in the room. Bellin rapidly explained what he'd already seen. Caldwell watched the tail end of the fight between the nursing mother and CDR woman in silence. *No More Lines!'* began. Lou reentered Bellin's office as the knife-belt fight started with Maria's husband. When it ended, Bellin spoke.

"Jeremy, we need your yacht."

Caldwell turned his head. "Say what?"

Bellin pointed to the monitor. "The Cuban people are entitled to know what happened today in Havana. If we can get a copy of this to Miami, it can be beamed back on TV Marti immediately."

Caldwell returned his attention to the monitor. At the conclusion of the taping, he heard gunfire and saw the camera come to the ground. Kristine had continued to shoot film after she'd fallen.

The last sequence was of the Cuban president kneeling before Maria, the brutal butt of the Uzi, then Castro carrying the young mother off the Plaza.

When Lou ejected the copy of the cassette and handed it to Caldwell, the British ambassador said:

"I'm driving this directly to my boat. When it reaches international waters, I'll raise your Coast Guard."

"I'll come with you," said Bellin.

Lou raised a hand. "I wouldn't do that, sir."

"Why not?" countered Bellin.

"This building is being watched," replied Lou. "If you leave, you'll be followed. When they report you've boarded a boat, I'm certain you will be stopped before you can get into international waters....and searched."

"He's right," commented Caldwell. "I'll detour to my embassy and pick up my wife and some others for my little trip. Make it look like a regular outing."

Swiss Embassy

While Bellin was occupied with his superiors in Washington, Fricke hurriedly gathered all available VCRs in the embassy.

Lou found Camille in her studio brushing out her hair, and he asked that she bring her own VCR to Bellin's office.

When Camille arrived, Lou had three sets of VCRs making copies of Kristine's cassette. As he hooked up Camille's machine, she asked him:

"What do you plan to do with the extra cassettes?"

"Distribute them back to the students," replied Lou.

"Why?"

"Maybe, one of them will get back to Kristine."

"That'll be a miracle," said Camille. "Havana University has more than 11,000 students."

Lou debated whether to remain vague or tell her that the copies would be delivered to the Canadian embassy for direct distribution to the students who'd organized the dissident chants at the Plaza.

He decided to remain vague. "We'll make enough copies to---"

"Louis!"

Bellin was at the door. From the alarm on his face, Lou thought the building might be on fire.

"Castro's here!" blurted Bellin. "He's told the lobby receptionist that he wants to speak with the President!"

Fighting an impulse to smile, Lou kept an inquisitive look on his face. So Castro wanted to talk. That possibility had been part of the contingency plans discussed with the President. It was surmised that Castro's first move---if *Havana Heat* managed to boil over---would be to release another mass emigration of refugees to Miami.

As far as President Steiner was concerned, that would be counter-productive. Allowing more Cubans to enter the United States would only strengthen

286

Castro's dictatorship by removing the very people most likely to overthrow it. Steiner already had decided to delay acceptance of such a plan.

Due to the criminals and psychopaths which Castro deliberately included in the 1980 boatlift, President Steiner felt he had an adequate reason for discouraging another mass emigration.

Castro would have to come up with some other alternative, and Lou wondered what it might be.

"I've already relayed Castro's request to Washington," said Bellin excitedly, adding: "I want you there when I meet with him."

Lou rose from his chair. "Why's he want to talk with Steiner?"

Bellin shrugged. "I haven't spoken with him yet."

"May I come also?" asked Camille.

"We may need you," Bellin nodded, "if he prefers to speak in Spanish."

Though Castro spoke English, on occasion he was known to refuse to use the language.

At the lobby, they found the Cuban president standing alone with his back to them, staring out the glass door of the entryway. Outside the embassy, Lou could see a sizeable contingent of white-uniformed bodyguards gathered.

Though the footsteps of the approaching Americans were plainly audible on the marble floor of the lobby, Castro did not turn to meet the Americans. They were forced to walk around to his front.

Fricke thought the flushed face of Fidel Castro displayed the rage of someone who had just vented great anger. The blood vessels across his forehead still bulged with his fury. Castro's eyes appeared enlarged; and, to Fricke, they displayed a savage malevolence not uncommon to other dictators he'd observed under stress. Though he had read the Cuban president was the same height as himself, Fricke was surprised to find that Castro towered over him.

As Bellin began introductions, Lou glanced at Castro's boots. Their heels were at least two inches thick.

"....and these are my assistants," continued Bellin. "Louis Fricke and Camille Fox."

Castro inspected Fricke without offering his hand. His cold gaze halted on the American's beard.

Surely, thought the CIA man, he knows who I am. Why else would I have been followed? Is he going to accuse me now of disrupting his rally? Lou waited.

Castro spoke gruffly to Lou.

"You look like a barbudo!"

Though he knew the word, Lou awkwardly smiled as he inquired: "What's a barbudo?"

"When we fought in the Sierra Maestra," replied Castro, "that is what the peasants called us. It meant *the bearded ones*."

Lou was impressed by Castro's English. Though grammatically correct and evenly-delivered, a heavy accent added a venomous tone to his voice.

The CIA man thought to thank Castro for what he considered to be a compliment; but he remained mute, finding himself intimidated by the menacing mood of the Cuban leader.

Castro's cruel countenance remained immobile as he glared into the eyes of Fricke, forcing the lesser man to look away.

Angered by his loss of composure, Lou dropped his eyes to the whipcord blouse of Castro's uniform. By the dried blood on the uniform, Lou knew it was the same one Castro had worn in the Plaza. Camille had noticed the blood earlier and she broke the silence.

"How is Maria?"

Castro raised an eyebrow to Camille, his eyes coming alert.

It occurred to Lou that Castro might suspect Maria of being an operative of the CIA from the question, and he wanted to tell Camille to say no more.

"She's the young woman you carried from the Plaza," Lou broke in.

Shifting his dubious stare to the CIA man, Castro curtly inquired: "You know this woman?"

I was right, thought Fricke. He will suspect Maria. But then the CIA man decided that Castro would certainly submit Maria to a chemical interrogation, and that would clear her of suspicion.

Before speaking, Lou forced himself to lock eyes with Castro. "Camille and I met Maria for the first time today at the dolphin fountain in the Plaza. Her husband happened to be sitting beside us when she arrived with her baby."

The face of the Cuban president remained skeptical.

Lou slowed his voice: "Her husband was killed by a member of the Rapid-Action-Brigade."

Instead of his last words angering Castro, Lou was relieved to see the face of the Cuban president soften.

"So that is why," observed Castro, bringing his hand up to stroke his beard. He repeated himself in a solemn whisper. "So....that is why."

The Cuban president turned away from the Americans to look pensively out the glass door of the lobby. The husband's fate explained the woman's actions. It explained everything.

Castro came back to Camille, and this time he spoke in a compassionate, almost reverent voice.

"The woman, Maria, has recovered....but will not speak." Castro wrinkled his brow. "Her child did not live."

His last words hung in the air for a time as the three people stood silently. Abruptly, Castro acquired his earlier sternness and spoke to Bellin.

"I must speak to President Steiner as soon as possible!"

Bellin led the way to an elevator for the top floor. His earlier message to Washington had already been received at the White House, and a response was waiting for Bellin in the embassy radio room, instructing him to inquire concerning the purpose of Castro's request.

The Cuban president simply repeated his desire to talk directly with Steiner. He would not reveal more.

Upon being informed President Steiner would speak with him shortly, Castro told Bellin: "I do not wish to be addressed by name or title. Please ask President Steiner to refer to me by the codename, *Hector*."

Bellin hesitated. "They're going to ask why."

"This is an unofficial communication," explained Castro, "and I assume it will be taped. By using a codename, I can speak more freely."

And no one can prove it was you later, thought Lou with an admiring grin. Afterwards, if need be, you can deny the entire conversation.

Castro, noticing Fricke's expression, raised a finger to Bellin. "If President Steiner has no objections, I will refer to him as *Louis*."

After explaining the Cuban president's unusual request, Bellin offered him a receiver to the satellite transmitter.

Castro spoke tentatively. "Hello....Louis."

The transmitter returned a business-like: "Hello to you, Hector."

Castro spoke haltingly, composing each word.

"This conversation is....an historic occasion."

A pause.

"I would have preferred....that the circumstances....were more agreeable."

Steiner waited, declining to respond.

Castro's voice became severe without being louder.

"The interference by the United States....in the affairs of the Cuban nation during the last 24 hours is....most ungracious."

The mildness of the reproach surprised President Steiner.

"And constitute illegal acts," continued Castro. "I am reminded of the tricks you Americans play on one another during national elections."

Having concluded the necessary unpleasantries, Castro paused at length before resuming a friendlier tone.

"I have often wondered why the United States did not make Cuba a state on one of the many occasions in which your military invaded this island."

Steiner was beginning to understand the warning he'd received that any conversation with Fidel Castro would be primarily one way and of a lecturing nature.

"Your country," Castro buoyantly went on, "has considerable reason to be grateful to the Cuban people. If we had not started an insurrection against the Spanish in 1895, there would have been no Spanish-American War. The United States would not have acquired Hawaii, Puerto Rico, Guam, and temporarily, the Philippines. And your country might not have had Theodore Roosevelt for a president."

Though Castro was enjoying his discourse, he decided it was finally time to draw Steiner into the discussion.

"Louis, do you know why President McKinley declined to acquire Cuba after the Spanish-American War?"

President Steiner, his voice congenial, asked: "What is your answer to that question?"

Castro lightly snickered to himself, assuming Steiner didn't know his own history.

"In 1895," began Castro, "the first riots in Havana against Spanish rule were touched off by a recession....due to dropping demand for our sugar in the United States. After the war ended, President McKinley and your Congress determined that Cuba would be an economic burden if annexed."

Castro made a short, self-deprecating laugh.

"We have a saying here in Cuba. Sugar is our greatest asset....and our greatest curse. The climate and soil make sugarcane our most productive crop; yet, dependence on only one product has caused us many problems."

Having set up his witness, the lawyer in Castro now cast the dagger. His tone remained sincere, but it was no longer lecturing.

"Louis....since Cuba's economic problems are chronically severe....and the United States has no interest in acquiring Cuba....why do American presidents continue to interfere in our affairs?"

President Steiner thought to explain the strategic nature of Cuba's location off the coast of the Florida, then he realized that any attempt to answer the question---any response at all---would be tantamount to an admission of guilt in the Che stratagems. Steiner also wasn't ready to publicly, or even privately, warn Castro not to harbor a portion of Algeria's suspected nuclear arsenal. The American president let the silence build, patiently waiting out his counterpart.

After a long twenty seconds, Steiner thought he'd won the contest of silence....when Castro gladly resumed his solitary dialogue.

"Louis, I have always believed the reason for this aggression is that the White House is poorly informed by your State Department and Central Intelligence Agency. Before the Bay of Pigs, Kennedy was furnished false information from these sources. Your CIA also led LBJ and Nixon down a deceitful path in Vietnam."

Castro paused significantly. "In the last 30 years, the only well-informed president in the White House has been Carter. In fact, he and I were making progress, before the voters removed him. His error was his honesty---a fatal flaw for any politician in a democracy."

The Cuban president paused at the jibe.

In the Oval Office, President Steiner cautiously smiled at Secretary of State Clayton Walters. As far as Steiner was concerned, Castro had said nothing of note yet. And Walters had forewarned him not to challenge the intellect of the Cuban leader, for Castro relished overwhelming opponents with recitations of lengthy and indisputable facts on virtually any political subject.

292

"Another question," began Castro, "that has puzzled me for many years is how the American presidents ignore their press. Your newspaper and television reporters are among the world's finest. Yet, the White House relies on second-rate information from Langley and, as you say, Foggy Bottom."

Though he was thoroughly enjoying his remonstrations to the American president, Castro stopped to consider how to draw him in again.

"Louis, have you ever been briefed concerning Cuba by anyone who has met me personally?"

Steiner had to think it over and didn't like his admission. "No, Hector. To the best of my knowledge, I have not."

"Then, Louis....may I recommend an American to you? Do you know Tad Szulc?"

"I have not met Szulc, but I've heard of him."

Castro's voice became enthusiastic. "Szulc lives in your Washington and has known me for 35 years. When I first met him in 1959, he was a 'New York Times' reporter. He has visited Cuba many times since and written a long biography of my life."

"Perhaps, I'll give him a call, Hector."

"Louis, there are many more important Americans who know me well. Also at the 'Times,' there was Herbert Mathews. And, of course, C L Sulz---"

Steiner broke in. "I'm familiar with Mathews, Hector. He's the reporter you hoodwinked into believing 18 men were a guerrilla army of hundreds."

In the Oval Office, Steiner raised a thumb to his Secretary of State who had briefed him thoroughly on the erroneous 'Times' articles by Mathews.

Steiner quickly added: "That's an instance where the American press printed many falsehoods. Mathews said you were defeating Batista's army--- when, in fact, you'd lost three-quarters of your men in the previous three months."

Castro snorted. "I did not have to hoodwink Mathews. He was a disillusioned man....from covering the Spanish Civil War. He did not wish to see the same tragedies inflicted on Cuba."

"I understand," countered Steiner, "that your brother, Raul, marched the same ragged band of rebels repeatedly across Mathews' line of sight....to create the illusion of many more."

Steiner paused to see if Castro would deny it.

"I think you would have done the same in my place," Castro finally stated. "After that interview appeared in the papers, many volunteers came into the mountains to join me. And money was no longer a problem. I remember....Mathews called me *the Robin Hood of the Sierra Maestra.*"

"I suppose we Americans," began Steiner dryly, "have done our part for your Cuba. Mathews claimed his articles altered the course of Cuban history, that they led to your assumption of power."

Castro goodnaturedly laughed. "I am not the only person who became a world leader due to a New York paper. Do you recall what John Kennedy said after his election?"

Steiner clearly remembered the 'Times' endorsement of JFK, though he didn't recall the former president's words.

"He said," Castro recited, *"In part, at least, I am one person who can truthfully say: I got my job through the New York Times."*

Castro paused meaningfully.

"It's amusing," offered Steiner, "that the 'Times' endorsed both of you. The two of you were so dissimilar."

"I cannot agree with that," Castro cordially countered. "President Kennedy and I shared many concerns for the common worker, the minorities, the disadvantaged."

As an afterthought, Castro added: "It was his misfortune to inherit the Bay of Pigs operation from Eisenhower and Nixon."

Steiner could not dispute either statement of the Cuban president, for they were both true.

Anxious to make another point, Castro switched back to his previous subject. "Louis, did you know---at the time of the Mathews interview---that

Batista opposed me with a standing army, navy, and air force of 40,000 regulars?"

Steiner hadn't realized the disparity was that great.

"To survive," reflected Castro, "I have found it necessary to manage the press no less than the politicians do in your country. I believe you Americans call it 'giving the news a spin,' do you not?"

As Steiner pondered the point, he found himself beginning to enjoy the conversation. He was gaining a sense that meeting Castro might be somewhat of a pleasant, if not rewarding experience. The man was certainly a shrewd politician to have survived so long.

"I've always meant to personally thank my friends at the CIA," continued Castro, "for their assistance in 1958. Your vice-consul in Santiago funneled $50,000 to us and later shipped me a powerful radio transmitter for broadcasting to the Cuban people."

In the Oval Office, Steiner shot a glance at his CIA Director. Rolle returned a shrug.

"An amazing result," Castro went on, "of the Mathews' articles was that three sons of American servicemen stationed at Guantanamo Bay came into the mountains to enlist in my cause."

"Is that so?" said Steiner doubtfully. He'd also been warned that Castro often exaggerated his accomplishments.

"Yes, they were among the first 90 rebels who joined me in the Sierra Maestra. I remember their names---Victor Buehlman, Michael Garney, and Charles Ryan. And many more Americans joined later. Twenty-six flights of arms from Florida were piloted to me by Americans."

With details that specific, mused Steiner, it must be true.

Castro deliberated a moment. "It is proper that Americans should have helped my Revolution because Cubans assisted in yours. In 1779, a Cuban expeditionary force captured Mobile and Pensacola. We brought 2,000 British soldiers back to Havana and held them until the end of your war."

Steiner shot a questioning glance at Clayton Walters, who nodded agreement with the statement.

"And just before your Battle of Yorktown," Castro went on, "the ladies of Havana society pawned their jewelry for your cause. We raised enough to pay the salaries of 5,000 American soldiers for a period of four months. Your historian, Stephen Bonsal, wrote that this contribution *may with truth be regarded as the bottom dollars upon which the edifice of American independence was erected.*"

"I am impressed by your prodigious memory," commented Steiner. He added somewhat defensively: "In 1898, the United States contributed to Cuba's independence also."

Castro made another of his short derisive laughs.

"We traded independence from Spain," he began, "for economic domination by the United States. After the Spanish governor left, American businessmen invaded Cuba. Nine of Cuba's ten largest sugar mills were acquired by U.S. corporations. IT&T came to own both our telephone system and electric utilities....and they charged higher rates than in the United States. Texaco owned one of our two oil refineries. Much of the best farmland was bought up by United Fruit. Later, the TV network and transportation systems were American-controlled."

Castro paused to catch his breath before asking:

"How would you Americans feel if Japan came to own and control that much of the United States?"

Steiner saw no harm in being candid. "I don't suppose we'd stand for it, Hector."

"Neither could Cuba," replied Castro swiftly. "Especially the poor, who suffered the most by this exploitation. They had no hope of improving their meager existences."

"At least....in 1898," offered President Steiner, "the United States saw to it that the Cuban people enjoyed self-determination for the first time in their history."

296

Steiner paused himself, carefully selecting his words to chide the Cuban leader. "It's unfortunate Cuba has maintained a democratic form of government for such short periods in this century."

There was a bitterness in Castro's finely-enunciated reply.

"You Americans had five-hundred years of British tradition before you established your democracy! What did Cuba have?"

Castro delivered his answer with an eloquence acquired from years of repetition.

"We had four-hundred years of corrupt governors, appointed by a cruel Spanish monarchy, guided by an intolerant religion---all of whom sought only to enrich themselves!"

It was a point he made with immense satisfaction, particularly to proponents of democracy who understood little of Latin America's Spanish heritage.

"In 1898," Castro vociferously went on, "the Cuban people were not equipped to govern themselves. They have proven that over and over. When exposed to unbridled freedoms, Cuba has always reverted to an autocracy. One-man rule is the only way Cuba can be governed. Sometimes, this man is enlightened, sometimes not."

"When I was a boy in school," continued Castro, "I wondered why South America was not one great nation---like the United States. Later, I learned that our Latin nature is more volatile, more unstable than your North American mentality. To avoid chaos, we Latins require a stronger central government. Look at Mexico. They have essentially a one-party government, and their leadership is preplanned years in advance. That is the only manner in which Mexicans can---."

President Steiner cut in. "Aren't Mexico's freedoms a good example of what you could do in Cuba?"

"A good example of *what*?" Castro coldly responded. "Poverty? Crime? Disease? Pollution? Corruption? Of which example do you speak?"

In the strained silence, Steiner recalled his Secretary of State's caution about engaging the Cuban president in debate.

Steiner spoke, but his voice lacked conviction. "I meant Mexico's freedom of speech, their freedom of the press, and other such freedoms."

With an unaccustomed grace, Castro decided not to recite the number of Mexican politicians and other officials who were gunned down on the streets during the average year. Instead, he returned to the subject of his own country.

"Before 1959, Cuba was full of poverty, disease, and corruption. That is why the people joined me in our Revolution. They wanted a better life....and now they have one."

Again, it was a practiced response of the Cuban president.

Steiner fought himself to keep from taking the opening. He wanted to inquire why the Cubans were rioting then....if they had a better life? But Steiner didn't care to risk being accused of starting the riots. He spoke in a tired voice.

"Hector, why did you wish to speak with me?"

There was prolonged silence before Castro's words came---measured, calm, and humble.

"Tonight, I would speak on Cuban television. I plan to offer a concession---a solution. I will discuss it with you immediately after the telecast, but I wish to speak to my people first."

Realizing Castro was requesting noninterference for a television broadcast, President Steiner looked to Walters. His Secretary of State kept a poker-face for a long moment, then nodded, giving a smile of encouragement.

Steiner spoke into his phone. "I will look forward to hearing your speech, Hector."

"And I shall look forward to discussing it with you afterwards, Louis.

"It's been a pleasure talking with you," Steiner genuinely said.

"One more matter," cautioned Castro in an even tone. "There has been a violation of Cuban airspace by aircraft flying out of Guantanamo Bay."

Steiner was caught off guard. "As I understand it," he replied, "my planes were on a training flight over international waters when they came under attack."

Castro hesitated a moment, uncertain himself of the precise facts. His Air Force generals had claimed the Harriers opened fire first.

"A training flight would not have flown all the way to Cienfuegos," contended Castro. "That is beyond the range of your Harriers."

"When I learned of the flight," offered Steiner, "it was ordered back to its base. I believe one or two of my planes were crippled though and had to make forced-landings in your country."

Debating whether the American president was lying or ignorant, Castro decided it made little difference. "The pilots shall be returned to you. I suggest we discuss this matter further after we have gathered more facts."

"That's a good idea. I agree, Hector."

Castro voice quieted as he voiced a thought which he'd never dared to share before.

"Perhaps, if the United States had made Cuba a state many years ago, I would still have become a politician....maybe even a senator in your Congress."

And Steiner couldn't resist the compliment.

"I'm sure you would have made a formidable one."

Plaza De La Revolucion

For three hours---since State Security had cleared the vast Plaza---Vilma Espin supervised the removal of the injured and the gathering of the dead.

The lifeless were arranged in orderly rows. A separate area behind the Jose Marti platform, cordoned off from prying eyes, was reserved for children.

Vilma had seen death before. In the Sierra Maestra, it was not uncommon....but that was more than half a lifetime ago. And then it was adults who had died in her arms, men for whom death was an accepted, daily risk.

Now, they are dying again, thought Vilma, as she gazed down the rows of motionless bodies. One of Fidel's favorite slogans, *The Revolution is ongoing,* ran through her mind. Didn't Fidel boast that his was the longest revolution of any nation in history? But this is not right, she decided. The bodies of women outnumber the men. And, worse, those of children outnumber both women and men.

After the first row of 50 children was gathered, Vilma found she could no longer bear to view the small faces frozen in their final moments of terror. When the second row began, she had moved away from the Jose Marti memorial, distancing herself from their lifeless forms. By the time the third row started, Vilma---a grandmother six times---began talking to herself.

"The children are only napping."

"With no signs of injury, they cannot be dead."

Vilma was repeating these phrases to others when a white-uniformed officer of Fidel Castro's bodyguard appeared at her side. He clicked his heels to gain attention.

"Comadre Espin," began the peacock of an officer, "El Presidente requests your presence in his office."

Vilma wordlessly followed the man into the Palacio de la Revolucion. When she entered the broad reception hall which served as Castro's office, her vacant face and unsteady gait gave her the appearance of a sleepwalker.

As Vilma strode toward the seated Castro, he was mildly amused by the manner in which her .38 pistol rode her right hip.

Years earlier, in the Sierra Maestra, Vilma had been a slim beauty who'd captivated Fidel's brother Raul. She took the same risks as the men and handled the same weapons. Now....the pistol rode too high on her wide, paunchy hips, its muzzle pointing out at a 45-degree angle to the floor. Only Vilma and Raul Castro were permitted to enter the office of the Maximum Leader armed.

Looking up, Vilma halted midway across the broad hall---still 60 feet from the desk of the Cuban president---thinking that the man sitting behind the desk could not be Fidel. There was no beard. She could not fully see the upper half of the man's face, for his fingers were crisscrossed just below his eyes. A pistol rested on the desk within his reach.

The man's hands dropped, revealing the dark, bushy eyebrows and eagle-beaked nose of Fidel Castro.

"Your beard!" exclaimed Vilma.

She thought the bare face of Fidel might have looked younger, had it not hung so dejectedly. Except in old photographs taken before the Sierra Maestra years, Vilma had never seen him without a beard.

In a distraught tone, she announced: "There are 148 bodies of dead children in the Plaza. More were carried away by their families."

When Fidel made no comment nor gave any reaction to this news, she completed her report. "And 119 adult bodies, 83 of whom died by knives."

"Sit."

Fidel hissed the single word as if speaking to a dog.

No concern for the dead children, thought Vilma. He cares only for himself. She took a chair before his desk.

"Raul," mumbled Fidel, "is dead."

Vilma rapidly blinked.

"A bullet," said Fidel.

The face of the woman started to come undone. Her jaw dropped, without opening the mouth, and her eyes wandered to the floor and back.

Fidel went on in a raspy voice. "Raul was killed by a stray bullet while leading troops to block General Diaz's column from Santa Clara."

It was a half-lie, but Fidel could not bring himself to repeat the full truth. Raul had been leading an army column to oppose Diaz; however, the barrage of bullets that killed him were not stray. They had been deliberately released by the gunner in a tank behind Raul's jeep.

Vilma gradually closed her eyes under a tightened brow. Her breathing slowed. Another person might have thought she was praying, but Fidel knew Vilma too well to think that. His harsh voice heightened.

"Because of your knives, he died!"

Vilma came alive, jerking upright in her chair.

"Because of your knives," Fidel lashed out again, "the husband of the woman who carried the flag in the Plaza was killed."

Fidel paused before hoarsely adding:

"That is why she led the students against me! That is why the crowd went out of control!"

Staring open-mouthed at the accusation, Vilma started to protest. "But---"

"I did not need your knives at my rally," Fidel cut in. "I could have dominated the dissidents with my voice and the counter-chants."

"But you agreed to the knives!" insisted Vilma. "You said it was an excellent---"

"Hah!" grunted Fidel, dismissing her words. "I never said that."

Vilma's eyes narrowed at the open lie.

"That is not how---"

"You also killed my brother!" interrupted Fidel again, pointing a finger at her. "What happened in the Plaza today was *your* fault!"

Vilma visibly quaked. Never before had Fidel directed his wrath upon her.

Fidel glared at his former sister-in-law. His words were not for her sole benefit. In their repeating, he would find the best phrases, the proper nuances to use in explaining the events in the Plaza to his people over the next few days.

Vilma's mind raced.

She had been a frequent and active participant in *accusation sessions* conducted by Fidel before, and it did not take her long to realize what was happening. Whenever a disaster or crisis occurred of Fidel's making, he quickly shifted the blame to someone else....before the people could fix in their minds the true responsibility. And now she would be his sacrificial lamb..

Yes, Vilma thought, I suggested the knives. But it was your insistence that the rally be held immediately. And that everybody come. You are responsible for the children being there. And you lost control of the crowd.

Vilma wanted to shout out her thoughts, but the shock of his accusations stilled her tongue. If I am to be assigned the fault for the tragedy in the Plaza, she asked herself, then what will be my fate? What does he have in store for me?

Checking his watch, Fidel jumped up from his desk. He grabbed the remote control of his TV and switched on its screen.

"Watch!" he commanded. "I have made a videotape which will be shown on Cuba-Vision now."

Vilma twisted around to view the screen of Cuba's only TV station.

Fidel Castro's bare face appeared in the picture. So he shaved for the telecast, observed Vilma.

As Fidel spoke on the screen, his strained voice often reverted to a loud whisper.

303

"People of Cuba! I speak to each of you as your brother. We must not fight each other. We must not shed our own precious blood."

Castro's expression became earnest, losing much of its tiredness.

"I have personally investigated today's tragedy in the Plaza de la Revolucion. This needless bloodshed was caused by ruffians improperly ordered into the crowd by my half-brother, Raul. I would have countermanded his orders; but, as you saw, I had lost my voice."

So, now he blames Raul, Vilma told herself. Anybody but himself. She jumped from her chair.

Never before had Vilma heard Fidel refer to Raul as a half-brother in public. To lend truth to the rumor that Raul was the result of a brief liaison between Fidel's mother and the Batista officer, Captain Felipe Mirabel, would now discredit Raul. Vilma knew it was another subtle way of Fidel distancing himself from what had happened in the plaza.

"You lie! You lie!" Vilma shouted.

Fidel turned his back on the protesting woman and increased the television's volume.

"Therefore, I ordered the Revolutionary Army to arrest those responsible for the deaths in the Plaza....including Raul Castro."

Vilma watched as the offscreen camera came closer to Castro's despondent face. He withdrew a handkerchief and dabbed at an eye.

Switching her attention to the real person, Vilma detected a satanic smile on Fidel's face as he raptly watched his own image. Could he be serious? she wondered. Surely, he does not intend to have me arrested also.

"My half-brother resisted his arrest. And in the struggle---"

The face of Castro cringed on screen, as if he were struggling to control his emotions.

"---Raul was accidentally shot....and killed."

And with these words, Fidel assumed his government had atoned for the deaths of those in the Plaza.

Eyewitnesses to Raul's demise would not refute the version furnished by the Cuban president. All of them---even those loyal to Castro---had been imprisoned. It was vitally important that as few people as possible knew the Revolutionary Army had murdered its own Chief of Staff.

On television, Fidel again wiped at his eyes. After coughing to clear his throat, he lowered his chin in a penitent manner. When he came up, his countenance had altered to one of determination.

"It is time for radical change in Cuba! It is time that we join with the democracies of the world. And it is time for Cubans to learn to govern themselves."

"You are lying!" exclaimed Vilma, knowing the consummate actor in her brother-in-law.

"It is time for Cubans to learn how to elect their future leaders."

"You are lying!" she shouted again, angered then frightened at Fidel's proclamation. In her mind, Vilma knew free elections would spell the end of the Marxist state to which she and Raul had dedicated their lives.

On the screen, Castro gave his viewers a plaintive smile.

"Yes, my brothers and sisters, it is time to think ahead. I will be 70 soon. I cannot live forever. It is my desire that Cubans elect a new President within a year. For I wish to retire....to end my days at my birthplace in Biran. The burden of the Revolution has consumed too much of my life."

Vilma heard polite applause in the background of the TV studio. Castro was then surrounded by a somber cluster of people. After each of them warmly embraced him, Castro bent down to pick up a child, a young girl.

The child had a concerned look. When applause in the studio suddenly quieted, she finally spoke.

"Long live Fidel."

Though she recited the words with little conviction, the others in the TV studio immediately picked it up.

"Long live Fidel! Long live Fidel!"

In the Palacio de la Revolucion, the real Castro lowered the sound a few notches with his remote control. He continued to admire his image and voice for a moment before glancing at Vilma.

Her entire attention was already focused on him.

A wave of nausea washed over Castro at what he saw.

Vilma stood in a wide stance, at a distance of ten feet. In both hands, she gripped the .38 that had been on her hip. It was pointed at his chest.

"You were always an opportunist," she told him in an agitated voice.

Fidel waved at the gun. "Put that away."

"You were never a good Communist!" she bitterly exclaimed.

Lifting his hand to her, Fidel took a step forward.

"Give me the gun."

The pistol came higher, freezing on his face.

He let his hand slowly drop to his side.

"Yes, Fidel. You are right. I am responsible for the knives."

Fidel smirked. "So put the gun away."

"But you are also responsible for the deaths in the Plaza."

Vilma gave him a grim smile as she paused.

"Who will arrest you, Fidel?"

"I have killed no one," he replied.

Vilma shook her head back-and-forth. "In 35 years, you have ordered the killing of more than a thousand persons!"

Fidel placed the TV remote control on his desk to free up his gun hand.

Vilma continued. "And you have told the Cuban people more thousands of lies."

Spreading his hands expansively, Fidel spoke in a sympathetic tone. "You are upset, Vilma. Please, sit down."

"Yes," she willingly nodded. "I am upset."

He pointed to her chair. "You need rest."

"It was I who suggested knives," she repeated, "but it was your rally. You gathered the people to save your skin. And Raul told you it was too soon. There was no time to plan it....to control it."

There was a nervous edge to Fidel's brief laugh.

"Come now, Vilma. It was to save your skin, too. We ruled together."

In her mind's eye, Vilma again saw the pallid expressions on the bodies lying in the Plaza. She shook her head. "I will not rule over the bodies of dead children!"

Fidel's face hardened.

Vilma nodded toward the television. Her tone became hopeful. "You told lies just then....yes?"

"I told the truth," stated the Cuban president.

"You will not retire," countered Vilma. "You will manipulate any election to re-elect yourself. You would not be less than a king....as long as you live."

"You misjudge me, Vilma."

She disregarded his comment. "How did my husband die?"

Fidel paused.

He thought to remind Vilma that Raul Castro had not been her husband in nine years, but he had seen the hurt on her face earlier. And it might be foolish to further aggravate the woman. Fidel decided to tell the truth.

"He was shot in the back by his own men."

"Did you have your brother killed?" she immediately asked.

Fidel widened his eyes in feigned surprise.

"No," he said in a quieted voice. "An army sergeant killed him."

Too often, Vilma had seen Fidel contort and corrupt the truth with the greatest of ease. With an open-eyed grace, he would invite listeners to believe falsehoods; and in their repetition---though she knew they were lies---even she had come to accept and believe them. Many times, Fidel had told her: *The truth is only what each person perceives, and reality varies with the beholder.*

"I don't know whether to believe you," uttered Vilma.

"It is the truth," said Fidel with calm assurance.

She studied him for several seconds, not surprised that he demonstrated no fear at the weapon trained on his chest.

"You had Camilo Ceinfuegos, your finest military leader in the Sierra Maestra, killed," began Vilma. "And before that, I helped you kill Frank Pais. You sent Che to his death in Bolivia. It was the same with General Ochoa. Whoever gets in your way is removed, even those closest to you."

"But I would not kill my own brother," replied Castro in a firm voice.

"A half-brother, perhaps?" offered Vilma, and when this solicited no reply, she asked:

"Am I to be next?"

He shook his head with a short laugh. "Of course not. I need you. Now, more than ever."

Vilma eye's narrowed. "I am afraid of what you need me for."

"Put your gun back in its holster," said Fidel matter-of-factly, walking behind his desk.

Vilma turned with him, keeping aim.

Sitting at his desk, Fidel shook his head, eyes down. "I do not understand you, Vilma."

She moved to the front of the desk. Vilma almost smiled at the idea that came to her. It would save Fidel....and herself.

"Fidel, I understand you all too well," she began. "Tomorrow, you will call for the National Assembly to convene. Then, before your most loyal party members, you will publicly offer to resign. But your compadres will refuse to accept your resignation. Right? Then, reluctantly, you will agree to serve another year. And, after that, two more years, then three. Right? Everything will be the same."

Having voiced what she fervently wished, Vilma watched Fidel closely, waiting for some sign that he liked the idea, that he would agree to keep their Marxist state.

Fidel stared at Vilma for a long moment.

"You were always the smartest," he silently told her. And he began to consider her proposal. Yes, it might do. Nasser had tried the ploy after losing to the Israelis, and it had worked quite well for him. Perhaps....

Fidel shook his head. His people had spoken, and he had clearly heard them. More important, the Cuban president had fought a losing battle long enough. It was true that the burden of ruling his island nation had become tiresome....even irksome.

"No, Vilma," he gently told her, "it is time for a change. And, if I am careful, I can lead the Cubans through a transition to some form of democracy."

Fidel meant to add: "That way, I can preserve the gains of my Revolution."

But his eyes and mind were concentrating on another matter far more compelling. The knuckles of Vilma's fingers were going white around the butt of her .38.

"You will not be a traitor," Vilma said softly, almost sweetly.

Fidel, pushing a button under the lip of his desk to summon his bodyguards, mustered a sardonic smile. The irony of the occasion was amusing. This woman had always accepted his lies. Now, when he told her the inevitable truth, she would not accept it.

Vilma finished compressing the trigger.

Seeing the final squeeze, Fidel threw up his hands to block her line of sight and twisted to dive under his desk.

The pistol discharged.

With both hands, he caught the bullet. The short passage of hot metal through the soft tissue and thin bones of his hands did little to deflect the lead-alloy slug.

Initially, the Cuban president did not feel what hit him. A bullet moving near the speed of sound deadens the tissue and organs it crushes.

The slug met its first real obstacle at the enamel of his molars, shattering two of them. Widened to twice its original size, the bullet then ripped through the meaty flesh of Fidel's tongue, neatly shearing it.

A wide jagged hole through his opposite jaw was created by the growing mass of bullet as it tore a ragged opening out his right cheek.

Fidel's head, rocked by the blow, roughly hit against the back of his chair. When his head rebounded forward again, his jaw came open and the severed tongue fell to the floor.

In a daze, Fidel viewed the scene before him.

From a side door, a trio of bodyguards burst into his office. They were armed with Uzis, at the ready. What they saw gave them pause.

Vilma Espin's hands were still raised, the pistol pointing at their Commandante. Its report had been unmistakable. The face of Castro revealed her target.

His jaw, gushing blood from both sides, hung open disbelievingly. With his wounded hands held up before him, Castro appeared to be catching the blood spurting from his face.

The Uzis were fired from the hip.

A volley from the first Uzi lifted Vilma off her feet. Firepower of the second Uzi spun her body before it hit the floor. Multiple volleys then slammed into her torso, rolling it across the marble floor. Vilma was dead before her body came up against the wall under the live TV screen.

The face of Fidel Castro on the television screen displayed both compassion and concern as he explained to his people, in detail, how the rally in the Plaza had gone array. The blame was set entirely on Raul and the ruffians of the Rapid-Action-Brigades.

In their haste to rush their leader to medical care, Castro's bodyguards failed to notice and bring the detached portion of his tongue.

When the office of the Cuban president was again empty, except for the torn body of Vilma Espin, the only sound came from the television set directly above Vilma.

Fidel's image on the TV screen was earnestly paying tribute to the brave students who had

310

displayed courage in the face of the RAB thugs....and he particularly lauded the magnificent blonde who had stood above the crowd, bearing the flag of Cuba.

On the way to the hospital, Castro attempted to speak but could only emit an unintelligible, throaty gargle at best....before choking on his own blood. Angrily, he tried again and again to communicate. Each time, he only sputtered more blood.

When Castro thought to write out orders, he found the wounds in both his hands prevented the use of a pen. For the first time in 35 years, Castro found himself unable to control events around him.

At the hospital, the physicians had difficulty restraining their patient on the operating table to administer an anesthetic. Four nurses were required to hold down just his head and neck.

As he went under, Fidel Castro once again heard the howl of the rabid dog. This time---the first time---he felt the teeth clamp around his neck.

Epilogue

In the chaos immediately following the incapacitation of the Cuban president, most of those who ruled with Fidel Castro were quick to repudiate him. Others fled or faded into anonymity.

TV Marti played the tape filmed by the student, Kristine, over and over....without commentary. Rioting against State Security and RAB units spread across the Cuban island.

General Diaz, with the air cover he'd acquired at Santa Clara, continued his march on Havana. By nightfall, Diaz and the two other commanders of Cuba's three military districts declared martial law throughout the island nation.

Captain "Iron Balls" Barragan is now carried on the rolls of the U.S. Marine Corps as an advisor on liaison tour with the Cuban Air Force. His Cuban pilot friends have assigned him a new call sign, "King Cobra."

Colonel Hemingway, taking early disability retirement, acquired the bluff overlooking Lake Tahoe. A rough-hewn home is being expanded for an expected child. He fully intends to play in the Citadel's next alumni-varsity contest.

Lou Fricke's presence in Havana became an embarrassment to the CIA for two reasons, and he was pulled out within 10 days. The stated reason was Lou's growing substance-abuse problem. Visions of the broken bodies in the Plaza would not go away unless blurred with alcohol. The other reason, unstated, was to remove evidence of CIA involvement in the fall of Fidel. Other camcorders had filmed the frozen rows of trampled children. The mind-searing scenes in the Plaza de la Revolucion were repeated for days on CNN. Instead of rallying Cubans against Castro (which was no longer necessary), the scenes in the Plaza became a symbol to the world of the excesses of the CIA.

After recovering from his wounds, Fidel Castro was forcibly returned to his childhood home in Biran ---the same one he'd threatened to burn down as a child. He did learn to speak again. After several months, through therapy and a throat device, he is able to make himself understood....providing his listener has patience and is nearby. Since his conversations are still one-sided, the listeners are scarce.

No statue or other monuments to the 35-year dominance of Communism in Cuba survived the fall of its leader....other than the murals of Che Guevara.

An outpouring of compassion from the affectionate Cuban populace brought Maria out of seclusion after eight months. Ambitious politicos have begun seeking her endorsement of their plans for Cuba's future.

REVIEWER'S COMMENTS on **GOOD FRIDAY,**
a *New York Times* bestseller in 1988

"As readable as Tom Clancy . . . a smashingly good story that grabs you and never lets go!"
—*Pacific Flyer Aviation News*

"Holt has the mIddle East in flames and he takes no prisoners. A crackling fast read."
---*Stephen Coonts, author Flight of the Intruder*

"Even more action-packed than Holt's first novel ....paints a hardnosed picture of political necessity ....breakneck action....Holt moves his drama deftly and believably over a broad terrain...tension is maintained at a high level."   ---*Publishers Weekly*

"The one thing the author does know is flying and he takes the reader on a few wild acrobatics."
---*The New York Times*

"Holt has written an explosive and frightening scenario. Tension is the key word in this fast-paced narrative!"   --*Waldenbooks Newsletter*

"A first-rate adventure yarn that previews combat abilities in the 1990s...timely...provocative."
--*Marine Corps Gazette*

"Although I am a voracious reader, I usually can't sit down and read any book from cover to cover in anything less than a week. Not true with **Good Friday**. I read it on the plane from California to Washington D.C. and loved every minute of it."
---*Dale Brown, author Flight of the Old Dog.*

"Holt's plot weaves intrigue, suspense, and lots of military action to create a plausible plot. This novel is exceptional!"   ---*Midwest Book Review*

"**Good Friday** is tautly written, plunging ahead at supersonic speed."   --*Library Journal*

"A spectacular novel of conflict in the Star Wars era. It's about killer satellites, super-accelerating rockets, and lethal thermonuclear-powered chemical lasers, and it's not fantasy."
--Oceanside Blade-Tribune

"In 1998, Star Wars research has culminated in the ultimate defense system, a series of space platforms armed with laser weaponry. But Peacemaker can think for itself, and all the superpowers are equally uneasy. An updated plot told with modern pace and action."
--SF & Fantasy, Summer 1991

"This is a page-turner, of that there is no doubt."
--Martyn Taylor, Vector

"What first struck me about this novel was the dramatic changes which the past ten years have brought, both technical and political. Technically, the ideas here would once have been the realm of pure sf: a satellite defense system, whose fusion-powered lasers are capable of pinpoint destruction of targets the size of a single vehicle on the surface of the Earth; and controlled by a computer with an inbuilt ability to act on its own initiative, overriding commands from the ground control. Thanks to Ronald Reagan, such concepts are now acceptable fodder for cold-war techno-thrillers."
--Dreamberry Wine, Spring 1991

"I found Peacemaker a fascinating read."
--Anne Williams, Headline Publishing

*movie rights optioned by Bernhard/Robson

REVIEWER'S COMMENTS on **THE CHRISTMAS RUBY**----a San Diego-based Christmas story

"....a novel for the holidays....meant to be read aloud ...the players read like a Damon Runyon piece. *Deuce*, the young homeless hero whose mother picked his name from a racing form; *Earl the Whirl*, an aging con man; and *Tanya Toogood*, a well-to-do widow."
              ----**San Diego Union-Tribune**

"The Christmas Ruby is a jewel!" —**Barnaby Conrad,** Director, Santa Barbara Writer's Conference, and author of **Matador**

"....a light-hearted book....intended for the whole family....features several unique characters, who learn lifelong lessons about the value and reward of honesty and giving." ---**Encinitas Coast Dispatch**

"....full of well-developed and interesting characters. Makes you feel good, and encourages us to help others at Christmastime." ---**Evelyn Kooperman,** *San Diego city librarian.*

"...this inherently bittersweet story on the streets of downtown San Diego is difficult to resist....a wonderful find at anytime of year. Read it aloud---it will make you glow." ---**Annie Flanigan, Waldenbooks**

"....colorful characters abound as Earl the Whirl, con man extraordinaire, stacks the deck and changes the lives of those he meets. **The Christmas Ruby** is an alternately funny, alluring, bizarre, frightening, and sweet story full of surprises." –**Patricia Valiton, UCSD**

"....based in San Diego....the street-smart Deuce makes his bed on a row of chairs under a table at the City Library....Earl the Whirl is an expert at any game of chance....by Christmas Eve, in a surprising twist of events, these two scam artists inadvertently teach each other the art of giving." ---**The Beach News**

For Loved Ones, Friends, and Others who return books slowly, additional copies of this book can be purchased from:

Pacific Rim Press
Playa del Pacifica
Post Office Box 220
Carlsbad, CA 92018

Please enclose $19.95, plus $1.20 tax if you live in California. We'll pay the shipping. Be sure to specify how you wish your book *autographed.*

Autographed editions of other books by Robert Lawrence Holt also can be purchased from Pacific Rim Press. They include:

Christmas Ruby	(hardbound)	$14.95
Good Friday	(hardbound)	14.95
Sweetwater	(hardbound)	14.95
Peacemaker	(hardbound)	17.95
Peacemaker	(trade paperback)	14.95
Bonds	(softbound)	7.95
Straight Teeth	(softbound)	8.95